2025 Easy ANTI-INFLAMMATORY

DIET COOKBOOK for Beginners

Mette A. Nilsson

2000 Days of Tasty and Healthy Recipes Book with Science-Backed Guide
for Better Eating | A No-Stress 30-Day Meal Plan

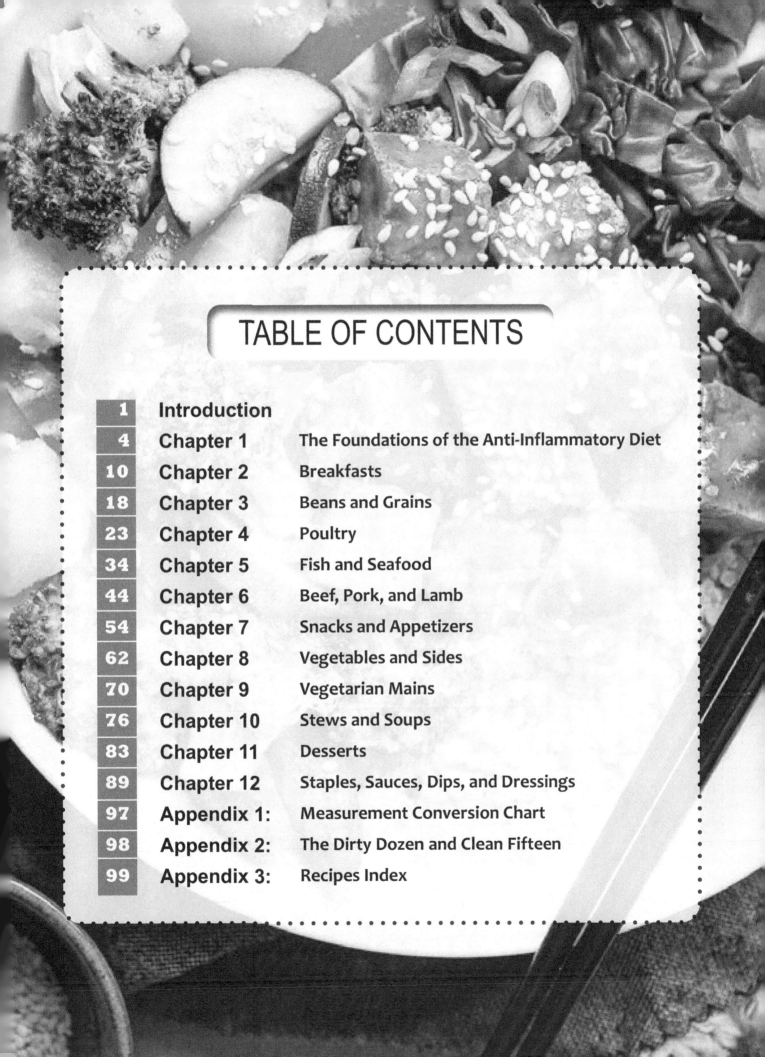

TABLE OF CONTENTS

1	Introduction	
4	Chapter 1	The Foundations of the Anti-Inflammatory Diet
10	Chapter 2	Breakfasts
18	Chapter 3	Beans and Grains
23	Chapter 4	Poultry
34	Chapter 5	Fish and Seafood
44	Chapter 6	Beef, Pork, and Lamb
54	Chapter 7	Snacks and Appetizers
62	Chapter 8	Vegetables and Sides
70	Chapter 9	Vegetarian Mains
76	Chapter 10	Stews and Soups
83	Chapter 11	Desserts
89	Chapter 12	Staples, Sauces, Dips, and Dressings
97	Appendix 1:	Measurement Conversion Chart
98	Appendix 2:	The Dirty Dozen and Clean Fifteen
99	Appendix 3:	Recipes Index

INTRODUCTION

In a world where our lives are increasingly fast-paced, it's easy to overlook the impact that our daily food choices have on our overall health. Chronic inflammation, often called the "silent killer," is a condition that many of us unknowingly battle due to the modern lifestyle. It is linked to a host of diseases, including heart disease, diabetes, arthritis, and even certain types of cancer. The good news is that what we eat can be a powerful tool in the fight against inflammation. This is where the Anti-Inflammatory Diet comes into play.

This cookbook is not just another collection of recipes; it is a guide to transforming your relationship with food and your body. By choosing the right foods, you can significantly reduce inflammation, boost your energy levels, improve your mood, and lower your risk of chronic diseases. The Anti-Inflammatory Diet is about more than just eliminating harmful foods; it's about embracing a way of eating that supports and nourishes your body from the inside out.

Understanding Inflammation and Its Impact on Health

Before diving into the delicious recipes this book has to offer, it's essential to understand what inflammation is and why it's so detrimental to our health. Inflammation is a natural response by the body's immune system to injury or infection. When you cut yourself or catch a cold, your body sends white blood cells to the affected area to fight off the threat. This is known as acute inflammation, and it's a crucial part of the healing process.

However, when inflammation persists over time, even when there is no injury or illness to fight, it becomes chronic. Chronic inflammation can damage healthy cells, tissues, and organs, leading to serious health issues. Factors such as poor diet, stress, lack of exercise, and exposure to environmental toxins can all contribute to chronic inflammation. This is where diet becomes a critical factor.

The Power of the Anti-Inflammatory Diet

The Anti-Inflammatory Diet focuses on whole, unprocessed foods that are rich in nutrients and antioxidants, which help combat inflammation at the cellular level. Instead of focusing on restriction, this diet encourages abundance—abundant fruits, vegetables, whole grains, lean proteins, and healthy fats. These foods are not only delicious but are also scientifically proven to reduce inflammation and promote overall health.

For example, leafy greens like spinach and kale are packed with vitamins A, C, and K, which have powerful anti-inflammatory properties. Berries, such as blueberries and strawberries, are rich in antioxidants that protect your cells from damage. Fatty fish like salmon and mackerel are high in omega-3 fatty acids, which have been shown to reduce inflammatory markers in the body. The diet also emphasizes the importance of spices like turmeric and ginger, which have been used for centuries for their anti-inflammatory and healing properties.

What to Expect from This Cookbook

This cookbook is designed to be your companion on the journey to better health. It is filled with a variety of recipes that are not only anti-inflammatory but also delicious and easy to prepare. Whether you're a seasoned home cook or someone just starting to explore the kitchen, you'll find recipes that fit your skill level and your taste preferences.

The recipes are divided into sections to help you easily find what you're looking for, whether it's a quick breakfast, a satisfying lunch, a hearty dinner, or a sweet treat that won't derail your health goals. Each recipe includes detailed instructions, nutritional information, and tips on how to make the dish even more anti-inflammatory.

Beyond just recipes, this cookbook also provides guidance on how to stock your pantry with anti-inflammatory staples, tips for meal planning, and suggestions for making sustainable changes to your diet and lifestyle. The goal is not just to provide you with meals for today but to empower you with knowledge and skills that will last a lifetime.

A Lifestyle Change, Not a Temporary Fix

It's important to approach the Anti-Inflammatory Diet as more than just a temporary change. This is not a fad diet that promises quick fixes or miraculous results in a short period. Instead, it's a sustainable way of eating that promotes long-term health and well-being. By consistently choosing foods that reduce inflammation, you'll likely notice a gradual improvement in how you feel, from better digestion to clearer skin to more stable energy levels.

One of the most significant aspects of this diet is its flexibility. It's not about deprivation or strict rules. Instead, it's about making informed choices that align with your health goals. This cookbook encourages you to listen to your body, experiment with new foods, and discover what works best for you. The recipes are versatile, allowing you to adapt them to your dietary preferences, whether you're vegetarian, gluten-free, or simply looking to eat more plant-based meals.

Conclusion: Embrace the Journey to Wellness

Embarking on an Anti-Inflammatory Diet is a journey towards wellness that goes beyond just the physical benefits. As you start to nourish your body with wholesome, healing foods, you'll likely find that your relationship with food shifts. Instead of viewing meals as just something to get through the day, you'll begin to see them as an opportunity to nurture yourself and those you care about.

This cookbook is here to support you every step of the way, providing you with the tools, recipes, and inspiration you need to succeed. Remember, the journey to better health is not about perfection but about progress. Every small step you take towards reducing inflammation and improving your diet is a step towards a healthier, happier you.

So, open up this cookbook, explore the recipes, and enjoy the process of cooking and eating in a way that truly supports your well-being. Here's to a future filled with vibrant health and delicious, anti-inflammatory meals!

Chapter 1

The Foundations of the Anti-Inflammatory Diet

Chapter 1: The Foundations of the Anti-Inflammatory Diet

The journey to better health begins with understanding the foundations of the Anti-Inflammatory Diet. This chapter will explore the key principles of the diet, the science behind its benefits, and practical steps to incorporate anti-inflammatory foods into your daily life. By the end of this chapter, you'll have a clear understanding of how to make food choices that support your body's natural healing processes and reduce inflammation.

What is the Anti-Inflammatory Diet?

The Anti-Inflammatory Diet is not a rigid set of rules or a temporary eating plan. Instead, it's a flexible approach to eating that emphasizes whole, nutrient-dense foods that help reduce chronic inflammation in the body. The diet is based on the idea that certain foods can either promote or reduce inflammation, and by choosing the right ones, you can help your body function optimally.

At its core, the Anti-Inflammatory Diet is about balance. It encourages the consumption of a wide variety of fruits, vegetables, whole grains, lean proteins, and healthy fats, while limiting or avoiding foods that are known to trigger inflammation, such as processed foods, refined sugars, and trans fats. The goal is to create a diet that is rich in anti-inflammatory compounds, such as antioxidants, omega-3 fatty acids, and phytochemicals, while minimizing pro-inflammatory ingredients.

The Science Behind the Diet

Chronic inflammation is a key contributor to many diseases, including heart disease, diabetes, arthritis, and even certain cancers. When the body is in a state of chronic inflammation, it is constantly trying to repair damage, which can lead to a range of health problems. The foods we eat play a significant role in either promoting or reducing this inflammation.

For example, omega-3 fatty acids, found in fatty fish like salmon, are known to reduce the production of inflammatory molecules called cytokines. On the other hand, trans fats and refined sugars can increase inflammation by promoting the release of these harmful molecules. By choosing foods that are high in anti-inflammatory compounds, you can help reduce the overall inflammatory burden on your body.

Key Components of the Anti-Inflammatory Diet

1. Fruits and Vegetables: These are the cornerstone of the Anti-Inflammatory Diet. Rich in vitamins, minerals, fiber, and antioxidants, fruits and vegetables help neutralize free radicals that cause oxidative stress and inflammation. Aim to fill half your plate with a colorful variety of these foods at every meal.

2. Whole Grains: Unlike refined grains, whole grains retain their nutrient-rich bran and germ. They provide fiber, which helps regulate blood sugar levels and supports a healthy gut, both of which are important for controlling inflammation. Examples include brown rice, quinoa, and whole-wheat products.

3. Healthy Fats: Not all fats are created equal. The Anti-Inflammatory Diet emphasizes healthy fats, particularly those rich in omega-3 fatty acids. Sources include fatty fish, nuts, seeds, and olive oil. These fats have been shown to reduce inflammation and support heart health.

4. Lean Proteins: Protein is essential for repairing tissues and supporting the immune system. The diet encourages lean sources of protein, such as fish, poultry, legumes, and plant-based options like tofu and tempeh. Red meat, while not strictly forbidden, should be consumed in moderation, and processed meats should be avoided.

5. Herbs and Spices: Spices like turmeric, ginger, cinnamon, and garlic are potent anti-inflammatory agents. They not only add flavor to your meals but also contribute to the overall anti-inflammatory properties of your diet. Incorporate these spices regularly into your cooking.

6. Beverages: What you drink is just as important as what you eat. Water should be your primary beverage of choice, but green tea and herbal teas are also great options due to their antioxidant properties. Avoid sugary drinks and limit alcohol consumption, as they can contribute to inflammation.

Practical Steps to Get Started

Transitioning to an Anti-Inflammatory Diet doesn't have to be overwhelming. Here are some practical steps to help you get started:

1. Start Slow: If you're new to this way of eating, start by making small changes. For example, begin by adding more vegetables to your meals or swapping out refined grains for whole grains.

2. Plan Your Meals: Meal planning is key to staying on track. Take some time each week to plan your meals and snacks, focusing on incorporating anti-inflammatory foods. This will also help you avoid reaching for unhealthy options when you're short on time.

3. Shop Smart: When grocery shopping, stick to the perimeter of the store where fresh produce, lean meats, and whole grains are

typically located. Avoid the processed food aisles as much as possible.

4. Cook at Home: Preparing your own meals gives you control over the ingredients you use. Experiment with new recipes and try to cook at home as often as you can. This not only ensures that your meals are anti-inflammatory but also allows you to enjoy the process of cooking and eating.

5. Listen to Your Body: Pay attention to how different foods make you feel. Everyone's body reacts differently to certain foods, so it's important to listen to your body's signals. If a particular food makes you feel sluggish or bloated, it may be worth cutting back or eliminating it from your diet.

Overcoming Common Challenges

As with any dietary change, there can be challenges along the way. You might find it difficult to give up certain comfort foods, or you may struggle with meal planning and preparation. The key is to be patient with yourself and to view this as a long-term lifestyle change rather than a quick fix.

One common challenge is dealing with social situations where unhealthy foods are prevalent. In these cases, try to focus on the social aspect rather than the food. You can also bring a healthy dish to share, so you know there will be something you can eat. Another challenge might be cravings for sweets or processed snacks. To overcome this, try to keep healthy snacks on hand, such as nuts, fruits, or yogurt, and allow yourself the occasional treat in moderation.

Conclusion: Building a Strong Foundation

The Anti-Inflammatory Diet is more than just a way to eat—it's a commitment to nourishing your body in a way that supports overall health and well-being. By focusing on whole, nutrient-dense foods and making informed choices, you can reduce chronic inflammation and set the stage for a healthier future. This chapter has provided you with the foundational knowledge you need to get started. As you move forward in this book, you'll find a variety of recipes and tips to help you implement these principles in your daily life, making the Anti-Inflammatory Diet an enjoyable and sustainable part of your routine.

30-Day Meal Plan

DAYS	BREAKFAST	LUNCH	DINNER	SNACK/DESSERT
1	Golden Beet and Spinach Frittata 11	Chicken Salad with Green Apples and Grapes 25	Pan-Seared Haddock with Beets 37	Pecan and Date Snack Bars 57
2	Chia Pudding with Oats, Strawberries, and Kiwi 11	Basic Beans 19	Mediterranean Chicken Bake 28	Maple-Glazed Pears with Hazelnuts
3	Protein Scotch Eggs 16	General Tso's Chicken 24	Spiced Trout and Spinach 40	Cinnamon-Spiced Apple Chips 57
4	Nutmeg and Cherry Breakfast Quinoa 12	Balsamic-Glazed Chicken Thighs with Steamed Cauliflower 31	Seared Scallops with Greens 38	Mini Dark Chocolate-Almond Butter Cups 86
5	Tropical Coconut Delight 11	Indian Butter Chickpeas 19	Coconut-Braised Curried Chicken 25	Blueberry Parfait with Lemon-Coconut Cream 86
6	Ground Beef Breakfast Skillet 11	Spicy Chicken Drumsticks 29	Roasted Salmon and Asparagus 35	Smooth Chia Pudding 57
7	Meditteranean Vegetable Frittata 12	Turkey Sloppy Joes 26	Roasted Leg of Lamb 45	Pumpkin and Carrot Crackers 59
8	Allergen-Free Breakfast Cookies 12	Coconutty Brown Rice 20	Coconut-Braised Chicken 26	Coconut-Crusted Cod with Mango-Pineapple Salsa 41
9	German Chocolate Cake Protein Oats 14	Tuscan Chicken 27	Fish En Papillote 36	Lime Sorbet
10	Chia-Coconut Porridge 13	Red Lentil Curry with Cauliflower and Yams 21	Grilled Chipotle Shrimp Skewers	Roasted Apricots 58
11	Persian Herb Frittata 14	Apple-Turkey Burgers 30	Baked Salmon with Oregano Pistou 37	Mini Snack Muffins 60
12	Morning Millet 13	Chicken Skewers with Mint Sauce 24	Seared Honey-Garlic Scallops 41	Sweet and Spicy Pepitas 56
13	Maple-Tahini Oatmeal 13	Fricase De Pollo 32	Five-Spice Cod Broth 40	Coconut-Almond Bake 67
14	Garlicky Tofu Scramble 13	Country Captain's Chicken	Fish and Vegetable Casserole 40	Spiced Nuts 59
15	Chia Breakfast Pudding 13	Chicken Bone Broth 26	Salmon Baked with Leeks and Fennel 36	Parsley Chimichurri 95
16	Blueberry-Millet Breakfast Bake 14	Korean Beef Lettuce Wraps 47	Fennel Baked Salmon 42	Baked Apple and Walnut Chips 59

DAYS	BREAKFAST	LUNCH	DINNER	SNACK/DESSERT
17	Avocado Toast with Greens 12	Beefy Lentil and Tomato Stew 48	Shrimp with Cinnamon Sauce 43	Strawberry Jam Thumbprint Cookies 84
18	Lulu's Iced Coffee 12	Lentils with Tomatoes and Turmeric 20	Spicy Lime-Chicken "Tortilla-Less" Soup	Tangy Lemon Mousse 85
19	Avocado Boat Breakfast 17	Turkey Meatballs in a Muffin Tin 24	Sesame Mahi-Mahi and Fruit Salsa 40	Chocolate-Coconut Brownies 84
20	Buckwheat Granola 14	Black Bean Chili with Garlic and Tomatoes 20	Grilled Rib-Eye and Summer Succotash 47	Coconut Rice with Blueberries 84
21	Turkey-Cranberry Sausage with Sage 17	Sesame Chicken Stir-Fry 28	Sardine Donburi 35	Warm Cinnamon-Turmeric Almond Milk 86
22	Mini Fruit Muffins 16	Pork Chops with Gingered Applesauce 49	Herbed Lamb Fillets with Cauliflower Mash 50	Coconut-Blueberry Popsicles 85
23	Maple-Cinnamon Granola 16	Chicken Cacciatore	Sole with Vegetables in Foil Packets 42	Seedy Cookie Dough Bites 87
24	Vegan "Frittata"	Shrimp with Spicy Spinach 35	Roast Chicken with Lemon and White Beans 28	Honey Panna Cotta with Blackberry-Lime Sauce 86
25	Golden Coconut Pancakes 17	Mushroom Turkey Thighs 33	Pecan-Crusted Trout 42	Maple Carrot Cake 85
26	Santa Barbara Migas 15	Chicken and Broccoli Stir-Fry 27	Sweet Potato-Ground Turkey Hash 15	Chocolate Fondue 87
27	Sweet Potato-Ground Turkey Hash 15	Lemon Zoodles with Shrimp	Orange Chicken Skewers	Vanilla Ice Cream 88
28	Simple Steel-Cut Oats 15	Garlic-Mustard Steak 51	White Fish with Mushrooms 42	Cranberry Compote 87
29	Smoked Salmon Scrambled Eggs 15	Balsamic-Glazed Turkey Wings 30	Coconut Crab Cakes 37	Lemon Lavender and Strawberry Compote 85
30	Warming Gingerbread Oatmeal 15	Thai Coconut Soup 78	Salmon and Asparagus Skewers 39	Blueberry Crisp 87

Chapter
2

Breakfasts

Chapter 2 Breakfasts

Tropical Coconut Delight

Prep time: 2 minutes | Cook time: 10 minutes | Serves 4

- 2 cups wholemeal oats
- 1 tablespoon milled chia seeds
- 3 cups coconut milk
- 3 teaspoons raw cacao
- (optional)
- ½ teaspoon stevia
- 1 teaspoon coconut shavings
- 6 fresh cherries (optional)

1. In a pan mix the oats, cacao, stevia and coconut milk. 2. Heat on a medium heat and then simmer until the oats are fully cooked through (5 to 10 minutes). 3. Pour into your favorite breakfast bowl and sprinkle the coconut shavings, cherries, and milled chia seeds on top. 4. Serve and Enjoy!

Per Serving:
calories: 349 | fat: 27g | protein: 7g | carbs: 24g | fiber: 4g | sugar: 5g | sodium: 16mg

Ground Beef Breakfast Skillet

Prep time: 20 minutes | Cook time: 20 minutes | Serves 4

- 1 tablespoon olive oil
- 1 pound (454 g) lean ground beef
- 2 teaspoons bottled minced garlic
- 2 cups chopped cauliflower
- 1 cup diced carrots
- 1 zucchini, diced
- 2 scallions, white and green parts, chopped
- Sea salt, to taste
- Freshly ground black pepper, to taste
- 2 tablespoons chopped fresh parsley

1. Place a large skillet over medium-high heat and add the olive oil. 2. Add the ground beef and garlic. Sauté for about 8 minutes, or until cooked through. 3. Stir in the cauliflower, carrots, and zucchini. Sauté for about 10 minutes, or until tender. 4. Stir in the scallions and sauté for 1 minute more. 5. Season the mixture with sea salt and pepper. Serve topped with the parsley.

Per Serving:
calories: 214 | fat: 9g | protein: 26g | carbs: 7g | fiber: 2g | sugar: 2g | sodium: 111mg

Golden Beet and Spinach Frittata

Prep time: 15 minutes | Cook time: 5 to 7 hours | Serves 4 to 6

- 1 tablespoon extra-virgin olive oil
- 8 large eggs
- 1 cup packed fresh spinach leaves, chopped
- 1 cup diced peeled golden beets
- ½ medium onion, diced
- ¼ cup unsweetened almond milk
- ¾ teaspoon sea salt
- ½ teaspoon garlic powder
- ½ teaspoon dried basil leaves
- Freshly ground black pepper, to taste

1. Coat the slow cooker with the olive oil. 2. In a large bowl, combine the eggs, spinach, beets, onion, almond milk, salt, garlic powder, and basil, and season with pepper. Whisk together and pour the custard into the slow cooker. 3. Cover the cooker and set to low. Cook for 5 to 7 hours, or until the eggs are completely set, and serve.

Per Serving:
calories: 202 | fat: 14g | protein: 13g | carbs: 6g | fiber: 1g | sugar: 4g | sodium: 606mg

Chia Pudding with Oats, Strawberries, and Kiwi

Prep time: 25 minutes | Cook time: 0 minutes | Serves 2

- 2 cups unsweetened almond milk
- ⅓ cup chia seeds
- ¼ cup maple syrup
- ½ teaspoon vanilla extract
- ½ cup toasted oats
- 4 large strawberries, sliced
- 1 kiwi, peeled and sliced

1. In a quart-size jar with a tight-fitting lid, combine the milk, chia seeds, maple syrup, and vanilla. Cover and shake well, then set aside for at least 15 minutes for the pudding to thicken. (This can even be done the night before and refrigerated overnight.) 2. Divide the pudding between two serving dishes, top with the toasted oats, strawberries, and kiwi, and serve.

Per Serving:
calories: 360 | fat: 11g | protein: 8g | carbs: 60g | fiber: 12g | sugar: 31g | sodium: 190mg

Nutmeg and Cherry Breakfast Quinoa

Prep time: 2 minutes | Cook time: 20 minutes | Serves

- ½ cup quinoa
- ½ cup unsweetened fresh cherries
- 1 cup water
- ¼ teaspoon ground nutmeg
- ½ teaspoon vanilla extract

1. Get a pan and combine all of the ingredients, cooking over medium to high heat until boiling. 2. Once boiling, cover and simmer for 15 minutes or until the quinoa is soft and the liquid has been absorbed. 3. Pour into serving bowls and enjoy.

Per Serving:
calories: 162 | fat: 3g | protein: 6g | carbs: 28g | fiber: 3g | sugar: 0g | sodium: 5mg

Lulu's Iced Coffee

Prep time: 5 minutes | Cook time: 0 minutes | Serves 2

- 2 cups cold brewed coffee
- ½ cup unsweetened almond milk
- ¼ teaspoon vanilla extract
- 1 cup ice

1. Combine the coffee, milk, and vanilla in a pitcher. 2. Divide the ice between two tall glasses. 3. Pour the iced coffee over the ice and serve.

Per Serving:
calories: 10 | fat: 1g | protein: 1g | carbs: 0g | fiber: 0g | sugar: 0g | sodium: 50mg

Allergen-Free Breakfast Cookies

Prep time: 10 minutes | Cook time: 12 minutes | Makes 10 cookies

- 3 very ripe bananas
- ½ cup almond butter
- 2 tablespoons raw honey
- 1 tablespoon coconut oil, melted
- 2 teaspoons vanilla extract
- 1 teaspoon baking powder
- 1 teaspoon ground cinnamon
- ½ teaspoon salt
- 2½ cups rolled oats
- ¾ cup dairy-free semi-sweet chocolate chips (optional)

1. Preheat the oven to 350ºF (180ºC). 2. Line a large baking sheet with parchment paper. 3. In a large bowl, mash the bananas with a potato masher or a fork. 4. Stir in the almond butter, honey, coconut oil, and vanilla until well mixed. 5. Sprinkle in the baking powder, cinnamon, and salt. Add the oats and chocolate chips (if using) in batches, stirring after each addition until all ingredients are incorporated. 6. Place heaping tablespoons of dough onto the prepared sheet, leaving at least 1 inch between dough balls. Bake for 10 to 12 minutes. 7. Let the cookies rest in the pan for 5 minutes, and then transfer to a cooling rack. These cookies will keep refrigerated in a sealed container for several days.

Per Serving:
calories: 306 | fat: 16g | protein: 7g | carbs: 39g | fiber: 5g | sugar: 8g | sodium: 119mg

Avocado Toast with Greens

Prep time: 5 minutes | Cook time: 4 minutes | Serves 1

- 2 slices gluten-free bread
- 1 ripe avocado, halved and pitted
- 1½ tablespoons freshly squeezed lemon juice, plus
- additional as needed
- ⅛ teaspoon salt, plus additional as needed
- 2 cups lightly packed spinach leaves

1. Toast the bread. 2. Fill a medium pot with 2 inches of water and insert a steamer basket. Bring the water to a boil over high heat. 3. Into a small bowl, scoop the avocado flesh from the peel with a spoon. 4. Add the lemon juice and salt. Mash together with a fork. Taste, and adjust the seasoning with more lemon juice or salt, if necessary. 5. When the water boils, add the spinach to the steamer basket. Cover and steam for 3 to 4 minutes, or until wilted. 6. Divide the avocado mixture between the two pieces of toast. Top each with half of the wilted greens.

Per Serving:
calories: 589 | fat: 44g | protein: 6g | carbs:46 g | fiber: 2g | sugar: 18g | sodium: 219mg

Meditteranean Vegetable Frittata

Prep time: 10 minutes | Cook time: 25 minutes | Serves 2

- 1 tablespoon coconut or extra virgin olive oil
- 4 free range eggs
- 1 sweet potato, peeled and
- 1 peeled and sliced zucchini
- 2 teaspoons parsley
- 1 teaspoon cracked black pepper

1. Preheat broiler on a medium heat. 2. Heat the oil in a skillet under the broiler until hot. 3. Spread the potato slices across the skillet and cooking for 8 to 10 minutes or until soft. 4. Add the zucchini to the skillet and cook for a further 5 minutes. 5. Meanwhile, whisk the eggs and parsley in a separate bowl, and season with pepper before pouring mixture over the veggies in the skillet. 6. Cook for 10 minutes on a low heat until golden. 7. Remove and turn over onto a plate or serving board.

Per Serving:
calories: 214 | fat: 11g | protein: 12g | carbs: 15g | fiber: 2g | sugar: 3g | sodium: 222mg

Chia-Coconut Porridge

Prep time: 5 minutes | Cook time: 0 minutes | Serves 4

- ¾ cup water
- ¾ cup unsweetened almond milk
- 1 teaspoon pure vanilla extract
- ¼ cup chia seeds
- ¼ cup unsweetened shredded coconut
- 2 tablespoons raw honey
- ½ cup sliced fresh strawberries

1. In a medium bowl, whisk the water, almond milk, and vanilla until well blended. 2. Stir in the chia seeds, cover the bowl, and refrigerate it for a minimum of 30 minutes and up to overnight. 3. Stir the coconut and honey into the chilled porridge. Spoon the porridge into four bowls. 4. Serve topped with the strawberries.

Per Serving:

calories: 124 | fat: 7g | protein: 2g | carbs: 15g | fiber: 4g | sugar: 10g | sodium: 22mg

Morning Millet

Prep time: 15 minutes | Cook time: 7 to 8 hours | Serves 4

- 1 cup millet
- 2 cups water
- 2 cups full-fat coconut milk
- ½ teaspoon sea salt
- ½ teaspoon ground cinnamon
- ½ teaspoon ground ginger
- ¼ teaspoon vanilla extract
- ½ cup fresh blueberries

1. In your slow cooker, combine the millet, water, coconut milk, salt, cinnamon, ginger, and vanilla. Stir well. 2. Cover the cooker and set to low. Cook for 7 to 8 hours. 3. Stir in the blueberries to warm at the end and serve.

Per Serving:

calories: 276 | fat: 22g | protein: 3g | carbs: 18g | fiber: 1g | sugar: 3g | sodium: 323mg

Maple-Tahini Oatmeal

Prep time: 5 minutes | Cook time: 15 minutes | Serves 2

- 2 cups water
- 1 cup gluten-free rolled oats
- ⅛ teaspoon salt
- ⅓ cup tahini
- 2 tablespoons maple syrup, divided

1. In a medium pot set over medium-high heat, stir together the water, oats, and salt. Bring to a boil. Reduce the heat to low and cover. Simmer for about 10 minutes, stirring occasionally, and checking for tenderness. 2. Stir in the tahini, letting it melt into

the oatmeal. Cook for 3 to 4 minutes more, or until the oatmeal is cooked through. 3. Divide the oatmeal between two bowls. Drizzle each with 1 tablespoon of maple syrup.

Per Serving:

calories: 500 | fat: 28g | protein: 15g | carbs: 55g | fiber: 12g | sugar: 9g | sodium: 131mg

Garlicky Tofu Scramble

Prep time: 10 minutes | Cook time: 8 minutes | Serves 4

- 3 tablespoons fresh-pressed coconut oil or extra-virgin olive oil
- 3 green onions, white and green parts, thinly sliced
- 3 garlic cloves, peeled and thinly sliced
- 1 (15 ounces / 425 g) package firm tofu, thoroughly drained and diced into ½-inch pieces
- Kosher salt, to taste
- 1 cup mung bean sprouts
- 2 tablespoons chopped mint
- 2 tablespoons chopped parsley
- 1 tablespoon lime juice, plus more as needed
- Fish sauce for serving (optional)
- Cooked brown rice for serving (optional)

1. Place the coconut oil, white parts of the green onions, and garlic in a cold sauté pan. Turn the heat to low. As the aromatics warm, stir occasionally until they are lightly browned and softened, about 4 minutes. 2. Add the tofu and a pinch of salt and turn the heat to medium. Cook, stirring occasionally, until the tofu is well coated with the oil and warmed, about 3 minutes. Stir in the mung bean sprouts and warm for 1 minute. Add the green parts of the green onions and the mint, parsley, and lime juice. Stir to combine. Taste, adding fish sauce or additional lime juice, if desired. 3. Serve.

Per Serving:

calories: 393 | fat: 31g | protein: 19g | carbs: 14g | fiber: 5g | sugar: 4g | sodium: 312mg

Chia Breakfast Pudding

Prep time: 5 minutes | Cook time: 0 minutes | Serves 4

- ¾ cup chia seeds
- ½ cup hemp seeds
- 2¼ cups coconut milk
- ½ cup dried cranberries
- ¼ cup maple syrup

1. In a medium bowl, stir together the chia seeds, hemp seeds, coconut milk, cranberries, and maple syrup, ensuring that the chia is completely mixed with the milk. 2. Cover the bowl and refrigerate overnight. 3. In the morning, stir and serve.

Per Serving:

calories: 483 | fat: 41g | protein: 9g | carbs: 25g | fiber: 6g | sugar: 17g | sodium: 22mg

German Chocolate Cake Protein Oats

Prep time: 15 minutes | Cook time: 6 to 8 hours | Serves 4 to 6

- 1 tablespoon coconut oil
- 2 cups rolled oats
- 2½ cups water
- 2 cups full-fat coconut milk
- ¼ cup unsweetened cacao powder
- 2 tablespoons collagen peptides
- ¼ teaspoon sea salt
- 2 tablespoons pecans
- 2 tablespoons unsweetened shredded coconu

1. Coat the slow cooker with the coconut oil. 2. In your slow cooker, combine the oats, water, coconut milk, cacao powder, collagen peptides, and salt. Stir to combine. 3. Cover the cooker and set to low. Cook for 6 to 8 hours. 4. Sprinkle the pecans and coconut on top and serve.

Per Serving:
calories: 457 | fat: 33g | protein: 10g | carbs: 36g | fiber: 7g | sugar: 3g | sodium: 191mg

Persian Herb Frittata

Prep time: 10 minutes | Cook time: 20 minutes | Makes 1 frittata

- 4 tablespoons avocado oil or olive oil, divided
- 1 large onion, diced
- 2 cloves garlic, minced
- 1 green onion, white part only, minced
- 6 large eggs
- 1 teaspoon baking powder
- 1 teaspoon dried dill weed
- 1 teaspoon turmeric powder
- ½ teaspoon fine Himalayan salt
- ½ teaspoon ginger powder
- 1 cup minced fresh cilantro
- 1 cup minced fresh parsley
- ½ cup minced fresh basil

1. Heat an 8-inch skillet over medium or medium-low heat. If your stove runs hot, adjust the temperature; you don't want the bottom of the frittata to burn. When the skillet is hot, pour in 2 tablespoons of the avocado oil. Add the onions, garlic, and green onions and cook, stirring often, for 8 minutes, or until tender, translucent, and aromatic. Remove the onion mix from the skillet and set aside to cool. Put the skillet back on the stove over medium heat. 2. In a large bowl, whisk together the eggs, baking powder, seasonings, and fresh herbs. Add the cooled onion mix. 3. Turn on the broiler and set an oven rack just below it. 4. Drizzle the remaining 2 tablespoons of avocado oil into the skillet and pour in the egg mixture. Cover with a tight-fitting lid. Cook for 7 minutes, or until the edges of the frittata begin to separate from the skillet and the frittata is almost set but still wet in the center. Then remove the lid and place the skillet under the broiler for 1 to 2 minutes. Watch it carefully; you only need to broil it until the center is just set. 5.

Remove the frittata from the oven. Run a spatula around the edge of the frittata and carefully shake it out of the skillet and onto a cutting board. Cut into four pieces, serve, and share. 6. Once the frittata has cooled to room temperature, you can store it in an airtight container in the refrigerator for up to 5 days. Enjoy the leftovers cold or gently warmed up in a 300°F (150°C) oven for 5 minutes.

Per Serving:
calories: 365 | fat: 22g | protein: 11g | carbs: 8g | fiber: 2g | sugar: 2g | sodium: 278mg

Blueberry-Millet Breakfast Bake

Prep time: 10 minutes | Cook time: 55 minutes | Serves 8

- 2 cups millet, soaked in water overnight
- 2 cups fresh or frozen blueberries
- 1¾ cups unsweetened applesauce
- ⅓ cup melted coconut oil
- 2 teaspoons grated fresh ginger
- 1½ teaspoons ground cinnamon

1. Preheat the oven to 350°F (180°C). 2. In a fine-mesh sieve, drain and rinse the millet for 1 to 2 minutes. Transfer to a large bowl. 3. Gently fold in the blueberries, applesauce, coconut oil, ginger, and cinnamon. 4. Pour the mixture into a 9-by-9-inch casserole dish. Cover with aluminum foil. 5. Place the dish in the preheated oven and bake for 40 minutes. Remove the foil and bake for 10 to 15 minutes more, or until lightly crisp on top.

Per Serving:
calories: 323 | fat: 13g | protein: 6g | carbs: 48g | fiber: 6g | sugar: 9g | sodium: 4mg

Buckwheat Granola

Prep time: 15 minutes | Cook time: 10 minutes | Serves 6

- 3 cups buckwheat groats
- ½ cup coarsely chopped pecans
- ⅓ cup extra-virgin olive oil
- ¼ cup maple syrup
- 1 teaspoon vanilla extract
- ¼ teaspoon salt

1. Preheat the oven to 350°F (180°C). 2. In a medium bowl, combine the buckwheat, pecans, oil, maple syrup, vanilla, and salt. Mix well to evenly coat the buckwheat with the oil and maple syrup. 3. Spread the mixture on a rimmed baking sheet and place in the oven. 4. After 5 minutes, remove the baking sheet from the oven. Using a spatula, stir the mixture around so it will bake evenly. Return to the oven and bake until the granola is lightly toasted, about 5 minutes more. 5. Allow to cool completely before serving.

Per Serving:
calories: 490 | fat: 21g | protein: 11g | carbs: 71g | fiber: 9g | sugar: 8g | sodium: 110mg

Sweet Potato-Ground Turkey Hash

Prep time: 10 minutes | Cook time: 26 minutes | Serves 4

- 1½ pounds (680 g) extra-lean ground turkey
- 1 sweet onion, chopped, or about 1 cup precut packaged onion
- 2 teaspoons bottled minced garlic
- 1 teaspoon ground ginger
- 2 pounds (907 g) sweet potatoes, peeled, cooked, and diced
- Pinch sea salt
- Pinch freshly ground black pepper
- Pinch ground cloves
- 1 cup chopped kale

1. In a large skillet over medium-high heat, sauté the turkey for about 10 minutes, or until it is cooked through. 2. Add the onion, garlic, and ginger. Sauté for 3 minutes. 3. Add the sweet potatoes, sea salt, pepper, and cloves. Reduce the heat to medium. Sauté for about 10 minutes, stirring until the sweet potato is heated through. 4. Stir in the kale. Cook for about 3 minutes, stirring until it has wilted. 5. Divide the hash among four bowls and serve.

Per Serving:
calories: 467 | fat: 14g | protein: 34g | carbs: 50g | fiber: 8g | sugar: 7g | sodium: 153mg

Simple Steel-Cut Oats

Prep time: 15 minutes | Cook time: 6 to 8 hours | Serves 4 to 6

- 1 tablespoon coconut oil
- 4 cups boiling water
- ½ teaspoon sea salt
- 1 cup steel-cut oats

1. Coat the slow cooker with the coconut oil. 2. In your slow cooker, combine the boiling water, salt, and oats. 3. Cover the cooker and set to warm (or low if there is no warm setting). Cook for 6 to 8 hours and serve.

Per Serving:
calories: 172 | fat: 6g | protein: 6g | carbs: 27g | fiber: 4g | sugar: 0g | sodium: 291mg

Smoked Salmon Scrambled Eggs

Prep time: 5 minutes | Cook time: 8 minutes | Serves 4

- 2 tablespoons extra-virgin olive oil
- 6 ounces (170 g) smoked salmon, flaked
- 8 eggs, beaten
- ¼ teaspoon freshly ground black pepper

1. In a large nonstick skillet over medium-high heat, heat the olive oil until it shimmers. 2. Add the salmon and cook for 3 minutes, stirring. 3. In a medium bowl, whisk the eggs and pepper. Add them to the skillet and cook for about 5 minutes, stirring gently, until done.

Per Serving:
calories: 236 | fat: 18g | protein: 19g | carbs: 0g | fiber: 0g | sugar: 0g | sodium: 411mg

Santa Barbara Migas

Prep time: 15 minutes | Cook time: 10 minutes | Serves 4

- 1 tablespoon avocado oil
- ½ onion, diced
- 8 eggs
- ¾ teaspoon salt
- ½ teaspoon garlic powder
- ½ teaspoon freshly ground black pepper
- ½ cup plantain chips, crushed
- ½ cup salsa
- 2 avocados, sliced
- Splash of freshly squeezed lime juice
- Fresh cilantro leaves, for garnish (optional)

1. In a small skillet over medium heat, add the avocado oil and sauté the onion until translucent, about 5 minutes 2. In a medium bowl, whisk the eggs, salt, garlic powder, and pepper. Add to the skillet, and stir until cooked to your desired doneness, 2 to 3 minutes. 3. Add the plantain chips to the egg mixture. Stir well and remove the skillet from the heat. 4. Top with the salsa and avocado. Sprinkle with the lime juice. Garnish with cilantro (if using) and serve immediately.

Per Serving:
calories: 374 | fat: 27g | protein: 14g | carbs: 22g | fiber: 6g | sugar: 3g | sodium: 508mg

Warming Gingerbread Oatmeal

Prep time: 2 minutes | Cook time: 8 minutes | Serves 4

- 3 cups water
- 2 cups steel cut or wholemeal oats
- 1 tablespoon ground cinnamon
- 1 teaspoon ground cloves
- ¼ teaspoon fresh ginger,
- grated
- ¼ teaspoon ground allspice
- ¼ teaspoon nutmeg
- ¼ teaspoon cardamom
- 1 teaspoon raw honey to taste (optional)

1. Mix the oats and water in a saucepan and gently heat on a medium heat for 5 to 8 minutes or until cooked through. 2. Whilst cooking stir in the spices. 3. When cooked and hot through, pour into your bowl. 4. Drizzle honey over the top if desired.

Per Serving:
calories: 315 | fat: 5g | protein: 13g | carbs: 55g | fiber: 9g | sugar: 2g | sodium: 6mg

Vegan "Frittata"

- 1½ cups garbanzo bean flour
- 1 teaspoon salt
- 1 teaspoon ground turmeric
- ½ teaspoon ground cumin
- 1 teaspoon chopped fresh sage
- 1½ cups water
- 2 tablespoons extra-virgin olive oil
- 1 zucchini, sliced
- 2 scallions, sliced

1. Preheat the oven to 350ºF (180ºC). 2. In a medium bowl, whisk together the garbanzo bean flour, salt, turmeric, cumin, and sage. 3. Slowly add the water, stirring constantly to prevent the batter from getting lumpy. Set aside. 4. In an oven-safe skillet, heat the oil over high heat. Sauté the zucchini until softened, 2 to 3 minutes. Stir in the scallions, then spoon the batter over the vegetables. 5. Place the skillet in the oven and bake until firm when jiggled slightly, 20 to 25 minutes. 6. Serve warm or at room temperature.

Per Serving:
calories: 140 | fat: 6g | protein: 6g | carbs: 15g | fiber: 3g | sugar: 3g | sodium: 410mg

Mini Fruit Muffins

- 1 cup almond meal
- 3 teaspoons stevia
- 2 tablespoons chopped crystalized ginger
- 1 tablespoon ground linseed meal
- ½ cup buckwheat flour
- ¼ cup brown rice flour
- 2 teaspoons gluten-free baking powder
- ½ teaspoon ground cinnamon
- 1 cup sliced rhubarb
- 1 apple, peeled and diced
- ⅓ cup almond milk
- ¼ cup extra virgin olive oil
- 1 free range egg
- 1 teaspoon vanilla extract

1. Preheat oven to 350ºF (180ºC). Line muffin tins with olive oil using a baking brush or kitchen towel. Put the almond meal, stevia, ginger, and the linseed into a bowl. 2. Sieve the flours over the mix along with the baking powder and spices and stir. Add the rhubarb and the apple into the flour mixture. 3. In a separate bowl, beat the egg, vanilla, milk, and oil until combined. Fold the wet ingredients into the dry ingredients until smooth. 4. Pour batter into the muffin tin, leaving a 1 cm gap at the top so that the muffin can rise and then bake for 20 minutes or until risen and golden. Remove and place on a cooling rack before serving.

Per Serving:
calories: 367 | fat: 16g | protein: 9g | carbs: 52g | fiber: 7g | sugar: 7g | sodium: 37mg

Maple-Cinnamon Granola

- 4 cups gluten-free rolled oats
- 1½ cups sunflower seeds
- ½ cup maple syrup
- ½ cup coconut oil
- 1½ teaspoons ground cinnamon

1. Preheat the oven to 325ºF (165ºC). 2. Line two baking sheets with parchment paper. 3. In a large bowl, stir together the oats, sunflower seeds, maple syrup, coconut oil, and cinnamon. Stir well so the oats and seeds are evenly coated with the syrup, oil, and cinnamon. 4. Divide the granola mixture evenly between the two sheets. 5. Place the sheets in the preheated oven and bake for 35 to 40 minutes, stirring every 10 minutes so everything browns evenly. 6. Cool completely, then store in large glass jars with tight-fitting lids.

Per Serving:
calories: 400 | fat: 22g | protein: 9g | carbs: 47g | fiber: 6g | sugar: 12g | sodium: 3mg

Protein Scotch Eggs

- 16 ounces (454 g) lean ground turkey
- ½ teaspoon black pepper
- ½ teaspoon nutmeg
- ½ teaspoon cinnamon
- ½ teaspoon cloves
- ½ teaspoon dried tarragon
- ½ cup fresh parsley, finely chopped
- ½ tablespoon dried chives
- 1 clove garlic, finely chopped
- 4 free range eggs, boiled and peeled

1. Preheat the oven to 375ºF (190ºC). 2. Cover a baking sheet with parchment paper. 3. Combine the turkey with the cinnamon, nutmeg, pepper, cloves, tarragon, chives, parsley and garlic in a mixing bowl and mix with your hands until thoroughly mixed. 4. Divide the mixture into 4 circular shapes with the palms of your hands. Flatten each one into a pancake shape using the backs of your hands or a rolling pin. 5. Wrap the meat pancake around 1 egg, until it's covered. (you can moisten the meat with water first to help prevent it from sticking to your hands). 6. Bake in the oven for 25 minutes or until brown and crisp. Check the meat is cooked through with a knife before serving.

Per Serving:
calories: 255 | fat: 15g | protein: 28g | carbs: 2g | fiber: 1g | sugar: 1g | sodium: 145mg

Golden Coconut Pancakes

Prep time: 10 minutes | Cook time: 10 minutes | Serves 4

- ½ cup almond flour
- ¼ cup coconut flour
- 1 teaspoon baking soda
- 3 eggs, beaten
- 2 bananas, mashed
- 1 teaspoon pure vanilla extract
- 1 tablespoon coconut oil
- Pure maple syrup, for serving (optional)
- Fresh fruit, for serving (optional)

1. In a medium bowl, stir together the almond flour, coconut flour, and baking soda until well mixed. 2. Make a well in the center and add the eggs, bananas, and vanilla. Beat together until well blended. 3. Place a large skillet over medium-high heat and add the coconut oil. 4. For each pancake, pour ¼ cup of batter into the skillet, four per batch. Cook for about 3 minutes, or until the bottom is golden and the bubbles on the surface burst. Flip and cook for about 2 minutes more until golden and cooked through. Transfer to a plate and repeat with any remaining batter. 5. Serve with a drizzle of maple syrup or top with fresh fruit (if using).

Per Serving:
calories: 218 | fat: 15g | protein: 8g | carbs: 17g | fiber: 4g | sugar: 8g | sodium: 78mg

Avocado Boat Breakfast

Prep time: 2 minutes | Cook time: 5 minutes | Serves 2

- 1 ripe avocado
- 2 free range eggs
- 1 tablespoon white wine vinegar

1. Place a large pan of water on a high heat and boil. 2. Once boiling add white wine vinegar (don't worry if you don't have it, it just helps with the poaching). 3. Lower the heat to a simmer and crack the eggs in. 4. Stir the water ever now and then around the eggs to keep them moving and cook for 2 minutes for a very runny yolk; 2 to 4 minutes for a soft to firm yolk and 5 for a hard yolk. 5. Whilst cooking, prepare your avocado by cutting through to the stone lengthways around the whole of the fruit. 6. Use your palms on each side to twist the avocado and it should come away into 2 halves. Using your knife, carefully wedge it into the stone and pull to remove the stone. Alternatively, cut around the stone with the knife and use the sharp end to coax it out. 7. Use your avocado halves as a dish for the eggs and serve.

Per Serving:
calories: 292 | fat: 24g | protein: 11g | carbs: 10g | fiber: 7g | sugar: 1g | sodium: 110mg

Turkey-Cranberry Sausage with Sage

Prep time: 20 minutes | Cook time: 30 minutes | Serves 6

- 2 teaspoons organic canola oil, plus 2 tablespoons
- ½ cup finely chopped yellow onion
- 1½ pounds (680 g) ground turkey
- ¾ cup dried berries, such as cranberries, blueberries, or cherries
- ¼ cup flat-leaf parsley leaves, chopped
- 1 egg, lightly beaten
- 1 tablespoon minced fresh sage
- 1 tablespoon thyme leaves
- 1 teaspoon grated lemon zest
- 1 teaspoon kosher salt
- ½ teaspoon ground black pepper
- ½ teaspoon ground allspice

1. In a small skillet over medium heat, warm the 2 teaspoons canola oil. Add the onion and cook, stirring frequently, until soft, 6 to 8 minutes. Let cool. 2. In a large bowl, combine cooked onion, ground turkey, dried berries, parsley, egg, sage, thyme, lemon zest, salt, pepper, and allspice. Stir gently to combine, being careful not to overmix. Cover and refrigerate the mixture for at least 1 hour, or up to overnight. 3. Shape the mixture into 12 patties, each about 2½ inch wide and ½ inch thick. 4. In a large nonstick skillet over medium-low heat, warm the 2 tablespoons canola oil. Arrange the patties in the pan so they are not touching (you will probably have to do two batches) and cook until they are browned and no longer pink in the center, 3 to 4 minutes per side. Serve immediately, or keep warm in a 200ºF (93ºC) oven for up to 30 minutes.

Per Serving:
calories: 262 | fat: 13g | protein: 24g | carbs: 14g | fiber: 1g | sugar: 7g | sodium: 159mg

Chapter 3

Beans and Grains

Chapter 3 Beans and Grains

Brown Rice with Bell Peppers

Prep time: 10 minutes | Cook time: 10 minutes | Serves 4

- 2 tablespoons extra-virgin olive oil
- 1 red bell pepper, chopped
- 1 green bell pepper, chopped
- 1 onion, chopped
- 2 cups cooked brown rice
- 2 tablespoons low-sodium soy sauce

1. In a large nonstick skillet over medium-high heat, heat the olive oil until it shimmers. 2. Add the red and green bell peppers and onion. Cook for about 7 minutes, stirring frequently, until the vegetables start to brown. 3. Add the rice and the soy sauce. Cook for about 3 minutes, stirring constantly, until the rice warms through.

Per Serving:
calories: 266 | fat: 8g | protein: 5g | carbs: 44g | fiber: 3g | sugar: 4g | sodium: 455mg

Indian Butter Chickpeas

Prep time: 15 minutes | Cook time: 6 to 8 hours | Serves 4 to 6

- 1 tablespoon coconut oil
- 1 medium onion, diced
- 1 pound (454 g) dried chickpeas, soaked in water overnight, drained, and rinsed
- 2 cups full-fat coconut milk
- 1 (14½-ounce / 411-g) can crushed tomatoes
- 2 tablespoons almond butter
- 2 tablespoons curry powder
- 1½ teaspoons garlic powder
- 1 teaspoon ground ginger
- ½ teaspoon sea salt
- ½ teaspoon ground cumin
- ½ teaspoon chili powder

1. Coat the slow cooker with coconut oil. 2. Layer the onion along the bottom of the slow cooker. 3. Add the chickpeas, coconut milk, tomatoes, almond butter, curry powder, garlic powder, ginger, salt, cumin, and chili powder. Gently stir to ensure the spices are mixed into the liquid. 4. Cover the cooker and set to low. Cook for 6 to 8 hours, until the chickpeas are soft, and serve.

Per Serving:
calories: 720 | fat: 30g | protein: 27g | carbs: 86g | fiber: 19g | sugar: 9g | sodium: 440mg

Basic Beans

Prep time: 30 minutes | Cook time: 7 to 8 hours | Makes 6 cups

- 1 pound (454 g) dried beans, any kind
- Water

1. Rinse the beans, and pick out any broken ones or possible rocks or dirt particles. 2. Put the beans in a large bowl or in your slow cooker and cover with water. Let soak for a minimum of 8 hours, or overnight, at room temperature. 3. Drain and rinse the beans well. Put them in your slow cooker and cover with 2 inches of fresh water. 4. Cover the cooker and set to low. Cook for 7 to 8 hours, or until soft and cooked through. Drain and serve

Per Serving:
calories: 259 | fat: 0g | protein: 15g | carbs: 48g | fiber: 19g | sugar: 2g | sodium: 0mg

Mediterranean Quinoa with Peperoncini

Prep time: 15 minutes | Cook time: 6 to 8 hours | Serves 4 to 6

- 1½ cups quinoa, rinsed well
- 3 cups vegetable broth
- ½ teaspoon sea salt
- ½ teaspoon garlic powder
- ¼ teaspoon dried oregano
- ¼ teaspoon dried basil leaves
- Freshly ground black
- pepper, to taste
- 3 cups arugula
- ½ cup diced tomatoes
- ⅓ cup sliced peperoncini
- ¼ cup freshly squeezed lemon juice
- 3 tablespoons extra-virgin olive oil

1. In your slow cooker, combine the quinoa, broth, salt, garlic powder, oregano, and basil, and season with pepper. 2. Cover the cooker and set to low. Cook for 6 to 8 hours. 3. In a large bowl, toss together the arugula, tomatoes, peperoncini, lemon juice, and olive oil. 4. When the quinoa is done, add it to the arugula salad, mix well, and serve.

Per Serving:
calories: 359 | fat: 14g | protein: 10g | carbs: 50g | fiber: 6g | sugar: 2g | sodium: 789mg

Coconutty Brown Rice

Prep time: 15 minutes | Cook time: 3 hours | Serves 4 to 6

- 2 cups brown rice, soaked in water overnight, drained, and rinsed
- 3 cups water
- 1½ cups full-fat coconut milk
- 1 teaspoon sea salt
- ½ teaspoon ground ginger
- Freshly ground black pepper, to taste

1. In your slow cooker, combine the rice, water, coconut milk, salt, and ginger. Season with pepper and stir to incorporate the spices. 2. Cover the cooker and set to high. Cook for 3 hours and serve.

Per Serving:
calories: 479 | fat: 19g | protein: 9g | carbs: 73g | fiber: 4g | sugar: 1g | sodium: 604mg

Herbed Harvest Rice

Prep time: 15 minutes | Cook time: 3 hours | Serves 4 to 6

- 2 cups brown rice, soaked in water overnight, drained, and rinsed
- ½ small onion, chopped
- 4 cups vegetable broth
- 2 tablespoons extra-virgin olive oil
- ½ teaspoon dried thyme leaves
- ½ teaspoon garlic powder
- ½ cup cooked sliced mushrooms
- ½ cup dried cranberries
- ½ cup toasted pecans

1. In your slow cooker, combine the rice, onion, broth, olive oil, thyme, and garlic powder. Stir well. 2. Cover the cooker and set to high. Cook for 3 hours. 3. Stir in the mushrooms, cranberries, and pecans, and serve.

Per Serving:
calories: 546 | fat: 20g | protein: 10g | carbs: 88g | fiber: 7g | sugar: 14g | sodium: 607mg

Quinoa Florentine

Prep time: 5 minutes | Cook time: 25 minutes | Serves 4

- 2 tablespoons extra-virgin olive oil
- 1 onion, chopped
- 3 cups fresh baby spinach
- 3 garlic cloves, minced
- 2 cups quinoa, rinsed well
- 4 cups no-salt-added vegetable broth
- ½ teaspoon sea salt
- ⅛ teaspoon freshly ground black pepper

1. In a large pot over medium-high heat, heat the olive oil until it shimmers. 2. Add the onion and spinach. Cook for 3 minutes, stirring occasionally. 3. Add the garlic and cook for 30 seconds, stirring constantly. 4. Stir in the quinoa, vegetable broth, salt, and pepper. Bring to a boil and reduce the heat to low. Cover and simmer for 15 to 20 minutes, until the liquid is absorbed. Fluff with a fork.

Per Serving:
calories: 403 | fat:12 g | protein: 13g | carbs: 62g | fiber: 7g | sugar: 2g | sodium: 278mg

Lentils with Tomatoes and Turmeric

Prep time: 10 minutes | Cook time: 10 minutes | Serves 4

- 2 tablespoons extra-virgin olive oil, plus extra for garnish
- 1 onion, finely chopped
- 1 tablespoon ground turmeric
- 1 teaspoon garlic powder
- 1 (14 ounces / 397 g) can lentils, drained
- 1 (14 ounces / 397 g) can chopped tomatoes, drained
- ½ teaspoon sea salt
- ¼ teaspoon freshly ground black pepper

1. In a large pot over medium-high heat, heat the olive oil until it shimmers. 2. Add the onion and turmeric, and cook for about 5 minutes, stirring occasionally, until soft. 3. Add the garlic powder, lentils, tomatoes, salt, and pepper. Cook for 5 minutes, stirring occasionally. Serve garnished with additional olive oil, if desired

Per Serving:
calories: 248 | fat: 8g | protein: 12g | carbs: 34g | fiber: 15g | sugar: 5g | sodium: 243mg

Black Bean Chili with Garlic and Tomatoes

Prep time: 10 minutes | Cook time: 20 minutes | Serves 4

- 2 tablespoons extra-virgin olive oil
- 1 onion, chopped
- 2 (28 ounces / 794 g) cans chopped tomatoes, undrained
- 2 (14 ounces / 397 g) cans black beans, drained
- 1 tablespoon chili powder
- 1 teaspoon garlic powder
- ½ teaspoon sea salt

1. In a large pot over medium-high, heat the olive oil until it shimmers. 2. Add the onion. Cook for about 5 minutes, stirring occasionally, until soft. 3. Stir in the tomatoes, black beans, chili powder, garlic powder, and salt. Bring to a simmer. Reduce the heat to medium and cook for 15 minutes, stirring occasionally.

Per Serving:
calories: 481 | fat: 10g | protein: 25g | carbs: 60g | fiber: 21g | sugar: 14g | sodium: 278mg

Spanish Rice

- 2 cups white rice
- 2 cups vegetable broth
- 2 tablespoons extra-virgin olive oil
- 1 (14½-ounce / 411-g) can crushed tomatoes
- 1 (4-ounce / 113-g) can Hatch green chiles
- ½ medium onion, diced
- 1 teaspoon sea salt
- ½ teaspoon ground cumin
- ½ teaspoon garlic powder
- ½ teaspoon chili powder
- ½ teaspoon dried oregano
- Freshly ground black pepper, to taste

1. In your slow cooker, combine the rice, broth, olive oil, tomatoes, chiles, onion, salt, cumin, garlic powder, chili powder, and oregano, and season with pepper. 2. Cover the cooker and set to low. Cook for 5 to 6 hours, fluff, and serve.

Per Serving:

calories: 406 | fat: 7g | protein: 8g | carbs: 79g | fiber: 2g | sugar: 5g | sodium: 1058mg

Red Lentil Curry with Cauliflower and Yams

- 2 tablespoons organic canola oil
- 1 yellow onion, diced
- 2 teaspoons grated fresh ginger
- 2 garlic cloves, minced
- 1 tablespoon red curry paste (optional if nightshade-sensitive)
- 1 teaspoon garam masala
- Kosher salt, to taste
- Freshly ground black pepper
- 4 cups water
- 1 (14 ounces / 397 g) can unsweetened coconut milk
- 2 tablespoons lime juice
- 1 tablespoon agave nectar
- 1½ cups red lentils
- 2 small garnet yams, diced
- 1 small head cauliflower, cut into small florets
- Steamed brown rice for serving (optional)
- Cilantro for garnish

1. In a Dutch oven or large stockpot over medium heat, warm the canola oil. Add the onion and cook, stirring frequently, until soft, 8 to 10 minutes. Turn the heat to low and add the ginger and garlic. Cook, stirring frequently, until fragrant, about 1 minute. Add the curry paste (if using), garam masala, 1 teaspoon salt, and ½ teaspoon pepper and cook, stirring frequently, for 1 minute. 2. Add the water, turn the heat to medium-high, and bring to a boil, scraping up the browned bits on the bottom of the pot. Add the coconut milk, lime juice, agave nectar, and lentils and bring to a boil. Cover, turn the heat to medium-low, and simmer for 10 minutes. 3. Add the yams and cauliflower to the pot, cover, and simmer until the lentils are cooked through, about 15 minutes. Season with salt and pepper. Serve over steamed brown rice, if desired, and garnish with cilantro.

Per Serving:

calories: 394 | fat: 22g | protein: 14g | carbs: 41g | fiber: 8g | sugar: 4g | sodium: 187mg

Basic Quinoa

- 2 cups quinoa, rinsed well
- 4 cups vegetable broth

1. In your slow cooker, combine the quinoa and broth. 2. Cover the cooker and set to low. Cook for 4 to 6 hours. Fluff with a fork, cool, and serve.

Per Serving:

calories: 335 | fat: 5g | protein: 12g | carbs: 61g | fiber: 7g | sugar: 2g | sodium: 550mg

Thai Red Curry with Tofu and Green Beans

Prep time: 35 minutes | Cook time: 25 minutes | Serves 8

- 8 (8 ounces / 227 g) green beans, trimmed and cut into 1-inch pieces
- 1 tablespoon organic canola oil
- 1 large red onion, sliced
- Kosher salt, to taste
- 1½ teaspoon minced garlic
- 1 teaspoon minced fresh ginger
- 1 Thai bird chile or small serrano chile, thinly sliced (optional if nightshade-sensitive)
- 4 tablespoons Thai red curry paste (2 tablespoons if nightshade-sensitive)
- 2 (14 ounces / 397 g) cans unsweetened coconut milk
- 1 cup chicken or vegetable stock
- ⅓ cup lime juice
- ¼ cup fish sauce, plus more as needed
- 3 tablespoons honey
- 2 pounds (907 g) extra-firm tofu, cut into 1-inch cubes
- 1½ cups cherry tomatoes, halved (optional if nightshade-sensitive)
- ¼ cup chopped basil
- 1 pound (454 g) dried brown rice noodles, such as Annie Chun's Pad Thai Brown Rice Noodles

1. Bring a pot of salted water to a boil and fill a medium bowl with ice water. Add the green beans to the boiling water and cook for 2 minutes. With a slotted spoon, transfer the beans to the ice-water bath to stop the cooking. Be careful not to overcook the beans, they should still have some bite. Dry the beans. 2. In a large stockpot or Dutch oven over medium heat, warm the canola oil. Add the onion and a pinch of salt and cook, stirring occasionally, until softened, 6 to 8 minutes. Add the garlic, ginger, chile (if using), and curry paste and cook, stirring, until fragrant, about 1 minute. Add the coconut milk, chicken stock, lime juice, fish sauce, and honey and bring to a boil. Turn the heat to medium-low and simmer, uncovered, to combine the flavors, about 10 minutes. 3. Turn the heat to medium-high, add the tofu, and simmer, stirring occasionally, for 3 minutes. Add the tomatoes (if using) and blanched green beans. Continue to simmer until the tofu is warmed through, the green beans are crisp-tender, and the sauce has thickened slightly, about 2 minutes. Stir in the basil. Taste and add more fish sauce or salt as desired. 4. Prepare the rice noodles according to the package instructions. Place a serving of noodles in the bottom of each bowl and top with a few ladlesful of the curry. Serve immediately.

Per Serving:

calories: 417 | fat: 10g | protein: 17g | carbs: 67g | fiber: 6g | sugar: 12g | sodium: 277mg

Mushroom Risotto with Spring Peas

Prep time: 15 minutes | Cook time: 2 to 3 hours | Serves 4 to 6

- 1½ cups Arborio rice
- 1 cup English peas
- 1 small shallot, minced
- ¼ cup dried porcini mushrooms
- 4½ cups broth of choice (choose vegetable to keep it vegan)
- 1 tablespoon freshly squeezed lemon juice
- ½ teaspoon garlic powder
- ½ teaspoon sea salt

1. In your slow cooker, combine the rice, peas, shallot, mushrooms, broth, lemon juice, garlic powder, and salt. Stir to mix well. 2. Cover the cooker and set to high. Cook for 2 to 3 hours and serve.

Per Serving:

calories: 382 | fat: 1g | protein: 12g | carbs: 79g | fiber: 3g | sugar: 4g | sodium: 934mg

Chapter
4

Poultry

Chapter 4 Poultry

Turkey Meatballs in a Muffin Tin

Prep time: 10 minutes | Cook time: 20 minutes | Makes 12 meatballs

- 1½ pounds (680 g) ground turkey
- 1 small white onion, minced
- 1 egg, whisked
- ¼ cup fresh mushrooms, minced
- 1 teaspoon garlic powder
- ½ teaspoon salt
- ½ teaspoon dried oregano
- ¼ teaspoon freshly ground black pepper
- ¼ teaspoon ground ginger
- 1 slice gluten-free bread, torn into small pieces

1. Preheat the oven to 400ºF (205ºC). 2. In a large bowl, add the turkey, onion, egg, mushrooms, garlic powder, salt, oregano, pepper, ginger, and bread, and mix thoroughly with your hands. 3. Form the turkey mixture into 12 balls and place 1 in each cup of a 12-cup muffin tin. 4. Bake for 20 minutes. Serve immediately.

Per Serving:
calories: 78 | fat: 3g | protein: 15g | carbs: 3g | fiber: 0g | sugar: 0g | sodium: 139mg

Chicken Skewers with Mint Sauce

Prep time: 20 minutes | Cook time: 20 minutes | Serves 4 to 6

Mint Sauce:
- 1 bunch fresh mint, stemmed
- ½ cup extra-virgin olive oil
- 1 garlic clove

Chicken:
- 6 boneless skinless chicken breasts, cut into 1½- to 2-inch cubes
- ¼ cup extra-virgin olive oil
- ¼ cup freshly squeezed lemon juice

- 2 teaspoons lemon zest
- ½ teaspoon salt
- Pinch freshly ground black pepper

- 1 teaspoon salt
- ¼ teaspoon freshly ground black pepper
- Pinch ground turmeric
- 2 fresh mint sprigs

Make the Mint Sauce: 1. In a blender or food processor, combine the mint, olive oil, garlic, lemon zest, salt, and pepper. Blend until smooth. 2. Refrigerate in an airtight container for no more than four or five days. Make the Chicken: 1. Soak 12 (6-inch) wooden skewers in water for at least 30 minutes so the skewers won't burn while on the grill. 2. In a large zip-top plastic bag, combine the chicken, olive oil, lemon juice, salt, pepper, turmeric, and mint. Close the bag, refrigerate, turn to coat, and let marinate at least 30 minutes, or overnight. 3. Preheat the grill, or place a stovetop grill over high heat. 4. Put 3 or 4 chicken cubes on each skewer. Discard the marinade and mint sprigs. 5. Reduce the grill to medium. Grill the chicken for 15 to 20 minutes, turning occasionally, until each skewer is marked on both sides and the chicken is cooked through. 6. Serve with the mint sauce.

Per Serving:
calories: 657 | fat: 51g | protein: 50g | carbs: 2g | fiber: 1g | sugar: 0g | sodium: 1024mg

General Tso's Chicken

Prep time: 15 minutes | Cook time: 15 minutes | Serves 4

Sauce:
- 1 tablespoon ghee
- ¼ teaspoon ground ginger
- 2 garlic cloves, minced
- 3 tablespoons coconut sugar
- 3 tablespoons coconut

Chicken:
- 2 tablespoons avocado oil
- 1 cup brown rice flour
- ¼ teaspoon salt

- aminos
- 2 tablespoons rice vinegar
- 1 tablespoon arrowroot powder
- ½ teaspoon red pepper flakes

- ¼ teaspoon garlic powder
- 1 pound (454 g) boneless, skinless chicken thighs, cut into 1-inch pieces

Make the Sauce: 1. In a small saucepan over medium heat, stir together the ghee and ginger. Cook, stirring frequently, for 2 minutes. 2. Add the garlic, coconut sugar, coconut aminos, vinegar, arrowroot powder, and red pepper flakes. Stir well and bring to a simmer. Reduce the heat to medium-low and cook for 5 minutes until the sauce begins to thicken and reduce slightly. Make the Chicken: 1. In a large skillet over medium-high heat, heat the avocado oil. 2. In a small bowl, mix the rice flour, salt, and garlic powder. 3. Dredge the chicken in the flour mixture and put in the hot skillet. Cook for 3 to 4 minutes per side. Transfer to a serving dish. 4. Pour the sauce over the chicken, and serve immediately.

Per Serving:
calories: 436 | fat: 16g | protein: 27g | carbs: 46g | fiber: 2g | sugar: 6g | sodium: 251mg

Coconut-Braised Curried Chicken

Prep time: 5 minutes | Cook time: 35 minutes | Serves 6

- 2 pounds (907 g) boneless, skinless chicken thighs
- 2 teaspoons fine Himalayan salt
- 2 teaspoons turmeric powder
- 1 teaspoon dry mustard
- 1 teaspoon ginger powder
- 1 teaspoon ground black pepper
- 1 teaspoon ground cumin
- Pinch of ground cloves
- 2 tablespoons ghee
- 3 sprigs fresh thyme
- 1 cup full-fat coconut milk
- 2 tablespoons coconut vinegar or red wine vinegar
- Fresh cilantro, for garnish (optional)

1. Heat a large skillet over medium heat. While it heats, place the chicken thighs and seasonings in a large bowl and mix until all the thighs are evenly coated. 2. Place the ghee in the hot skillet and add as many chicken thighs as you can without overcrowding the pan (the thighs shouldn't touch)—you'll probably need to cook the thighs in two batches. Brown for 5 minutes, then flip the chicken over and brown for another 5 minutes. If you're cooking the thighs in batches, remove the first batch, place the second batch in the skillet, and repeat. When all the chicken is browned, return it all to the skillet. 3. Add the thyme sprigs, coconut milk, and vinegar to the skillet. Cover with a tight-fitting lid and let it simmer for 15 minutes. 4. Stir well, scraping the bottom of the skillet to lift any flavorful bits that are stuck to it. Transfer the chicken to a serving platter and pour the pan sauce over it, or serve the sauce on the side. Garnish with fresh cilantro, if desired. 5. Store leftovers in an airtight container in the fridge for up to 5 days. To reheat, sauté over medium heat for 10 minutes.

Per Serving:

calories: 425 | fat: 25g | protein: 45g | carbs: 4g | fiber: 1g | sugar: 1g | sodium: 527mg

Russian Kotleti

Prep time: 10 minutes | Cook time: 10 minutes | Serves 4

- ¼ cup filtered water
- 1 pound (454 g) ground chicken
- ½ small white onion, diced
- 1 egg, whisked
- 1 teaspoon salt
- ½ teaspoon garlic powder
- ½ teaspoon dried dill
- ½ teaspoon freshly ground black pepper
- 1 slice gluten-free bread
- 2 teaspoons ghee

1. In a medium bowl, combine the chicken, onion, egg, salt, garlic powder, dill, and pepper. Mix well with your hands. 2. In a small bowl, soak the bread in the water for 1 minute. 3. Add the soaked bread to the chicken mixture. With your hands, work to break it up as you mix it in. If you prefer, mix the ingredients in a stand mixer. 4. Divide the chicken mixture into 8 portions and roll each into a ball. Press them slightly to form short, thick patties. 5. In a large skillet over medium heat, heat the ghee. Place the patties in the pan so they do not touch, and cook for 5 minutes per side. Cut into one to check for doneness (no longer pink) before removing from the heat.

Per Serving:

calories: 213 | fat: 9g | protein: 24g | carbs: 9g | fiber: 1g | sugar: 0g | sodium: 618mg

Chicken Salad with Green Apples and Grapes

Prep time: 20 minutes | Cook time: 0 minutes | Serves 4

- 1 large avocado, diced
- 2 tablespoons Dijon mustard
- ½ teaspoon garlic powder
- Dash salt
- Dash freshly ground black pepper
- 2 (8-ounce / 227-g) grilled boneless, skinless chicken breasts, chopped
- 2 small green apples, diced
- 1 cup grapes, halved
- ¼ cup sliced scallions
- 2 tablespoons minced celery

1. In a large bowl, combine the avocado, mustard, garlic powder, salt, and pepper, stirring until creamy. 2. Add the chicken, apples, grapes, scallions, and celery. Stir well to combine. 3. Serve chilled, if desired.

Per Serving:

calories: 234 | fat: 7g | protein: 24g | carbs: 19g | fiber: 5g | sugar: 13g | sodium: 644mg

Cilantro-Lime Chicken Drumsticks

Prep time: 15 minutes | Cook time: 2 to 3 hours | Serves 4 to 6

- ¼ cup fresh cilantro, chopped
- 3 tablespoons freshly squeezed lime juice
- ½ teaspoon garlic powder
- ½ teaspoon sea salt
- ¼ teaspoon ground cumin
- 3 pounds (1.4 kg) chicken drumsticks

1. In a small bowl, stir together the cilantro, lime juice, garlic powder, salt, and cumin to form a paste. 2. Put the drumsticks in the slow cooker. Spread the cilantro paste evenly on each drumstick. 3. Cover the cooker and set to high. Cook for 2 to 3 hours, or until the internal temperature of the chicken reaches 165°F (74°C) on a meat thermometer and the juices run clear, and serve.

Per Serving:

calories: 417 | fat: 12g | protein: 71g | carbs: 1g | fiber: 1g | sugar: 1g | sodium: 591mg

Turkey Sloppy Joes

Prep time: 15 minutes | Cook time: 4 to 6 hours | Serves 4 to 6

- 1 tablespoon extra-virgin olive oil
- 1 pound (454 g) ground turkey
- 1 celery stalk, minced
- 1 carrot, minced
- ½ medium sweet onion, diced
- ½ red bell pepper, finely chopped
- 6 tablespoons tomato paste
- 2 tablespoons apple cider vinegar
- 1 tablespoon maple syrup
- 1 teaspoon Dijon mustard
- 1 teaspoon chili powder
- ½ teaspoon garlic powder
- ½ teaspoon sea salt
- ½ teaspoon dried oregano

1. In your slow cooker, combine the olive oil, turkey, celery, carrot, onion, red bell pepper, tomato paste, vinegar, maple syrup, mustard, chili powder, garlic powder, salt, and oregano. Using a large spoon, break up the turkey into smaller chunks as it combines with the other ingredients. 2. Cover the cooker and set to low. Cook for 4 to 6 hours, stir thoroughly, and serve.

Per Serving:
calories: 251 | fat: 12g | protein: 24g | carbs: 14g | fiber: 3g | sugar: 9g | sodium: 690mg

Chicken Bone Broth

Prep time: 15 minutes | Cook time: 6 to 8 hours | Makes about 12 cups

- 1 chicken carcass
- About 12 cups filtered water (enough to cover the bones)
- 2 carrots, roughly chopped
- 2 garlic cloves, roughly chopped
- 1 celery stalk, roughly chopped
- ½ onion, roughly chopped
- 2 bay leaves
- 1 parsley sprig
- ¾ teaspoon sea salt
- ½ teaspoon dried oregano
- ½ teaspoon dried basil leaves
- 1 tablespoon apple cider vinegar

1. In your slow cooker, combine the chicken carcass, water, carrots, garlic, celery, onion, bay leaves, parsley, salt, oregano, basil, and vinegar. 2. Cover the cooker and set to low. Cook for 6 to 8 hours. 3. Skim off any scum from the surface of the broth, and pour the broth through a fine-mesh sieve into a large bowl, discarding the chicken and veggie scraps. Refrigerate the broth in an airtight container for up to 5 days, or freeze it for up to 3 months.

Per Serving:
calories: 50 | fat: 1g | protein: 9g | carbs: 1g | fiber: 0g | sugar: 0g | sodium: 145mg

Coconut-Braised Chicken

Prep time: 15 minutes | Cook time: 35 minutes | Serves 4

- 1½ cups canned lite coconut milk
- 2 tablespoons grated fresh ginger
- Juice of 1 lime (1 or 2 tablespoons)
- Zest of 1 lime (optional)
- 1 tablespoon raw honey
- ½ teaspoon ground cardamom
- 1 tablespoon olive oil
- 1 pound (454 g) bone-in skin-on chicken thighs
- 1 scallion, white and green parts, chopped

1. In a medium bowl, whisk the coconut milk, ginger, lime juice, lime zest (if using), honey, and cardamom. Set it aside. 2. Place a large skillet over medium-high heat and add the olive oil. 3. Add the chicken thighs and pan-sear for about 20 minutes, or until golden, turning once. 4. Pour the coconut milk mixture over the chicken, and bring the liquid to a boil. Reduce the heat to low, cover, and simmer for about 15 minutes, or until the chicken is tender and cooked through. 5. Serve garnished with the scallions.

Per Serving:
calories: 480 | fat: 34g | protein: 35g | carbs: 12g | fiber: 3g | sugar: 4g | sodium: 104mg

Turkey Larb Lettuce Wraps

Prep time: 10 minutes | Cook time: 20 minutes | Serves 4

- 1 pound (454 g) ground turkey
- 1 small red onion, diced
- 2 garlic cloves, minced
- 4 scallions, sliced
- 2 tablespoons freshly squeezed lime juice
- 2 tablespoons fish sauce
- 2 tablespoons minced fresh cilantro
- 1 tablespoon minced fresh mint (optional)
- 1 tablespoon coconut sugar
- ¼ teaspoon red pepper flakes
- 8 small romaine lettuce leaves

1. In a large skillet over medium-high heat, cook the turkey for 10 minutes, stirring and breaking up the meat. 2. Add the onion and garlic, and cook for about 10 minutes, stirring, until the onions soften and the meat is cooked. 3. Remove from the heat. Stir in the scallions, lime juice, fish sauce, cilantro, mint (if using), coconut sugar, and red pepper flakes until well incorporated. 4. Fill each romaine leaf with the meat mixture. Serve warm or cold.

Per Serving:
calories: 143 | fat: 2g | protein: 24g | carbs: 9g | fiber: 1g | sugar: 4g | sodium: 781mg

Chicken and Broccoli Stir-Fry

Prep time: 15 minutes | Cook time: 15 minutes | Serves 4 to 6

- 2 tablespoons coconut oil
- 1 pound (454 g) boneless, skinless chicken thighs, cut into thin strips
- 2 cups broccoli florets
- 2 garlic cloves, thinly sliced
- 1 teaspoon minced fresh ginger root
- 1 teaspoon salt
- ¼ teaspoon red pepper flakes
- ¾ cup chicken broth
- 1 teaspoon toasted sesame oil (optional)
- 1 tablespoon sesame seeds (optional)

1. In a Dutch oven, heat the coconut oil over high heat. 2. Add the chicken and sauté until it starts to brown, 5 to 8 minutes. 3. Add the broccoli florets, garlic, ginger, salt, red pepper flakes, and broth. 4. Cover the pot, lower the heat to medium, and let the mixture steam until the broccoli turns bright green, about 5 minutes. 5. Remove from the heat, add the sesame oil and sesame seeds (if using), and serve.

Per Serving:

calories: 250 | fat: 14g | protein: 27g | carbs: 5g | fiber: 1g | sugar: 0g | sodium: 810mg

Chicken Satay and Grilled Zucchini

Prep time: 20 minutes | Cook time: 10 minutes | Serves 3

Satay:

- 1 pound (454 g) boneless, skinless chicken thighs
- 1 teaspoon fine Himalayan salt
- 1 teaspoon ground black pepper
- 1 teaspoon turmeric powder

Zucchini:

- 3 small zucchini, halved lengthwise
- 1 tablespoon avocado oil or olive oil
- Pinch of fine Himalayan salt
- Tahini Sauce:

- ½ teaspoon ground toasted cumin seeds or ground cumin
- 2 tablespoons coconut oil
- 1 tablespoon coconut vinegar
- 1 tablespoon toasted sesame oil
- Juice of 2 lemons
- 2 tablespoons tahini
- 1 tablespoon coconut aminos
- ½ teaspoon fish sauce
- ½ teaspoon ginger powder

1. Cut each chicken thigh lengthwise into two or three strips, then cut the strips in half to make thumb-sized chunks. Place the chicken chunks, salt, pepper, turmeric, cumin, coconut oil, vinegar, and sesame oil in a large bowl. Mix well, cover, and set in the refrigerator to marinate for at least an hour or up to 3 days. 2. If you are using bamboo or wooden skewers, soak them in water for 20 minutes before grilling. Thread four or five pieces of marinated chicken onto each skewer and set aside. 3. Preheat the grill to 450ºF (235ºC). 4. While the grill heats, prepare the zucchini and tahini sauce: Brush the zucchini with the oil and sprinkle with the salt. Place on a tray or cutting board that's large enough to hold everything after cooking. 5. Place all of the sauce ingredients in a small bowl and stir until smooth and well combined. Set aside. 6. When the grill has come to temperature, place the skewers on the hottest part of the grill and close the lid. Cook undisturbed for 3 minutes. Open the lid and turn the skewers over with tongs. Put the zucchini cut side down on the other side of the grill. Close the lid and lower the heat to 400ºF (205ºC). You may have to crack the lid periodically for temperature control. Grill for 5 to 8 minutes, until the chicken has a nice char to it and the internal temperature reaches 175ºF (79ºC). Flip the zucchini once halfway through. Remove the skewers and zucchini from the grill and place everything on the tray or cutting board. 7. Drizzle the tahini sauce over everything or serve on the side for dipping. 8. Store leftover skewers and sauce in separate airtight containers in the fridge for up to 5 days. To reheat the chicken, quickly sear in a hot skillet for 5 minutes.

Per Serving:

calories: 344 | fat: 19g | protein: 34g | carbs: 4g | fiber: 3g | sugar: g1 | sodium: 587mg

Tuscan Chicken

Prep time: 5 minutes | Cook time: 20 minutes | Serves 4

- 4 boneless, skinless chicken breast halves, pounded to ½- to ¾-inch thickness
- ½ teaspoon sea salt
- ⅛ teaspoon freshly ground black pepper
- 1 teaspoon garlic powder
- 2 tablespoons extra-virgin olive oil
- 1 zucchini, chopped
- 2 cups cherry tomatoes
- ½ cup sliced green olives
- ¼ cup dry white wine

1. Season the chicken breasts with the salt, pepper, and garlic powder. 2. In a large nonstick skillet over medium-high heat, heat the olive oil until it shimmers. Add the chicken and cook 7 to 10 minutes per side, until it reaches an internal temperature of 165ºF (74ºC). Remove the chicken and set aside on a platter, tented with foil. 3. In the same skillet, add the zucchini, tomatoes, and olives. Cook for about 4 minutes, stirring occasionally, until the zucchini is tender. 4. Add the white wine and use a wooden spoon to scrape any browned bits from the bottom of the pan. Simmer for 1 minute. Return the chicken and any juices that have collected on the platter to the pan and stir to coat with the sauce and vegetables.

Per Serving:

calories: 171 | fat: 11g | protein: 8g | carbs: 8g | fiber: 2g | sugar: 4g | sodium: 598mg

Southwest Turkey-Stuffed Bell Peppers

Prep time: 15 minutes | Cook time: 20 minutes | Serves 6

- 6 bell peppers, any color, tops and ribs removed, seeded
- 1 tablespoon avocado oil
- 1 pound (454 g) ground turkey
- 1 small white onion, diced
- 2 garlic cloves, minced
- 1 (16-ounce / 454-g) can diced tomatoes, drained
- ½ teaspoon ground cumin
- ½ teaspoon paprika
- ½ teaspoon dried oregano
- ½ teaspoon salt
- Freshly ground black pepper, to taste

1. Preheat the oven to 400ºF (205ºC). 2. Line a baking sheet with aluminum foil. 3. Arrange the bell peppers on the prepared pan. Drizzle with the avocado oil. 4. Bake for 20 minutes, or until softened and cooked. 5. Meanwhile, in a large skillet over medium-high heat, brown the turkey for 5 minutes, breaking up the meat with a spoon. 6. Add the onion and garlic. Cook for 10 minutes, stirring frequently, until the turkey is cooked. 7. Stir in the tomatoes, cumin, paprika, oregano, and salt, and season with pepper. 8. Fill each cooked pepper with the meat mixture. Enjoy warm.

Per Serving:
calories: 188 | fat: 9g | protein: 15g | carbs: 11g | fiber: 4g | sugar: 4g | sodium: 334mg

Sesame Chicken Stir-Fry

Prep time: 15 minutes | Cook time: 25 minutes | Serves 6

- ¾ cup warm water
- ½ cup tahini
- ¼ cup plus 2 tablespoons toasted sesame oil, divided
- 2 garlic cloves, minced
- ½ teaspoon salt
- 1 pound (454 g) boneless skinless chicken breasts, cut into ½-inch cubes
- 6 cups lightly packed kale, thoroughly washed and chopped

1. In a medium bowl, whisk together the warm water, tahini, ¼ cup of sesame oil, garlic, and salt. 2. In a large pan set over medium heat, heat the remaining 2 tablespoons of sesame oil. 3. Add the chicken and cook for 8 to 10 minutes, stirring. 4. Stir in the tahini-sesame sauce, mixing well to coat the chicken. Cook for 6 to 8 minutes more. 5. One handful at a time, add the kale. When the first handful wilts, add the next. Continue until all the kale has been added. Serve hot.

Per Serving:
calories: 417 | fat: 30g | protein: 27g | carbs: 12g | fiber: 3g | sugar: 0g | sodium: 311mg

Mediterranean Chicken Bake

Prep time: 15 minutes | Cook time: 20 minutes | Serves 4

- 4 (4-ounce / 113-g) boneless, skinless chicken breasts
- 2 tablespoons avocado oil
- 1 pint cherry tomatoes, halved
- 1 cup packed chopped fresh spinach
- 1 cup sliced cremini mushrooms
- ½ red onion, thinly sliced
- ½ cup chopped fresh basil
- 4 garlic cloves, minced
- 2 teaspoons balsamic vinegar

1. Preheat the oven to 400ºF (205ºC). 2. Place the chicken breasts in a glass baking dish. Brush with the avocado oil. 3. In a medium bowl, stir together the tomatoes, spinach, mushrooms, red onion, basil, garlic, and vinegar. 4. Top each chicken breast with one-fourth of the vegetable mixture. 5. Bake for about 20 minutes, or until the chicken is cooked through.

Per Serving:
calories: 219 | fat: 9g | protein: 28g | carbs: 7g | fiber: 2g | sugar: 2g | sodium: 193mg

Roast Chicken with Lemon and White Beans

Prep time: 15 minutes | Cook time: 1 hour 45 minutes | Serves 4 to 6

- 1 tablespoon extra-virgin olive oil
- 1 (3½- to 4-pound / 1.6- to 1.8-kg) chicken
- 1 teaspoon salt
- ¼ teaspoon freshly ground black pepper
- 1 onion, sliced
- 2 garlic cloves, thinly sliced
- ½ cup chicken broth
- ½ cup dry white wine
- 1 (15-ounce / 425-g) can white beans, drained and rinsed
- 2 tablespoons fresh lemon juice

1. Preheat the oven to 375ºF (190ºC). 2. Heat the olive oil in a large Dutch oven over high heat. 3. Pat the chicken dry with a paper towel and add the salt and pepper. 4. Place the chicken, breast-side down, in the Dutch oven and brown the skin for 4 to 5 minutes. Turn the chicken over and brown the back. 5. Scatter the onion and garlic slices around the chicken and add the broth and white wine. Cover the Dutch oven and bake for 1 hour. 6. Add the white beans and lemon juice, cover, and cook for an additional 30 minutes. 7. Uncover and let the chicken cool for 10 minutes before serving.

Per Serving:
calories: 460 | fat: 12g | protein: 57g | carbs: 27g | fiber: 6g | sugar: 2g | sodium: 700mg

Spicy Chicken Drumsticks

Prep time: 10 minutes | Cook time: 35 to 45 minutes | Serves 4 to 6

- 6 chicken drumsticks
- 1 cup unsweetened coconut yogurt
- ½ cup extra-virgin olive oil
- Juice of 2 limes
- 2 garlic cloves, smashed
- 1 tablespoon raw honey
- 1 teaspoon salt
- 1 teaspoon ground cumin
- ½ teaspoon paprika
- ½ teaspoon ground turmeric
- ¼ teaspoon freshly ground black pepper
- Olive oil cooking spray

1. Place the chicken in a shallow baking dish. 2. In a small bowl, whisk together the yogurt, olive oil, lime juice, garlic, honey, salt, cumin, paprika, turmeric, and pepper until smooth. 3. Pour the yogurt mixture over the chicken. Cover with plastic wrap and chill for 30 minutes, or overnight. 4. Preheat the oven to 375ºF (190ºC). 5. Line a rimmed baking sheet with aluminum foil and lightly grease it with cooking spray. 6. Remove the drumsticks from the marinade and place them on the prepared sheet. Discard the marinade. 7. Place the sheet in the preheated oven and bake the drumsticks for 25 to 35 minutes, or until they start to brown and are cooked through.

Per Serving:

calories: 380 | fat: 31g | protein: 19g | carbs: 9g | fiber: 2g | sugar: 5g | sodium: 686mg

Crispy Chicken Milanese with Hollandaise

Prep time: 15 minutes | Cook time: 20 minutes | Serves 4

Chicken:

- 2 boneless, skinless chicken breasts (about 1 pound / 454 g)
- 1 teaspoon fine Himalayan salt

Hollandaise:

- 3 large egg yolks (separated from the egg whites above)
- Juice of 1 lemon
- ⅛ teaspoon fine Himalayan salt
- 1 cup ghee, divided
- ½ cup coconut flour
- 3 large egg whites
- ½ cup avocado oil or coconut oil, divided, for frying
- ½ teaspoon ground black pepper
- 2 medium zucchini
- Chopped fresh parsley, for garnish

1. Put the chicken breasts on a cutting board. Place one hand flat on top of a breast and, with a sharp knife, cut into the side horizontally. Open the breast like a book. Repeat with the other chicken breast.

2. Place a piece of plastic wrap over the chicken breasts and gently pound them with the smooth side of a mallet until they are about ¼ inch thick. Cut the chicken into eight equal-sized pieces and sprinkle with the salt. 3. Heat an 8- or 10-inch skillet over medium heat. 4. Put the coconut flour in a shallow bowl. Crack the eggs into a medium-sized bowl. Carefully remove the egg yolks and set them aside for the hollandaise. Whisk the egg whites. 5. When the skillet is hot, pour ¼ cup of the avocado oil into the skillet. 6. Dredge one chicken piece in the coconut flour, then dip it in the egg whites and then back in the coconut flour. Shake off any excess flour and place the piece in the skillet. Repeat with three more pieces of chicken. Cook for 6 to 8 minutes, until the chicken is crispy and golden brown, turning over halfway through. Remove the chicken from the skillet and set on a cooling rack to drain. 7. Add the remaining ¼ cup of avocado oil to the skillet and cook the last four pieces of chicken in the same fashion. 8. While the last of the chicken cooks, make the hollandaise: Whisk the egg yolks in a small saucepan for 1 minute, or until they become light yellow. Add the lemon juice, salt, and 1 tablespoon of the ghee. 9. Heat the remaining ghee in the microwave for 30 to 40 seconds, until liquid and warm. 10. Set the saucepan over medium-low heat. Keep whisking the hollandaise at a moderate speed until the sauce thickens and you can see the bottom of the pot in streaks between stirs. 11. Lower the heat to low. Add the melted ghee a tablespoon at a time, mixing it in completely before adding in the next spoonful, until thick and creamy. Stir in the pepper. Remove from the heat. 12. By now the last of the chicken should be done. Remove the chicken pieces from the skillet and set them on the cooling rack. 13. With a vegetable peeler, shave the zucchini into ribbons. Divide the ribbons among four plates. 14. Place two pieces of chicken on each plate and spoon hollandaise liberally over them. Garnish with fresh parsley.

Per Serving:

calories: 424 | fat: 30g | protein: 29g | carbs: 12g | fiber: 10g | sugar: 1g | sodium: 451mg

Lemon and Garlic Chicken Thighs

Prep time: 15 minutes | Cook time: 7 to 8 hours | Serves 4 to 6

- 2 cups chicken broth
- 1½ teaspoons garlic powder
- 1 teaspoon sea salt
- Juice and zest of 1 large lemon
- 2 pounds (907 g) boneless skinless chicken thighs

1. Pour the broth into the slow cooker. 2. In a small bowl, stir together the garlic powder, salt, lemon juice, and lemon zest. Baste each chicken thigh with an even coating of the mixture. Place the thighs along the bottom of the slow cooker. 3. Cover the cooker and set to low. Cook for 7 to 8 hours, or until the internal temperature of the chicken reaches 165ºF (74ºC) on a meat thermometer and the juices run clear, and serve.

Per Serving:

calories: 290 | fat: 14g | protein: 43g | carbs: 3g | fiber: 0g | sugar: 0g | sodium: 1017mg

Turkey-Thyme Meatballs

Prep time: 20 minutes | Cook time: 15 minutes | Serves 4

- 1½ pounds (680 g) lean ground turkey
- ½ sweet onion, chopped, or about ½ cup precut packaged onion
- ¼ cup almond flour
- 1 tablespoon chopped fresh
- thyme
- 2 teaspoons bottled minced garlic
- 1 egg
- ¼ teaspoon ground nutmeg
- Pinch sea salt

1. Preheat the oven to 350ºF (180ºC). 2. Line a rimmed baking sheet with aluminum foil and set it aside. 3. In a large bowl, combine the turkey, onion, almond flour, thyme, garlic, egg, nutmeg, and sea salt until well mixed. Roll the turkey mixture into 1½-inch meatballs. Arrange the meatballs on the prepared baking sheet. 4. Bake for about 15 minutes, or until browned and cooked through.

Per Serving:
calories: 303 | fat: 16g | protein: 36g | carbs: 4g | fiber: 1g | sugar: 2g | sodium: 147mg

Balsamic-Glazed Turkey Wings

Prep time: 15 minutes | Cook time: 7 to 8 hours | Serves 4 to 6

- 1¼ cups balsamic vinegar
- 2 tablespoons raw honey
- 1 teaspoon garlic powder
- 2 pounds (907 g) turkey wings

1. In a small bowl, whisk the vinegar, honey, and garlic powder. 2. Put the wings in the bottom of the slow cooker, and pour the vinegar sauce on top. 3. Cover the cooker and set to low. Cook for 7 to 8 hours. 4. Baste the wings with the sauce from the bottom of the slow cooker and serve.

Per Serving:
calories: 501 | fat: 25g | protein: 47g | carbs: 20g | fiber: 0g | sugar: 9g | sodium: 162mg

Apple-Turkey Burgers

Prep time: 15 minutes | Cook time: 30 minutes | Serves 6

- 1 red onion, finely chopped
- 1 apple, washed and grated
- 1 pound (454 g) ground turkey
- ¼ cup chickpea flour, plus additional as needed
- ½ teaspoon salt

1. Preheat the oven to 350ºF (180ºC). 2. Line a baking sheet with parchment paper. 3. In a large bowl, combine the onion and apple. 4. Add the ground turkey, chickpea flour, and salt. Mix well. If your mixture seems too wet, add another 1 or 2 tablespoons of chickpea flour. 5. Using a ⅓-cup measure, scoop the turkey mixture onto the prepared sheet. Flatten the patties with the bottom of the measure so they are ¾ to 1 inch thick. 6. Place the sheet in the preheated oven and bake for 30 minutes, or until the burgers are cooked through, are opaque in the middle, and the internal temperature reaches 165ºF (74ºC).

Per Serving:
calories: 301 | fat: 13g | protein: 34g | carbs: 16g | fiber: 4g | sugar: 7g | sodium: 417mg

Country Captain'S Chicken

Prep time: 30 minutes | Cook time: 2 hours | Serves 8

- 1 (4- to 5-pound / 1.8- to 2.3-kg) chicken, cut into 8 pieces
- Kosher salt, to taste
- 2 tablespoons extra-virgin olive oil
- 1 large red onion, thinly sliced
- 3 celery stalks, sliced
- 1½ tablespoons curry powder
- Freshly ground black pepper
- 2 tablespoons tomato paste
- (optional if nightshade-sensitive)
- 1 (28 ounces / 794 g) can diced tomatoes (optional if nightshade-sensitive)
- 1 cup chicken or vegetable stock
- ½ cup raisins
- ½ cup raw almonds, toasted and coarsely chopped
- 4 cups cooked brown rice
- 2 tablespoons chopped parsley

1. Rinse the chicken pieces and pat dry thoroughly. Season with salt. 2. In a large Dutch oven or stockpot over medium-high heat, warm the olive oil until just smoking. Working in batches, sear the chicken until well browned on both sides, 8 to 10 minutes per batch. Transfer the chicken to a platter and pour off all but 2 tablespoons of the accumulated fat. (If the bottom of the pot is scorched, discard the oil, wipe it clean, and add another 2 tablespoons oil.) 3. Turn the heat to medium and add the onion and celery. Cook, stirring frequently, until the onion is soft, 5 to 7 minutes. Add the curry powder, ½ teaspoon black pepper, and tomato paste (if using) and cook, stirring constantly, until fragrant, about 30 seconds. Add the tomatoes with their juices (if using), chicken stock, and raisins and bring to a simmer, scraping the bottom of the pot to remove all the caramelized bits. 4. Nestle the chicken into the pot, cover, and turn the heat to medium-low. Simmer until chicken thighs are fork-tender, about 45 minutes. 5. Transfer the chicken to a platter, turn the heat to medium-high, and cook, stirring occasionally, until the sauce has reduced slightly, 5 to 7 minutes. Taste, adding more salt and pepper if necessary. 6. Stir the toasted almonds into the brown rice. Spoon on plates and top with the chicken and sauce. Finish with the parsley. Serve immediately.

Per Serving:
calories: 546 | fat: 26g | protein: 45g | carbs: 34g | fiber: 4g | sugar: 7g | sodium: 308mg

Balsamic-Glazed Chicken Thighs with Steamed Cauliflower

Prep time: 10 minutes | Cook time: 40 minutes | Serves 4

- ½ cup balsamic vinegar
- ¼ cup extra-virgin oil
- 2 tablespoons maple syrup
- 8 (2- to 3-ounce / 57- to 85-

- g) bone-in chicken thighs
- 2 cauliflower heads, broken or cut into florets
- Salt, for seasoning

1. In a small bowl, whisk together the balsamic vinegar, olive oil, and maple syrup. 2. In a medium dish, combine the chicken thighs and vinegar-maple mixture. Marinate the chicken for 30 minutes in the refrigerator. 3. Preheat the oven to 350ºF (180ºC). 4. Cover the chicken with aluminum foil and place it in the preheated oven. Bake for 30 to 35 minutes, or until the chicken is cooked through. The internal temperature should read 165ºF (74ºC). 5. If you've left the skin on the chicken, leave the chicken in the oven (uncovered) for an additional 10 minutes to crisp the skin. 6. Fill a large pot with 2 inches of water and insert a steamer basket. Bring to a boil over high heat. Add the cauliflower. Cover and steam for 8 minutes. 7. Serve the chicken with the cauliflower. Drizzle the extra marinade from the casserole dish over the cauliflower, and season with salt, if needed.

Per Serving:
calories: 535 | fat: 38g | protein: 33g | carbs: 14g | fiber: 3g | sugar: 9g | sodium: 170mg

Chicken Kofta Kebabs

Prep time: 10 minutes | Cook time: 20 minutes | Makes 6 skewers

- 2 pounds (907 g) ground chicken
- 1 sweet onion, minced
- 3 tablespoons flaxseed meal
- 2 tablespoons coconut vinegar
- 2 tablespoons dried parsley
- 2 tablespoons full-fat coconut milk

- 1 teaspoons fine Himalayan salt
- 1 teaspoon granulated garlic
- 1 teaspoon ground black pepper
- 1 teaspoon ground cumin
- 1 teaspoon turmeric powder
- Butter lettuce, for serving
- Lemon wedges, for serving

1. If you are using bamboo or wooden skewers, soak them in water for 20 minutes. Turn on the broiler and move an oven rack to just under it. 2. Place all of the ingredients in a large bowl and mix until thoroughly combined. Shape the chicken mixture into six large sausages, thread a skewer through each one, and place on a sheet pan. 3. Broil for 15 minutes. Open the oven, use a spatula to carefully unstick each skewer from the pan, and turn them over. Broil for another 5 minutes. The skewers should be nicely browned all over. Remove from the oven and let cool for 5 minutes before serving. 4. Serve with butter lettuce leaves, lemon wedges for dipping or smearing. 5. Store leftovers in an airtight container in the fridge for up to 5 days. Reheat in a preheated 350ºF (180ºC) oven for 10 minutes.

Per Serving:
calories: 556 | fat: 37g | protein: 57g | carbs: 8g | fiber: 6g | sugar: 1g | sodium: 534mg

Shredded Jerk Chicken

Prep time: 15 minutes | Cook time: 20 minutes | Serves 6

- 2 tablespoons avocado oil
- 2 tablespoons coconut aminos
- Juice of 1 lemon
- 2 teaspoons liquid smoke
- 2 teaspoons garlic powder
- 2 teaspoons ground black

- pepper
- 1 teaspoon fine Himalayan salt
- 1 teaspoon Chinese five-spice powder
- 2 pounds (907 g) boneless, skinless chicken thighs
- 3 sprigs fresh thyme

Make the Marinade: 1. Place the avocado oil, coconut aminos, lemon juice, liquid smoke, garlic powder, pepper, salt, and Chinese five-spice powder in a small bowl and whisk to combine. 2. Place the chicken in a large bowl and add the marinade and thyme sprigs. Mix well to combine. (You can also place the chicken, thyme, and marinade in a freezer bag and shake well to combine.) Cover and place in the fridge to marinate for at least 20 minutes or up to overnight. Stovetop instructions: 3. Heat a large pot over medium heat. When it's hot, add the marinated chicken thighs. Reserve the marinade. Brown the chicken, stirring occasionally, for 8 to 10 minutes. Once the chicken is browned, reduce the heat to low and stir in the reserved marinade. Cover with a tight-fitting lid and simmer for 20 to 30 minutes, until the chicken pulls apart easily. Check it halfway through cooking; if all of the liquid has evaporated, add a cup of bone broth or water. Pressure cooker instructions: 4. Set a pressure cooker to sauté mode. Add the marinated chicken thighs. Reserve the marinade. Brown the chicken, stirring occasionally, for 8 to 10 minutes. Cancel the sauté function, stir in the reserved marinade, and close the lid. Cook on high pressure (or the appliance's poultry setting) for 10 minutes. Slow cooker instructions: 5. Heat a large pot over medium heat. When it's hot, add the marinated chicken thighs. Reserve the marinade. Brown the chicken, stirring occasionally, for 8 to 10 minutes. Place the browned chicken and all of the reserved marinade in a slow cooker and cook on high for 4 to 6 hours. 6. When the chicken is done, use two forks or a pair of tongs to shred it. Serve hot, with the cooking liquid spooned over it. 7. Store in an airtight container in the fridge for up to 5 days. To reheat, sauté over medium heat for 10 minutes.

Per Serving:
calories: 505 | fat: 38g | protein: 37g | carbs: 5g | fiber: 1g | sugar: 1g | sodium: 588mg

Coconut Chicken

Prep time: 10 minutes | Cook time: 6 hours | Serves 4 to 6

- 1 tablespoon coconut oil
- 6 bone-in skin-on chicken thighs
- 1 onion, sliced
- 2 garlic cloves, smashed
- 2 teaspoons curry powder
- 1 teaspoon salt
- ¼ teaspoon freshly ground black pepper
- 1 (13½-ounce / 383-g) can coconut milk
- 3 cups chicken broth
- ¼ cup chopped fresh cilantro
- 2 scallions, sliced

1. Coat the slow cooker with the coconut oil. 2. Add the chicken, onion, garlic, curry powder, salt, pepper, coconut milk, and chicken broth. Cover the slow cooker and cook on high for 6 hours. 3. Garnish with the cilantro and scallions before serving.

Per Serving:
calories: 652 | fat: 56g | protein: 32g | carbs: 10g | fiber: 3g | sugar: 5g | sodium: 1087mg

Fricase De Pollo

Prep time: 10 minutes | Cook time: 35 minutes | Serves 3

- 4 tablespoons avocado oil or ghee, divided
- 2 large carrots, diced
- 4 ribs celery, diced
- 1 large onion, diced
- 2 cloves garlic, minced
- 2 bay leaves
- 2 pounds (907 g) boneless, skinless chicken thighs, cut into 3-inch strips
- 1 teaspoons fine Himalayan salt
- 1 teaspoon ground black pepper
- 1 teaspoon ground cumin
- 2 sprigs fresh oregano
- ½ cup bone broth
- 2 green onions, sliced, for garnish

1. Heat 2 tablespoons of the avocado oil in a large pot or skillet over medium heat. Add the carrots, celery, onions, garlic, and bay leaves. Sauté over medium heat for 8 to 10 minutes, until the sofrito is very fragrant and the onions have become tender and translucent. 2. Remove the sofrito from the pot and set aside. Heat the remaining 2 tablespoons of avocado oil in the pot and add the chicken strips. Add the salt, pepper, cumin, and oregano sprigs. Stir to combine. Cook until the chicken is browned, about 10 minutes, turning the pieces occasionally. 3. While the chicken browns, place half of the sofrito in a blender with the broth and blend until smooth. Once the chicken is browned, add the rest of the sofrito and the sauce you just blended back to the pot. 4. Stir well, cover the pot with a tight-fitting lid, and simmer for 10 minutes. You will hear bubbling and sizzling from the pot. Remove the lid; if the mixture has a lot of liquid, reduce over high heat for 5 minutes, stirring occasionally. If not, stir well, garnish with green onions, and serve hot! 5. Store leftovers in an airtight container in the fridge for up to 5 days. Sauté over medium heat for 5 minutes to reheat.

Per Serving:
calories: 408 | fat: 25g | protein: 33g | carbs: 8g | fiber: 4g | sugar: 2g | sodium: 573mg

Easy Chicken and Broccoli

Prep time: 10 minutes | Cook time: 10 minutes | Serves 4

- 3 tablespoons extra-virgin olive oil
- 1½ pounds (680 g) boneless, skinless chicken breasts, cut into bite-size pieces
- 1½ cups broccoli florets, or chopped broccoli stems
- ½ onion, chopped
- ½ teaspoon sea salt
- ⅛ teaspoon freshly ground black pepper
- 3 garlic cloves, minced
- 2 cups cooked brown rice

1. In a large nonstick skillet over medium-high heat, heat the olive oil until it shimmers. 2. Add the chicken, broccoli, onion, salt, and pepper. Cook for about 7 minutes, stirring occasionally, until the chicken is cooked. 3. Add the garlic. Cook for 30 seconds, stirring constantly. 4. Toss with the brown rice to serve.

Per Serving:
calories: 345 | fat: 14g | protein: 14g | carbs: 41g | fiber: 3g | sugar: 1g | sodium: 276mg

Sesame Miso Chicken

Prep time: 10 minutes | Cook time: 4 hours | Serves 4 to 6

- ¼ cup white miso
- 2 tablespoons coconut oil, melted
- 2 tablespoons honey
- 1 tablespoon unseasoned rice wine vinegar
- 2 garlic cloves, thinly sliced
- 1 teaspoon minced fresh ginger root
- 1 cup chicken broth
- 8 boneless, skinless chicken thighs
- 2 scallions, sliced
- 1 tablespoon sesame seeds

1. In a slow cooker, combine the miso, coconut oil, honey, rice wine vinegar, garlic, and ginger root, mixing well. 2. Add the chicken and toss to combine. Cover and cook on high for 4 hours. 3. Transfer the chicken and sauce to a serving dish. Garnish with the scallions and sesame seeds and serve.

Per Serving:
calories: 320 | fat: 15g | protein: 32g | carbs: 17g | fiber: 1g | sugar: 11g | sodium: 1020mg

Chicken Breast with Cherry Sauce

Prep time: 10 minutes | Cook time: 30 minutes | Serves 4

- 1 tablespoon coconut oil
- 4 boneless skinless chicken breasts
- Salt, to taste
- Freshly ground black pepper, to taste
- 2 scallions, sliced
- ¾ cup chicken broth
- 1 tablespoon balsamic vinegar
- ½ cup dried cherries

1. Preheat the oven to 375ºF (190ºC). 2. In a large ovenproof skillet over medium-high heat, melt the coconut oil. 3. Season the chicken with salt and pepper. Place the chicken in the pan and brown it on both sides, about 3 minutes per side. 4. Add the scallions, chicken broth, balsamic vinegar, and dried cherries. Cover with an ovenproof lid or aluminum foil and place the pan in the preheated oven. Bake for 20 minutes, or until the chicken is cooked through.

Per Serving:

calories: 379 | fat: 14g | protein: 43g | carbs: 17g | fiber: 5g | sugar: 9g | sodium: 308mg

Mushroom Turkey Thighs

Prep time: 15 minutes | Cook time: 4 hours | Serves 4

- 1 tablespoon extra-virgin olive oil
- 2 turkey thighs
- 2 cups button or cremini mushrooms, sliced
- 1 large onion, sliced
- 1 garlic clove, sliced
- 1 rosemary sprig
- 1 teaspoon salt
- ¼ teaspoon freshly ground black pepper
- 2 cups chicken broth
- ½ cup dry red wine

1. Drizzle the olive oil into a slow cooker. Add the turkey thighs, mushrooms, onion, garlic, rosemary sprig, salt, and pepper. Pour in the chicken broth and wine. Cover and cook on high for 4 hours. 2. Remove and discard the rosemary sprig. Use a slotted spoon to transfer the thighs to a plate and allow them to cool for several minutes for easier handling. 3. Cut the meat from the bones, stir the meat into the mushrooms, and serve.

Per Serving:

calories: 280 | fat: 9g | protein: 43g | carbs: 3g | fiber: 0g | sugar: 1g | sodium: 850mg

Rosemary Chicken

Prep time: 10 minutes | Cook time: 20 minutes | Serves 4

- 1½ pounds (680 g) chicken breast tenders
- 2 tablespoons extra-virgin olive oil
- 2 tablespoons chopped fresh rosemary leaves
- ½ teaspoon sea salt
- ⅛ teaspoon freshly ground black pepper

1. Preheat the oven to 425ºF (220ºC). 2. Place the chicken tenders on a rimmed baking sheet. Brush them with the olive oil and sprinkle with the rosemary, salt, and pepper. 3. Bake for 15 to 20 minutes, or until the juices run clear.

Per Serving:

calories: 389 | fat: 20g | protein: 49g | carbs: 1g | fiber: 0g | sugar: 0g | sodium: 381mg

Chapter
5

Fish and Seafood

Chapter 5 Fish and Seafood

Sardine Donburi

Prep time: 10 minutes | Cook time: 50 minutes | Serves 6

- 2 cups brown rice, rinsed well
- 4 cups water
- ½ teaspoon salt
- 3 (4-ounce / 113-g) cans sardines packed in water, drained
- 3 scallions, sliced thin
- 1 (1-inch) piece fresh ginger, grated
- 4 tablespoons sesame oil, or extra-virgin olive oil, divided

1. In a large pot, combine the rice, water, and salt. Bring to a boil over high heat. Reduce the heat to low. Cover and cook for 45 to 50 minutes, or until tender. 2. In a medium bowl, roughly mash the sardines. 3. When the rice is done, add the sardines, scallions, and ginger to the pot. Mix thoroughly. 4. Divide the rice among four bowls. Drizzle each bowl with 1 teaspoon to 1 tablespoon of sesame oil.

Per Serving:
calories: 604 | fat: 24g | protein: 25g | carbs: 74g | fiber: 4g | sugar: 0g | sodium: 499mg

Roasted Salmon and Asparagus

Prep time: 5 minutes | Cook time: 15 minutes | Serves 4

- 1 pound (454 g) asparagus spears, trimmed
- 2 tablespoons extra-virgin olive oil
- 1 teaspoon sea salt, divided
- 1½ pounds (680 g) salmon, cut into four fillets
- ⅛ teaspoon freshly cracked black pepper
- Zest and slices from 1 lemon

1. Preheat the oven to 425ºF (220ºC). 2. Toss the asparagus with the olive oil and ½ teaspoon of the salt. Spread in a single layer in the bottom of a roasting pan. 3. Season the salmon with the pepper and remaining ½ teaspoon of salt. Place skin-side down on top of the asparagus. 4. Sprinkle the salmon and asparagus with the lemon zest and place the lemon slices over the fish. 5. Roast in the preheated oven 12 to 15 minutes, until the flesh is opaque.

Per Serving:
calories: 308 | fat: 18g | protein: 36g | carbs: 5g | fiber: 2g | sugar: 2g | sodium: 545mg

Daring Shark Steaks

Prep time: 15 minutes | Cook time: 40 minutes | Serves 2

- 2 shark steaks, skinless
- 2 tablespoons onion powder
- 2 teaspoons chili powder
- 1 garlic clove, minced
- ¼ cup Worcestershire sauce
- 1 tablespoon ground black pepper
- 2 tablespoons thyme, chopped

1. In a bowl, mix all of the seasonings and spices to form a paste before setting aside. 2. Spread a thin layer of paste on both sides of the fish, cover and chill for 30 minutes (if possible). 3. Preheat oven to 325ºF (165ºC). 4. Bake the fish in parchment paper for 30 to 40 minutes, until well cooked. 5. Serve on a bed of quinoa or wholegrain couscous and your favorite salad.

Per Serving:
calories: 201 | fat: 5g | protein: 23g | carbs: 17g | fiber: 3g | sugar: 2g | sodium: 500mg

Shrimp with Spicy Spinach

Prep time: 10 minutes | Cook time: 15 minutes | Serves 4

- ¼ cup extra-virgin olive oil, divided
- 1½ pounds (680 g) peeled shrimp
- 1 teaspoon sea salt, divided
- 4 cups fresh baby spinach
- 6 garlic cloves, minced
- ½ cup freshly squeezed orange juice
- 1 tablespoon sriracha sauce
- ⅛ teaspoon freshly ground black pepper

1. In a large nonstick skillet over medium-high heat, heat 2 tablespoons of the olive oil until it shimmers. 2. Add the shrimp and ½ teaspoon salt. Cook for about 4 minutes, stirring occasionally, until the shrimp are pink. Transfer the shrimp to a plate, tent with aluminum foil to keep warm, and set aside. 3. Return the skillet to the heat and heat the remaining 2 tablespoons of olive oil until it shimmers. 4. Add the spinach. Cook for 3 minutes, stirring. 5. Add the garlic. Cook for 30 seconds, stirring constantly. 6. In a small bowl, whisk the orange juice, Sriracha, remaining ½ teaspoon of salt, and pepper. Add this to the spinach and cook for 3 minutes. Serve the shrimp with the spinach on the side.

Per Serving:
calories: 317 | fat: 16g | protein: 38g | carbs: 7g | fiber: 1g | sugar: 3g | sodium: 590mg

Salmon Baked with Leeks and Fennel

Prep time: 10 minutes | Cook time: 20 minutes | Serves 4

- 1 tablespoon extra-virgin olive oil, plus additional for brushing
- 1 leek, white part only, sliced thinly
- 1 fennel bulb, sliced thinly
- 4 (5- to 6-ounce / 142- to 170-g) salmon fillets
- 1 teaspoon salt
- ¼ teaspoon freshly ground black pepper
- ½ cup vegetable broth, or water
- 1 fresh rosemary sprig

1. Preheat the oven to 375ºF (190ºC). 2. In a shallow roasting pan, add 1 tablespoon of olive oil. Add the leek and fennel. Stir to coat with the oil. 3. Place the salmon fillets over the vegetables and sprinkle with salt and pepper. 4. Pour in the vegetable broth and add the rosemary sprig to the pan. Cover tightly with aluminum foil. 5. Place the pan in the preheated oven and bake for 20 minutes, or until the salmon is cooked through. 6. Remove and discard the rosemary sprig. Transfer the salmon and vegetables to a platter and serve.

Per Serving:
calories: 288 | fat: 14g | protein: 34g | carbs: 8g | fiber: 2g | sugar: 1g | sodium: 692mg

Fish En Papillote

Prep time: 30 minutes | Cook time: 20 minutes | Serves 4

- 4 (4 ounces / 113 g) fish fillets, such as halibut, salmon, or snapper, pin bones removed
- Kosher salt, to taste
- Freshly ground black pepper
- Extra-virgin olive oil for drizzling
- 2 lemons, preferably Meyer, ends trimmed, cut into 12 slices
- 16 asparagus spears, bottoms trimmed, sliced on the bias into ½-inch pieces
- 1 cup cherry tomatoes (optional if nightshade-sensitive)
- 2 tablespoons finely chopped assorted herbs, such as basil, chives, parsley, tarragon, and dill

1. Preheat the oven to 400ºF (205ºC). Cut four pieces of parchment paper each 18 inch long. 2. Place a fish fillet on the center of a piece of parchment. Season with a small pinch each of salt and pepper, then drizzle with olive oil. Place three lemon slices on the fillet, overlapping them slightly to cover the fish. Sprinkle asparagus, and tomatoes (if using) evenly around the fish, then drizzle with a little olive oil and season again with a small pinch each of salt and pepper. 3. Bring the long sides of the paper together, and fold the top edges down together to create a 1-inch seal, then continue to fold down tightly over the fish and vegetables. Twist the open ends of the parchment in opposite directions to prevent steam from escaping. 4. Repeat the process with the remaining ingredients and parchment. Place the packets on a baking sheet. (If not baking immediately, refrigerate for up to 4 hours.) 5. Bake until the packets are lightly browned and have puffed up, about 15 minutes. Transfer each packet to a plate and let stand for 5 minutes. Using sharp scissors, cut an X into the center of each packet and carefully pull back the parchment and sprinkle with the herbs. Serve immediately.

Per Serving:
calories: 93 | fat: 6g | protein: 6g | carbs: 3g | fiber: 1g | sugar: 1g | sodium: 133mg

Rosemary-Lemon Cod

Prep time: 10 minutes | Cook time: 11 minutes | Serves 4

- 2 tablespoons extra-virgin olive oil
- 1½ pounds (680 g) cod, skin and bones removed, cut into 4 fillets
- 1 tablespoon chopped fresh rosemary leaves
- ½ teaspoon freshly ground black pepper, or more to taste
- ½ teaspoon sea salt
- Juice of 1 lemon

1. In a large nonstick skillet over medium-high heat, heat the olive oil until it shimmers. 2. Season the cod with the rosemary, pepper, and salt. Add the fish to the skillet and cook for 3 to 5 minutes per side until opaque. 3. Pour the lemon juice over the cod fillets and cook for 1 minute.

Per Serving:
calories: 246 | fat: 9g | protein: 39g | carbs: 1g | fiber: 0g | sugar: 0g | sodium: 370mg

Whitefish Chowder

Prep time: 10 minutes | Cook time: 35 minutes | Serves 8

- 4 carrots, peeled and cut into ½-inch pieces
- 3 sweet potatoes, peeled and cut into ½-inch pieces
- 3 cups full-fat coconut milk
- 2 cups water
- 1 teaspoon dried thyme
- ½ teaspoon salt
- 10½ ounces (298 g) white fish, skinless and firm, such as cod or halibut, cut into chunks

1. In a large pot, combine the carrots, sweet potatoes, coconut milk, water, thyme, and salt. Bring to a boil over high heat. Reduce the heat to low. Cover and simmer for 20 minutes. 2. In a blender, purée half of the soup. Return the purée to the pot. Add the fish chunks. 3. Cook for 12 to 15 minutes more, or until the fish is tender and hot.

Per Serving:
calories: 451 | fat: 29g | protein: 14g | carbs: 39g | fiber: 8g | sugar: 7g | sodium: 251mg

Baked Salmon with Oregano Pistou

Prep time: 10 minutes | Cook time: 20 minutes | Serves 4

Pistou:

- 1 cup fresh oregano leaves
- ¼ cup almonds
- 2 garlic cloves
- Juice of 1 lime (1 or 2

tablespoons)
- Zest of 1 lime (optional)
- 1 tablespoon olive oil
- Pinch sea salt

Fish:

- 4 (6-ounce / 170-g) salmon fillets
- Sea salt, to taste
- Freshly ground black pepper, to taste
- 1 tablespoon olive oil

Make the Pistou: In a blender, combine the oregano, almonds, garlic, lime juice, lime zest (if using), olive oil, and sea salt. Pulse until very finely chopped. Transfer the pistou to a bowl and set it aside. Make the Fish: 1. Preheat the oven to 400°F (205°C). 2. Lightly season the salmon with sea salt and pepper. 3. Place a large ovenproof skillet over medium-high heat and add the olive oil. 4. Add the salmon and pan-sear for 4 minutes per side. 5. Place the skillet in the oven and bake the fish for about 10 minutes, or until it is just cooked through. 6. Serve the salmon topped with a spoonful of pistou.

Per Serving:

calories: 377 | fat: 22g | protein: 36g | carbs: 13g | fiber: 9g | sugar: 0g | sodium: 239mg

Wasabi Salmon Burgers

Prep time: 10 minutes | Cook time: 10 minutes | Serves 4

- ½ teaspoon raw honey
- 2 tablespoons reduced-salt soy sauce
- 1 teaspoon wasabi powder
- 1 beaten free range egg
- 2 cans of wild salmon, drained
- 2 scallions, chopped
- 2 tablespoons coconut oil
- 1 tablespoon fresh ginger, minced

1. Combine the salmon, egg, ginger, scallions and 1 tablespoon oil in a bowl, mixing well with your hands to form 4 patties. 2. In a separate bowl, add the wasabi powder and soy sauce with the honey and whisk until blended. 3. Heat 1 tablespoon oil over a medium heat in a skillet and cook the patties for 4 minutes each side until firm and browned. 4. Glaze the top of each patty with the wasabi mixture and cook for another 15 seconds before you serve. 5. Serve with your favorite side salad or vegetables for a healthy treat.

Per Serving:

calories: 253 | fat: 13g | protein: 32g | carbs: 3g | fiber: 0g | sugar: 1g | sodium: 588mg

Coconut Crab Cakes

Prep time: 15 minutes | Cook time: 12 minutes | Serves 4

- 2 pounds (907 g) cooked lump crab meat, drained and picked over
- ½ cup shredded unsweetened coconut
- ½ cup coconut flour, plus more as needed
- ½ cup shredded carrot
- 2 scallions, white and green parts, finely chopped
- 2 eggs
- 1 teaspoon freshly grated lemon zest (optional)
- 2 tablespoons olive oil

1. In a large bowl, stir together the crab, coconut, coconut flour, carrot, scallions, eggs, and lemon zest (if using) until the mixture holds together when pressed. Add more coconut flour if the mixture is too wet. 2. Divide the mixture into 8 portions and flatten them until they are about 1 inch thick. Cover the crab cakes and refrigerate for about 1 hour to firm up. 3. Place a large skillet over medium-high heat and add the olive oil. 4. Add the crab cakes and sear for about 6 minutes per side until cooked through and golden on both sides, turning just once. 5. Serve 2 crab cakes per person.

Per Serving:

calories: 406 | fat: 20g | protein: 50g | carbs: 5g | fiber: 2g | sugar: 1g | sodium: 859mg

Pan-Seared Haddock with Beets

Prep time: 20 minutes | Cook time: 30 minutes | Serves 4

- 8 beets, peeled and cut into eighths
- 2 shallots, thinly sliced
- 1 teaspoon bottled minced garlic
- 2 tablespoons olive oil, divided
- 2 tablespoons apple cider vinegar
- 1 teaspoon chopped fresh thyme
- Pinch sea salt
- 4 (5-ounce / 142-g) haddock fillets, patted dry

1. Preheat the oven to 400°F (205°C). 2. In a medium bowl, toss together the beets, shallots, garlic, and 1 tablespoon of olive oil until well coated. Spread the beet mixture in a 9-by-13-inch baking dish. Roast for about 30 minutes, or until the vegetables are caramelized and tender. 3. Remove the beets from the oven and stir in the cider vinegar, thyme, and sea salt. 4. While the beets are roasting, place a large skillet over medium-high heat and add the remaining 1 tablespoon of olive oil. 5. Panfry the fish for about 15 minutes, turning once, until it flakes when pressed with a fork. Serve the fish with a generous scoop of roasted beets.

Per Serving:

calories: 314 | fat: 9g | protein: 38g | carbs: 21g | fiber: 4g | sugar: 11g | sodium: 540mg

Grilled Salmon Packets with Asparagus

- 4 (4-ounce / 113-g) skinless salmon fillets
- 16 asparagus spears, tough ends trimmed
- 4 tablespoons avocado oil, divided
- 1 teaspoon garlic powder, divided
- ½ teaspoon salt, divided
- Freshly ground black pepper, to taste
- 1 lemon, thinly sliced

1. Preheat the oven to 400ºF (205ºC). 2. Cut 4 (12-inch) squares of parchment paper or foil and put on a work surface. 3. Place 1 salmon fillet in the center of each square and 4 asparagus spears next to each fillet. Brush the fish and asparagus with 1 tablespoon of avocado oil. 4. Sprinkle each fillet with ¼ teaspoon garlic powder and ⅛ teaspoon salt, and season with pepper. 5. Place the lemon slices on top of the fillets. Close and seal the parchment around each fillet so it forms a sealed packet. 6. Place the parchment packets on a baking sheet. Bake for 20 minutes. 7. Place a sealed parchment packet on each of 4 plates and serve hot.

Per Serving:
calories: 339 | fat: 23g | protein: 30g | carbs: 1g | fiber: 1g | sugar: 0g | sodium: 530mg

Sesame-Tuna with Asparagus

- 2 asparagus bunches, washed and trimmed
- 3 tablespoons toasted sesame oil, divided
- ½ teaspoon salt
- 4 (4-ounce / 113-g) tuna steaks
- 2 tablespoons sesame seeds

1. Preheat the oven to 375ºF (190ºC). 2. Line a baking sheet with parchment paper. 3. In a large bowl, combine the asparagus, 1½ tablespoons of sesame oil, and the salt. Spread the asparagus onto the prepared sheet. 4. Place the sheet in the preheated oven and bake for 15 minutes. 5. While the asparagus cooks, brush the tuna with the remaining 1½ tablespoons of sesame oil. 6. Place a sauté pan over medium heat. When the pan is hot, add the tuna. Depending on the size of your pan, you may need to cook the tuna steaks one or two at a time. 7. Sear the tuna for 3 to 4 minutes on each side, or longer if you like your tuna more well done. 8. Plate the tuna and the asparagus on four plates. Sprinkle 1½ teaspoons of sesame seeds over each serving.

Per Serving:
calories: 349 | fat: 20g | protein: 37g | carbs: 6g | fiber: 3g | sugar: 2g | sodium: 350mg

Seared Scallops with Greens

- 1½ pounds (680 g) sea scallops, cleaned and patted dry
- Sea salt, to taste
- Freshly ground black pepper, to taste
- 2 tablespoons olive oil, divided
- 2 garlic cloves, thinly sliced
- 2 cups chopped kale leaves
- 2 cups fresh spinach

1. Lightly season the scallops all over with sea salt and pepper. 2. Place a large skillet over medium-high heat and add 1 tablespoon of olive oil. 3. Pan-sear the scallops for about 2 minutes per side, or until opaque and just cooked through. Transfer to a plate and cover loosely with aluminum foil to keep them warm. Wipe the skillet with a paper towel and place it back on the heat. 4. Add the remaining 1 tablespoon of olive oil to the skillet and sauté the garlic for about 4 minutes, or until caramelized. 5. Stir in the kale and spinach. Cook, tossing with tongs, for about 6 minutes, or until the greens are tender and wilted. 6. Divide the greens with any juices equally among four plates and top each with the scallops.

Per Serving:
calories: 232 | fat: 8g | protein: 30g | carbs: 9g | fiber: 1g | sugar: 0g | sodium: 682mg

Lime-Salmon Patties

- ½ pound (227 g) cooked boneless salmon fillet, flaked
- 2 eggs
- ¾ cup almond flour, plus more as needed
- 1 scallion, white and green parts, chopped
- Juice of 2 limes (2 to 4
- tablespoons), plus more as needed
- Zest of 2 limes (optional)
- 1 tablespoon chopped fresh dill
- Pinch sea salt
- 1 tablespoon olive oil
- 1 lime, cut into wedges

1. In a large bowl, mix together the salmon, eggs, almond flour, scallion, lime juice, lime zest (if using), dill, and sea salt until the mixture holds together when pressed. If the mixture is too dry, add more lime juice; if it is too wet, add more almond flour. 2. Divide the salmon mixture into 4 equal portions, and press them into patties about ½ inch thick. Refrigerate them for about 30 minutes to firm up. 3. Place a large skillet over medium-high heat and add the olive oil. 4. Add the salmon patties and brown for about 5 minutes per side, turning once. 5. Serve the patties with lime wedges.

Per Serving:
calories: 243 | fat: 18g | protein: 18g | carbs: 5g | fiber: 2g | sugar: 0g | sodium: 84mg

Sautéed Sardines with Cauliflower Mash

Prep time: 10 minutes | Cook time: 15 minutes | Serves 4

- 2 heads cauliflower, broken into large florets
- 4 tablespoons extra-virgin olive oil, divided
- ¼ teaspoon salt
- 4 (4-ounce / 113-g) cans sardines packed in water, drained
- 1 cup fresh parsley, finely chopped

1. Fill a large pot with 2 inches of water and insert a steamer basket. Bring the water to a boil over high heat. 2. Add the cauliflower to the basket. Cover and steam for 8 to 10 minutes, or until the florets are tender. Transfer the cauliflower to a food processor. 3. Add 2 tablespoons of olive oil and the salt to the cauliflower. Process until the cauliflower is smooth and creamy. Depending on the size of your processor, you may need to do this in two batches. 4. In a medium bowl, roughly mash the sardines. 5. Add the remaining 2 tablespoons of olive oil to a medium pan set over low heat. When oil is shimmering, add the sardines and parsley. Cook for 3 minutes. You want the sardines to be warm, not scalding hot. 6. Serve the sardines with a generous scoop of cauliflower mash.

Per Serving:
calories: 334 | fat: 24g | protein: 26g | carbs: 8g | fiber: 4g | sugar: 3g | sodium: 465mg

Manhattan-Style Salmon Chowder

Prep time: 10 minutes | Cook time: 15 minutes | Serves 4

- ¼ cup extra-virgin olive oil
- 1 red bell pepper, chopped
- 1 pound (454 g) skinless salmon, pin bones removed, and chopped into ½-inch pieces
- 2 (28 ounces / 794 g) cans crushed tomatoes, 1 drained and 1 undrained
- 6 cups no-salt-added chicken broth
- 2 cups diced sweet potatoes
- 1 teaspoon onion powder
- ½ teaspoon sea salt
- ¼ teaspoon freshly ground black pepper

1. In a large pot over medium-high heat, heat the olive oil until it shimmers. 2. Add the red bell pepper and salmon. Cook for about 5 minutes, stirring occasionally, until the fish is opaque and the bell pepper is soft. 3. Stir in the tomatoes, chicken broth, sweet potatoes, onion powder, salt, and pepper. Bring to a simmer and reduce the heat to medium. Cook for about 10 minutes, stirring occasionally, until the sweet potatoes are soft.

Per Serving:
calories: 570 | fat: 39g | protein: 41g | carbs: 55g | fiber: 16g | sugar: 24g | sodium: 600mg

Salmon and Asparagus Skewers

Prep time: 20 minutes | Cook time: 10 minutes | Makes 8 skewers

- 2 tablespoons ghee, melted
- 1 teaspoon Dijon mustard
- 1 teaspoon garlic powder
- ½ teaspoon salt
- ¼ teaspoon red pepper flakes
- 1½ pounds (680 g) boned skinless salmon, cut into 2-inch chunks
- 2 lemons, thinly sliced
- 1 bunch asparagus spears, tough ends trimmed, cut into 2-inch pieces

1. Preheat the broiler. 2. Line a baking sheet with aluminum foil. 3. In a small saucepan over medium heat, heat the ghee. 4. Stir in the mustard, garlic powder, salt, and red pepper flakes. 5. On each skewer, thread 1 chunk of salmon, 1 lemon slice folded in half, and 2 pieces of asparagus. Repeat with the remaining skewers until all ingredients are used. Place the skewers on the prepared pan and brush each with the ghee-seasoning mixture. 6. Broil for 4 minutes. Turn the skewers and broil on the other side for about 4 minutes.

Per Serving:
calories: 250 | fat: 9g | protein: 38g | carbs: 4g | fiber: 2g | sugar: 0g | sodium: 433mg

Baked Halibut with Avocado Salsa

Prep time: 20 minutes | Cook time: 15 minutes | Serves 4

Salsa:
- 1 avocado, peeled, pitted, and diced
- ½ mango, diced, or about 1 cup frozen chunks, thawed
- ½ cup chopped fresh strawberries
- 1 teaspoon chopped fresh mint
- Juice of 1 lemon (3 tablespoons)
- Zest of 1 lemon (optional)

Fish:
- 4 (6-ounce / 170-g) boneless skinless halibut fillets, patted dry
- Sea salt, to taste
- Freshly ground black pepper, to taste
- 1 tablespoon olive oil

Make the Salsa: In a medium bowl, stir together the avocado, mango, strawberries, mint, lemon juice, and lemon zest (if using). Set it aside. Make the Fish: 1. Lightly season the halibut with sea salt and pepper. 2. Place a large skillet over medium heat and add the olive oil. 3. Add the fish and panfry for about 7 minutes per side, turning once, or until it is just cooked through. 4. Top with the avocado salsa and serve.

Per Serving:
calories: 354 | fat: 15g | protein: 43g | carbs: 12g | fiber: 4g | sugar: 7g | sodium: 282mg

Spiced Trout and Spinach

Prep time: 10 minutes | Cook time: 15 minutes | Serves 4

- Extra-virgin olive oil, for brushing
- ½ red onion, thinly sliced
- 1 (10-ounce / 283-g) package frozen spinach, thawed
- 4 boneless trout fillets
- 1 teaspoon salt
- ¼ teaspoon chipotle powder
- ¼ teaspoon garlic powder
- 2 tablespoons fresh lemon juice

1. Preheat the oven to 375ºF (190ºC). Brush a 9-by-13-inch baking pan with olive oil. 2. Scatter the red onion and spinach in the pan. 3. Lay the trout fillets over the spinach. 4. Sprinkle the salt, chipotle powder, and garlic powder over the fish. 5. Cover with aluminum foil and bake until the trout is firm, about 15 minutes. 6. Drizzle with the lemon juice and serve.

Per Serving:

calories: 160 | fat: 7g | protein: 19g | carbs: 5g | fiber: 2g | sugar: 1g | sodium: 670mg

Fish and Vegetable Casserole

Prep time: 25 minutes | Cook time: 30 minutes | Serves 4

- 2 cups diced sweet potato
- 2 cups diced carrot
- 2 cups diced parsnip
- 1 sweet onion, cut into eighths
- 1 cup (2-inch) asparagus pieces
- 2 teaspoons chopped fresh thyme
- 1 teaspoon bottled minced garlic
- ¼ teaspoon sea salt
- 1 tablespoon olive oil
- 4 (6-ounce / 170-g) skinless tilapia fillets
- Juice of 1 lemon (3 tablespoons)

1. Preheat the oven to 350ºF (180ºC). 2. Tear off four 18-by-24-inch pieces of aluminum foil and fold each piece in half to make four 18-by-12-inch pieces. 3. In a large bowl, toss together the sweet potato, carrot, parsnip, onion, asparagus, thyme, garlic, sea salt, and olive oil. Place one-fourth of the vegetables in the center of each foil piece. 4. Top each vegetable mound with one tilapia fillet. 5. Sprinkle the fish with lemon juice. 6. Fold the foil to create sealed packages that have a bit of space at the top, and arrange the packets on a baking sheet. 7. Bake for about 30 minutes, or until the fish begins to flake and the vegetables are tender. 8. Carefully open the packets, plate, and serve.

Per Serving:

calories: 353 | fat: 6g | protein: 36g | carbs: 43g | fiber: 9g | sugar: 10g | sodium: 259mg

Sesame Mahi-Mahi and Fruit Salsa

Prep time: 15 minutes | Cook time: 20 minutes | Serves 2

Salsa:
- 1 cup fresh pineapple, peeled and cubed
- ½ red chili, finely chopped
- 1 lime, juiced
- 2 teaspoons cilantro, chopped
- 1 onion, finely chopped

Fish:
- 2 mahi-mahi fillets
- 2 teaspoons coconut oil
- 2 tablespoons sesame seeds

1. Get a bowl and mix all of the ingredients for the salsa. 2. Drizzle 1 teaspoon coconut oil on the fillets and coat each side with the sesame seeds. 3. Heat 1 tablespoon oil over a medium heat and then sauté the fillets for about 8 minutes each side or until the flesh flakes away. 4. Serve with the salsa on the side.

Per Serving:

calories: 445 | fat: 25g | protein: 23g | carbs: g | fiber: 10g | sugar: 18g | sodium: 436mg

Five-Spice Cod Broth

Prep time: 20 minutes | Cook time: 20 minutes | Serves 4

- 2 black cod fillets
- A pinch of black pepper
- 1 teaspoon reduced-sodium soy sauce
- 2 cups homemade chicken broth (use vegetable if you've given up meat)
- 1 teaspoon coconut oil
- 1 teaspoon five-spice powder
- 1 tablespoon olive oil
- 3 heads of pak-choi
- 1 carrot, sliced
- 1 tablespoon ginger, minced
- 2 cups of udon noodles
- 1 green onion, thinly sliced
- 2 teaspoons cilantro, finely chopped
- 1 teaspoon sesame seeds

1. Rub the fish with pepper. 2. In a bowl, combine pepper, soy sauce, 1 cup chicken broth, coconut oil and spice blend. Mix together and place to one side. 3. In a large saucepan, heat the oil on a medium heat and cook the pak-choi, ginger and carrot for about 2 minutes until the pak-choi is green. 4. Add the rest of the reserved chicken stock and heat through. 5. Add the udon noodles and stir, bringing to a simmer. 6. Add the green onion and the fish and cook for 10 to 15 minutes until fish is tender. 7. Add the fish, noodles and vegetables into serving bowls and pour the broth over the top. 8. Garnish with the cilantro and sesame seeds and serve with chopsticks for real authenticity!

Per Serving:

calories: 360 | fat: 7g | protein: 22g | carbs: 58g | fiber: 14g | sugar: 18g | sodium: 493mg

Scrumptious Scallops with Cilantro and Lime

Prep time: 5 minutes | Cook time: 5 minutes | Serves 1

- 8 queen or king scallops (row on)
- 1 tablespoon extra sesame oil
- 2 large garlic cloves, finely

- chopped
- 1 red chili, finely chopped
- ½ lime juice
- 2 tablespoons of chopped cilantro

1. Heat oil in a skillet on a medium to high heat and fry scallops for about 1 minute each side until lightly golden. 2. Add the chopped chili and garlic cloves to the pan and squeeze the lime juice over the scallops. Saute for 2 to 3 minutes. 3. Remove the scallops and sprinkle the cilantro over the top to serve.

Per Serving:
calories: 236 | fat: 14g | protein: 16g | carbs: 12g | fiber: 1g | sugar: 3g | sodium: 477mg

Coconut-Crusted Cod with Mango-Pineapple Salsa

Prep time: 15 minutes | Cook time: 7 minutes | Serves 4

Salsa:
- 1 cup diced mango
- 1 cup diced pineapple
- ½ large avocado, diced

Cod:
- 1 egg
- 1 cup unsweetened dried coconut
- 2 tablespoons avocado oil
- 4 (4-ounce / 113-g) cod

- Juice of 1 lime
- Dash salt
- Dash chili powder

- fillets
- 1 teaspoon salt
- ½ teaspoon garlic powder
- ¼ teaspoon cayenne pepper

Make the Salsa: In a medium bowl, gently stir together the mango, pineapple, avocado, lime juice, salt, and chili powder. Make the Cod: 1. In a small shallow bowl, beat the egg. Put the coconut in another small shallow bowl. 2. Dip each cod fillet into the egg, then into the coconut until well coated, and place on a plate. 3. Sprinkle each fillet with the salt, garlic powder, and cayenne pepper. 4. In a large skillet over medium-high heat, heat the avocado oil. 5. Cook each fillet one at a time in the hot skillet for 4 to 5 minutes. Flip and cook on the other side for 1 to 2 minutes until the flesh begins to flake. Transfer to a plate. 6. Top each fillet with salsa and serve.

Per Serving:
calories: 369 | fat: 27g | protein: 18g | carbs: 18g | fiber: 5g | sugar: 12g | sodium: 1069mg

Seared Honey-Garlic Scallops

Prep time: 10 minutes | Cook time: 15 minutes | Serves 4

- 1 pound (454 g) large scallops, rinsed
- Dash salt
- Dash freshly ground black pepper
- 2 tablespoons avocado oil

- ¼ cup raw honey
- 3 tablespoons coconut aminos
- 2 garlic cloves, minced
- 1 tablespoon apple cider vinegar

1. Pat the scallops dry with paper towels and sprinkle with the salt and pepper. 2. In a large skillet over medium-high heat, heat the avocado oil. 3. Place the scallops in the skillet, and cook for 2 to 3 minutes per side until golden. Transfer to a plate, tent loosely with aluminum foil to keep warm, and set aside. 4. In the same skillet, stir together the honey, coconut aminos, garlic, and vinegar. Bring to a simmer, and cook for 7 minutes, stirring occasionally as the liquid reduces. 5. Return the scallops to the skillet with the glaze. Toss gently to coat and serve warm.

Per Serving:
calories: 383 | fat: 19g | protein: 21g | carbs: 26g | fiber: 1g | sugar: 17g | sodium: 496mg

Cod with Ginger and Black Beans

Prep time: 10 minutes | Cook time: 15 minutes | Serves 4

- 2 tablespoons extra-virgin olive oil
- 4 (6 ounces / 170 g) cod fillets
- 1 tablespoon grated fresh ginger
- 1 teaspoon sea salt, divided

- ¼ teaspoon freshly ground black pepper
- 5 garlic cloves, minced
- 1 (14 ounces / 397 g) can black beans, drained
- ¼ cup chopped fresh cilantro leaves

1. In a large nonstick skillet over medium-high heat, heat the olive oil until it shimmers. 2. Season the cod with the ginger, ½ teaspoon of the salt, and the pepper. Place it in the hot oil and cook for about 4 minutes per side until the fish is opaque. Remove the cod from the pan and set it aside on a platter, tented with aluminum foil. 3. Return the skillet to the heat and add the garlic. Cook for 30 seconds, stirring constantly. 4. Stir in the black beans and the remaining ½ teaspoon of salt. Cook for 5 minutes, stirring occasionally. 5. Stir in the cilantro and spoon the black beans over the cod.

Per Serving:
calories: 419 | fat: 2g | protein: 50g | carbs: 33g | fiber: 8g | sugar: 1g | sodium: 505mg

Sole with Vegetables in Foil Packets

Prep time: 15 minutes | Cook time: 15 minutes | Serves 4

- 4 (5-ounce / 142-g) sole fillets
- Salt, to taste
- Freshly ground black pepper, to taste
- 1 zucchini, sliced thinly, divided
- 1 carrot, sliced thinly, divided
- 2 shallots, sliced thinly, divided
- 2 tablespoons snipped fresh chives, divided
- 4 teaspoons extra-virgin olive oil, divided
- ½ cup vegetable broth, or water, divided
- Lemon wedges, for garnish

1. Preheat the oven to 425ºF (220ºC). 2. Tear off four 12-by-20-inch pieces of aluminum foil. 3. Place 1 fillet on one half of a foil piece. Season with salt and pepper. 4. Top the fillet with one-quarter each of the zucchini, carrot, and shallots. Sprinkle with 1½ teaspoons of chives. 5. Drizzle 1 teaspoon of olive oil and 2 tablespoons of vegetable broth over the vegetables and fish. 6. Fold the other half of the foil over the fish and vegetables, sealing the edges so the ingredients are completely encased in the packet and the contents won't leak. Place the packet on a large baking sheet. 7. Repeat steps 3 through 6 with the remaining ingredients. 8. Place the sheet in the preheated oven and bake the packets for 15 minutes, or until the fish is cooked through and the vegetables are tender. 9. Carefully peel back the foil (the escaping steam will be hot) and transfer the contents—the liquid, too—to a plate. Serve garnished with the lemon wedges.

Per Serving:
calories: 224 | fat: 7g | protein: 35g | carbs: 4g | fiber: 1g | sugar: 2g | sodium: 205mg

Pecan-Crusted Trout

Prep time: 15 minutes | Cook time: 15 minutes | Serves 4

- Extra-virgin olive oil, for brushing
- 4 large boneless trout fillets
- Salt, to taste
- Freshly ground black pepper, to taste
- 1 cup pecans, finely ground, divided
- 1 tablespoon coconut oil, melted, divided
- 2 tablespoon chopped fresh thyme leaves
- Lemon wedges, for garnish

1. Preheat the oven to 375ºF (190ºC). 2. Brush a rimmed baking sheet with olive oil. 3. Place the trout fillets on the baking sheet skin-side down. Season with salt and pepper. 4. Gently press ¼ cup of ground pecans into the flesh of each fillet. 5. Drizzle the melted coconut oil over the nuts and then sprinkle the thyme over

the fillets. 6. Give each fillet another sprinkle of salt and pepper. 7. Place the sheet in the preheated oven and bake for 15 minutes, or until the fish is cooked through.

Per Serving:
calories: 672 | fat: 59g | protein: 30g | carbs: 13g | fiber: 9g | sugar: 3g | sodium: 110mg

Fennel Baked Salmon

Prep time: 10 minutes | Cook time: 20 minutes | Serves 4

- 1 tablespoon extra-virgin olive oil
- 1 fennel bulb, thinly sliced
- ½ small red onion, thinly sliced
- 4 (3- to 4-ounce / 85- to
- 113-g) boneless salmon fillets
- 1 teaspoon salt
- ¼ teaspoon freshly ground black pepper
- ½ cup dry white wine

1. Preheat the oven to 375ºF (190ºC). Brush a 9-inch square baking pan with the olive oil. 2. Scatter the fennel and red onion slices in the bottom of the pan. 3. Add the salmon fillets and the salt and pepper. Pour in the wine. 4. Bake until the salmon is firm to the touch and flakes with a fork, about 20 minutes. 5. Let the salmon rest for 5 minutes before serving.

Per Serving:
calories: 250 | fat: 14g | protein: 20g | carbs: 6g | fiber: 2g | sugar: 3g | sodium: 670mg

White Fish with Mushrooms

Prep time: 15 minutes | Cook time: 18 minutes | Serves 4

- 1 leek, thinly sliced
- 1 teaspoon minced fresh ginger root
- 1 garlic clove, minced
- ½ cup sliced shiitake mushrooms
- ½ cup dry white wine
- 1 tablespoon toasted sesame oil
- 4 (6-ounce / 170-g) white fish fillets (such as cod, haddock, or pollock)
- 1 teaspoon salt
- ⅛ teaspoon freshly ground black pepper

1. Preheat the oven to 375ºF (190ºC). 2. Combine the leek, ginger root, garlic, mushrooms, wine, and sesame oil in a 9-by-13-inch baking pan. Toss well to combine. 3. Bake for 10 minutes. 4. Set the fish on top of the mushrooms. Add the salt and pepper, cover with aluminum foil, and bake until the fish is firm, 5 to 8 minutes. Serve.

Per Serving:
calories: 210 | fat: 5g | protein: 31g | carbs: 5g | fiber: 1g | sugar: 1g | sodium: 680mg

Salmon with Quinoa

- 1 tablespoon extra-virgin olive oil, plus additional for brushing
- 1 pound (454 g) salmon fillets
- Salt, to taste
- Freshly ground black pepper, to taste
- 1 red onion, diced

- 2 cups cooked quinoa
- 1 pint cherry tomatoes, halved
- ½ cup chopped fresh basil
- ¼ cup chopped green olives
- 1 tablespoon apple cider vinegar

1. Preheat the oven to 375ºF (190ºC). 2. Brush a rimmed baking sheet with olive oil. Place the salmon fillets on the prepared sheet and brush the top of each with olive oil. Season with salt and pepper. 3. Place the sheet in the preheated oven and bake for 20 minutes. 4. In a large pan over medium-high heat, heat 1 tablespoon of olive oil. Add the onion and sauté for 3 minutes. 5. Stir in the quinoa, cherry tomatoes, basil, olives, and cider vinegar. Cook for 1 to 2 minutes, or until the tomatoes and quinoa are warmed through. 6. Transfer the tomatoes, quinoa, and salmon to a serving platter and serve.

Per Serving:

calories: 396 | fat: 16g | protein: 30g | carbs: 36g | fiber: 6g | sugar: 4g | sodium: 395mg

Curry-Glazed Salmon with Quinoa

- ¼ cup raw honey
- 1 teaspoon curry powder, plus additional as needed
- 6 (4-ounce / 113-g) wild salmon fillets

- 2 cups quinoa, rinsed well
- 4 cups water
- ½ teaspoon salt

1. Preheat the oven to 350ºF (180ºC). 2. Line a baking sheet with parchment paper. 3. In a small bowl, mix together the honey and curry powder. Taste, and add more curry powder if needed. 4. Pat the fillets dry with a clean kitchen towel and place them on the prepared sheet. 5. Brush the fillets with the curry and honey mixture. 6. In a medium pot, combine the quinoa, water, and salt. Bring to a boil over high heat. Reduce the heat to low. Cover and cook for 15 minutes. 7. Put the salmon into the preheated oven and bake for 15 to 20 minutes, or until the flesh is opaque and flakes easily with a fork. 8. Fluff the quinoa and serve alongside the salmon.

Per Serving:

calories: 445 | fat: 13g | protein: 32g | carbs: 48g | fiber: 4g | sugar: 12g | sodium: 251mg

Shrimp with Cinnamon Sauce

- 2 tablespoons extra-virgin olive oil
- 1½ pounds (680 g) peeled shrimp
- 2 tablespoons Dijon mustard
- 1 cup no-salt-added chicken broth

- 1 teaspoon ground cinnamon
- 1 teaspoon onion powder
- ½ teaspoon sea salt
- ¼ teaspoon freshly ground black pepper

1. In a large nonstick skillet over medium-high heat, heat the olive oil until it shimmers. 2. Add the shrimp. Cook for about 4 minutes, stirring occasionally, until the shrimp is opaque. 3. In a small bowl, whisk the mustard, chicken broth, cinnamon, onion powder, salt, and pepper. Pour this into the skillet and continue to cook for 3 minutes, stirring occasionally.

Per Serving:

calories: 270 | fat: 11g | protein: 39g | carbs: 4g | fiber: 1g | sugar: 1g | sodium: 564mg

Beef, Pork, and Lamb

Chapter 6 Beef, Pork, and Lamb

Savory Beef Meatloaf

Prep time: 10 minutes | Cook time: 1 hour | Serves 4

- 1½ pounds (680 g) extra-lean ground beef
- ½ cup almond flour
- ½ cup chopped sweet onion
- 1 egg
- 1 tablespoon chopped fresh
- basil
- 1 tablespoon chopped fresh parsley
- 1 teaspoon grated fresh horseradish, or prepared horseradish
- ⅛ teaspoon sea salt

1. Preheat the oven to 350ºF (180ºC). 2. In a large bowl, combine the ground beef, almond flour, onion, egg, basil, parsley, horseradish, and sea salt until well mixed. Press the meatloaf mixture into a 9-by-5-inch loaf pan. 3. Bake for about 1 hour until cooked through. 4. Remove the meatloaf from the oven, and let it rest for 10 minutes.

Per Serving:
calories: 407 | fat: 18g | protein: 56g | carbs: 4g | fiber: 2g | sugar: 2g | sodium: 215mg

Lazy Moco

Prep time: 10 minutes | Cook time: 15 minutes | Serves 4

- 4 cups riced cauliflower
- 2 tablespoons ghee, divided
- 1½ teaspoons fine

Gravy:
- 3 tablespoons ghee
- 2 tablespoons coconut flour
- 1 cup bone broth
- 1 tablespoon coconut vinegar
- 3 sprigs fresh thyme or

- Himalayan salt, divided
- 1 pound (454 g) 85% lean ground beef

- rosemary
- ½ teaspoon fine Himalayan salt
- ½ teaspoon ground black pepper
- 4 large eggs

1. Preheat the oven to 425ºF (220ºC). 2. Spread the cauliflower on a sheet pan so that it takes up about three-quarters of it. Drizzle 1 tablespoon of the ghee over the cauliflower and sprinkle with 1 teaspoon of the salt. 3. Form the beef into four patties about ¼ inch thick and make an indentation in the center of each patty. Coat the

patties with the remaining tablespoon of ghee and sprinkle with the remaining teaspoon of salt. Line them up next to the riced cauliflower in the empty space on the sheet pan. Place in the oven and roast for 15 minutes. 4. Meanwhile, make the gravy: Melt the ghee in a small saucepan over medium-high heat. Whisk in the coconut flour and keep whisking until the flour is browned and smells toasty, almost like popcorn. This will take only a few minutes. Then pour in the broth and vinegar and stir until the mixture is smooth and fluid. Add the thyme sprigs, salt, and pepper and bring to a boil. Reduce the gravy for 5 to 8 minutes, whisking occasionally, until it becomes thick. When it's ready, it will coat a back of a spoon. Remove the gravy from the heat and discard the thyme sprigs. 5. When the patties have about 5 minutes left to cook, heat a large skillet over medium heat. When it's hot, lightly grease the skillet, then crack in the eggs. Cook, undisturbed, until the whites are cooked through. Remove from the heat. Use the edge of the spatula to separate the eggs. 6. Assemble four plates, each with a cup of riced cauliflower topped with a burger patty, a generous amount of gravy over the patty, and a fried egg. Enjoy! 7. Store leftovers in an airtight container in the fridge for up to 5 days. To reheat, place in a skillet over medium heat, and fry the egg to order.

Per Serving:
calories: 541 | fat: 45g | protein: 31g | carbs: 9g | fiber: 5g | sugar: 1g | sodium: 598mg

Roasted Leg of Lamb

Prep time: 15 minutes | Cook time: 5 to 6 hours | Serves 4 to 6

- 1½ teaspoons sea salt
- ½ teaspoon freshly ground black pepper
- 1 teaspoon garlic powder
- 1 teaspoon dried thyme leaves
- 1 teaspoon dried rosemary

- 1 teaspoons Dijon mustard
- 1 (4-pound / 1.8-kg) bone-in lamb leg
- 2 cups broth of choice
- 1 small onion, roughly chopped

1. In a small bowl, stir together the salt, pepper, garlic powder, thyme, rosemary, and mustard to make a paste. Rub the paste evenly onto the lamb, and put it in the slow cooker. 2. Add the broth and onion around the lamb in the cooker. 3. Cover the cooker and set to low. Cook for 5 to 6 hours and serve.

Per Serving:
calories: 780 | fat: 41g | protein: 93g | carbs: 3g | fiber: 0g | sugar: 1g | sodium: 1023mg

Lentil-Lamb Ragu

Prep time: 10 minutes | Cook time: 30 minutes | Serves 4

- 2 tablespoons extra-virgin olive oil
- 1 red onion, chopped
- 4 garlic cloves, minced
- 1 pound (454 g) lean ground lamb
- 1 (14-ounce / 397-g) can chopped tomatoes
- 1 cup chicken broth, plus additional as needed
- ½ cup green lentils
- 1 teaspoon salt
- 1 teaspoon dried oregano
- 1 teaspoon ground cumin
- ½ teaspoon freshly ground black pepper

1. In a large pan over high heat, heat the olive oil. Add the onion and sauté for 3 minutes. Add the garlic and sauté for 1 minute. 2. Add the ground lamb, breaking it up with a spoon. Cook for 3 to 4 minutes, or until the lamb is browned. 3. Stir in the tomatoes, chicken broth, lentils, salt, oregano, cumin, and pepper. Simmer for 20 minutes, or until the lentils are cooked and most the liquid has evaporated. If the lentils are not yet tender and most of the liquid has evaporated, stir in a little more broth or some water.

Per Serving:
calories: 402 | fat: 16g | protein: 41g | carbs: 23g | fiber: 10g | sugar: 5g | sodium: 867mg

Party Meatballs

Prep time: 20 minutes | Cook time: 10 minutes | Serves 5

- 2 pounds (907 g) 85% lean ground beef
- 3 large egg whites, beaten
- 2 tablespoons red wine vinegar
- 1 tablespoon nutritional yeast
- 2 teaspoons dried dill weed
- 2 teaspoons dried parsley
- 1½ teaspoons fine Himalayan salt
- 2 teaspoons garlic powder
- 2 teaspoons ground black pepper
- 2 teaspoons onion powder
- 1 cup coconut oil, or more if needed, for frying

1. Arrange the oven racks in the middle and bottom positions. Preheat the oven to 400ºF (205ºC). Line two sheet pans with parchment paper. 2. Place all the ingredients except the coconut oil and dressing in a large bowl. Mix well with your hands. Shape the meat mixture into ½-inch meatballs. Use a small scoop or teaspoon to measure, then roll them between your hands to shape them. Place on the prepared sheet pans and bake for 10 minutes. 3. While the meatballs bake, heat a large pot over medium-high heat. Pour in the coconut oil—it should be 1 inch deep—and heat until the oil sizzles around the end of a wooden spoon handle when it's inserted in the oil. Add about fifteen meatballs at a time to the pot and cook for 3

to 5 minutes, using a slotted spoon to move and turn the meatballs as they cook. Then use the spoon to remove them from the oil and set on a paper towel–lined plate to drain. Repeat until all of the meatballs are browned and crispy. 4. Serve the meatballs with toothpicks, if desired. 5. Store leftovers in an airtight container in the fridge for up to 5 days. To reheat, bake in a preheated 350ºF (180ºC) oven for 10 minutes.

Per Serving:
calories: 305 | fat: 25g | protein: 20g | carbs: 1g | fiber: 1g | sugar: 0g | sodium: 574mg

Protein Fried Rice

Prep time: 10 minutes | Cook time: 25 minutes | Serves 6

- 1 pound (454 g) 85% lean ground beef
- 1 pound (454 g) ground pork
- 3 tablespoons sesame oil, divided
- 3 tablespoons coconut aminos, divided
- 1 tablespoon coconut oil
- 3 ribs celery, diced
- 3 cloves garlic, minced
- 2 green onions, sliced
- 1 tablespoon peeled and minced fresh ginger
- ½ cup chopped asparagus spears
- 1 tablespoon fish sauce
- 1 teaspoon fine Himalayan salt
- 1 teaspoon ground black pepper
- 1 teaspoon onion powder
- 1½ cups riced cauliflower
- Sesame seeds, for garnish (optional)

1. In a large bowl, mix together the ground beef and pork using your hands. Pour in 1 tablespoon of the sesame oil and 1 tablespoon of the coconut aminos. Gently mix and set aside. 2. Heat a large skillet over medium heat. When it's hot, melt the coconut oil in the skillet. Add the celery, garlic, green onions, and ginger. Sauté, stirring often, for 5 minutes, then remove the mixture from the skillet and set aside. Don't wash the skillet. 3. Add the meat mixture to the skillet, using your fingers to crumble it. Cook, using a whisk to break it up and stir it frequently, until browned and crumbled, 3 to 5 minutes. Continue to cook, stirring occasionally, until any fluid the meat released has evaporated, about another 10 minutes. It will smell divine, and there will be dark brown bits among the meat. 4. Add the cooked aromatics to the skillet, along with the asparagus, the remaining 2 tablespoons of sesame oil, the remaining 2 tablespoons of coconut aminos, the fish sauce, salt, pepper, and onion powder. Immediately mix in the riced cauliflower, stir, and cook for another 5 minutes, until the rice is thoroughly combined and heated. Garnish with sesame seeds, if desired. 5. Serve hot! Store leftovers in an airtight container in the fridge for up to 5 days. To reheat, sauté in a skillet over medium heat.

Per Serving:
calories: 463 | fat: 35g | protein: 30g | carbs: 7g | fiber: 3g | sugar: 1g | sodium: 600mg

Korean Beef Lettuce Wraps

- 2 pounds (907 g) beef chuck roast
- 1 small white onion, diced
- 1 cup broth of choice
- 3 tablespoons coconut aminos
- 2 tablespoons coconut sugar
- 1 tablespoon rice vinegar
- 1 teaspoon garlic powder
- 1 teaspoon sesame oil
- ½ teaspoon ground ginger
- ¼ teaspoon red pepper flakes
- 8 romaine lettuce leaves
- 1 tablespoon sesame seeds (optional)
- 2 scallions (both white and green parts), diced (optional)

1. In your slow cooker, combine the beef, onion, broth, coconut aminos, coconut sugar, vinegar, garlic powder, sesame oil, ginger, and red pepper flakes. 2. Cover the cooker and set to low. Cook for 7 to 8 hours. 3. Scoop spoonfuls of the beef mixture into each lettuce leaf. Garnish with sesame seeds and diced scallion (if using) and serve.

Per Serving:

calories: 428 | fat: 23g | protein: 46g | carbs: 12g | fiber: 1g | sugar: 10g | sodium: 425mg

Grilled Rib-Eye And Summer Succotash

- 1 pound (454 g) boneless rib-eye steak
- Olive oil for brushing
- Kosher salt, to taste
- Freshly ground black pepper
- 1 small shallot, minced
- 3 tablespoons lime juice
- 1 tablespoon sherry vinegar
- 1 tablespoon Dijon mustard
- 1 tablespoon honey
- ¼ cup extra-virgin olive oil
- 3 tablespoons finely chopped herbs, such as basil, mint, and chives
- 3 zucchini, ends trimmed, and sliced lengthwise into strips ½ inch thick
- 2 summer squash, ends trimmed, and sliced lengthwise into strips ½ inch thick
- 2 red or yellow bell peppers, halved and seeds, core and stem removed (optional if nightshade-sensitive)
- 2 cups cherry tomatoes, halved (optional if nightshade-sensitive)
- 1 cup edamame, fava beans, or other shelled fresh beans, blanched

1. Rinse the steak and thoroughly pat dry. Place on a plate and brush both sides with olive oil. Season generously with salt and pepper and let rest at room temperature for 1 hour. 2. In a small bowl, whisk together the shallot, lime juice, vinegar, mustard, and honey. Slowly whisk in the extra-virgin olive oil to form a vinaigrette. Gently stir in the herbs, then taste and season with salt and pepper. Set aside. 3. Prepare a grill for direct cooking over high heat. 4. Brush the zucchini strips, summer squash strips, and bell pepper halves on both sides with olive oil, then sprinkle with salt and pepper. Grill the zucchini and squash until just cooked through, about 2 minutes per side. Transfer to a cutting board. Grill the bell peppers, turning occasionally, until charred and blistered, 5 to 7 minutes. Place in a small bowl and cover with plastic wrap. Allow the vegetables to cool. 5. While the vegetables cool, grill the steak until well seared and an instant-read thermometer inserted into the center reads 130ºF (55ºC) for medium-rare, 3 to 4 minutes per side, or grill longer to reach the desired doneness. Allow the steak to rest on a cutting board for 5 to 10 minutes before slicing across the grain. 6. Remove the skins from the cooled bell peppers. Cut the zucchini, squash, and peppers into ½-inch dice. Place the vegetables in a large bowl and add the tomatoes (if using) and edamame. Pour half of the vinaigrette over the vegetables and toss to coat, adjusting with more vinaigrette as desired. 7. Place several generous spoonsful of the succotash on each plate, then pair with a fourth of the sliced steak. Serve immediately.

Per Serving:

calories: 223 | fat: 15g | protein: 16g | carbs: 9g | fiber: 3g | sugar: 6g | sodium: 62mg

Thin-Cut Pork Chops with Mustardy Kale

- 4 thin-cut pork chops
- 1 teaspoon sea salt, divided
- ¼ teaspoon freshly ground black pepper, divided
- 4 tablespoons Dijon mustard, divided
- 3 tablespoons extra-virgin olive oil
- ½ red onion, finely chopped
- 4 cups stemmed and chopped kale
- 2 tablespoons apple cider vinegar

1. Preheat the oven to 425ºF (220ºC). 2. Season the pork chops with ½ teaspoon of the salt and ⅛ teaspoon of the pepper. Spread 2 tablespoons of the mustard over them and put them on a rimmed baking sheet. Bake for about 15 minutes, or until the pork registers an internal temperature of 165ºF (74ºC) on an instant-read meat thermometer. 3. While the pork cooks, in a large nonstick skillet over medium-high, heat the olive oil until it shimmers. 4. Add the red onion and kale. Cook for about 7 minutes, stirring occasionally, until the vegetables soften. 5. In a small bowl, whisk the remaining 2 tablespoons of mustard, the cider vinegar, the remaining ½ teaspoon of salt, and the remaining ⅛ teaspoon of pepper. Add this to the kale. Cook for 2 minutes, stirring.

Per Serving:

calories: 504 | fat: 39g | protein: 28g | carbs: 10g | fiber: 2g | sugar: 0g | sodium: 595mg

Beefy Lentil and Tomato Stew

Prep time: 10 minutes | Cook time: 10 minutes | Serves 4

- 2 tablespoons extra-virgin olive oil
- 1 pound (454 g) extra-lean ground beef
- 1 onion, chopped
- 1 (14 ounces / 397 g) can lentils, drained
- 1 (14 ounces / 397 g) can chopped tomatoes with garlic and basil, drained
- ½ teaspoon sea salt
- ⅛ teaspoon freshly ground black pepper

1. In a large pot over medium-high heat, heat the olive oil until it shimmers. 2. Add the beef and onion. Cook for about 5 minutes, crumbling the beef with a wooden spoon until it browns. 3. Stir in the lentils, tomatoes, salt, and pepper. Bring to a simmer. Reduce the heat to medium. Cook for 3 to 4 minutes, stirring, until the lentils are hot.

Per Serving:
calories: 461 | fat: 15g | protein: 44g | carbs: 37g | fiber: 17g | sugar: 2g | sodium: 321mg

Pan-Seared Rib-Eye with Arugula

Prep time: 5 minutes | Cook time: 15 minutes | Serves 4

- 1 (1½- to 2-pound / 680- to 907-g) bone-in rib-eye steak
- 2 tablespoons ghee, divided
- 1½ teaspoons fine Himalayan salt
- 5 cloves garlic, peeled
- 3 sprigs fresh oregano, thyme, or sage
- 2 cups fresh arugula

1. Set the rib-eye out to come to room temperature about 30 minutes before you begin cooking. 2. Place a large cast-iron skillet in the oven and preheat the oven to 425ºF (220ºC). 3. While the oven heats, brush the steak with 1 tablespoon of the ghee and sprinkle it with the salt. 4. When the oven has come to temperature, remove the skillet and set it on the stovetop over medium heat. Place the steak in the skillet and sear for 2 minutes. Flip the steak with tongs and top it with the garlic and herbs. Sear for 2 minutes on the other side, then place the skillet with the steak in the oven for 8 to 10 minutes, depending on the thickness of the steak and the desired doneness. 5. Remove the skillet from the oven and return it to the stovetop over medium heat. Move the herbs and garlic to the side of the pan and dollop the remaining tablespoon of ghee over them. 6. Carefully tilt the skillet so the fat pools with the garlic and herbs. Using a small spoon, repeatedly pour this pooled fat over the steak as it cooks for 2 minutes. 7. Remove the steak from the skillet and set it on a cutting board to rest for 5 minutes. When ready to serve, run a sharp knife along the inside of the bone to separate the meat, then slice the steak against the grain in very thin slices. 8. Divide the steak slices among four plates. Add ½ cup arugula to each plate and spoon the pan sauce all over the arugula. Enjoy! 9. It's a shame to eat meat this good as leftovers—it's just not the same. But if you have extra, cut it up into small pieces and store in an airtight container in the fridge for up to 4 days. Reheat in a hot skillet. Rib-eye is fatty, so it will be nice and crispy; toss it with eggs or greens for a beef hash.

Per Serving:
calories: 586 | fat: 47g | protein: 38g | carbs: 2g | fiber: 0g | sugar: 0g | sodium: 592mg

Beef and Bell Pepper Fajitas

Prep time: 5 minutes | Cook time: 10 minutes | Serves 4

- 3 tablespoons extra-virgin olive oil
- 1½ pounds (680 g) flank steak, cut against the grain into ½-inch strips
- 2 green bell peppers, sliced
- 1 onion, sliced
- 1 cup store-bought salsa
- 1 teaspoon garlic powder
- ½ teaspoon sea salt

1. In a large nonstick skillet over medium-high heat, heat the olive oil until it shimmers. 2. Add the beef, bell peppers, and onion. Cook for about 6 minutes, stirring occasionally, until the beef browns. 3. Stir in the salsa, garlic powder, and salt. Cook for 3 minutes, stirring.

Per Serving:
calories: 470 | fat: 25g | protein:49 g | carbs: 12g | fiber: 3g | sugar: 6g | sodium: 562mg

Garlic-Mustard Lamb Chops

Prep time: 30 minutes | Cook time: 20 minutes | Serves 4

- 8 (4- to 5-ounce / 113- to 142-g) lamb loin chops
- 2 tablespoons chopped fresh oregano
- 4 garlic cloves, mashed
- ¼ cup extra-virgin olive oil
- 1 teaspoon Dijon mustard
- 1 teaspoon salt
- ¼ teaspoon freshly ground black pepper

1. Place the lamb chops in a shallow baking dish. 2. In a small bowl, whisk together the oregano, garlic, olive oil, Dijon mustard, salt, and pepper. 3. Rub the mixture over the lamb chops. Cover the dish with plastic wrap and marinate the chops at room temperature for 30 minutes. 4. Preheat the oven to 425ºF (220ºC). 5. Remove the plastic wrap and place the dish in the preheated oven. Bake the lamb chops for 15 to 20 minutes, or until they are sizzling and browned. 6. Let the chops sit for 5 minutes before serving.

Per Serving:
calories: 648 | fat: 34g | protein: 80g | carbs: 3g | fiber: 1g | sugar: 0g | sodium: 812mg

Carne Molida

Prep time: 5 minutes | Cook time: 20 minutes | Serves 4

- 2 tablespoons avocado oil
- 2 pounds (907 g) 85% lean ground beef
- 1 tablespoon granulated garlic
- 2 teaspoons dried parsley
- 1½ teaspoons fine Himalayan salt
- 2 teaspoons ground black pepper
- 2 teaspoons onion powder
- 1 teaspoon ground cumin
- Juice of 1 lime
- Chopped fresh cilantro, for garnish (optional)

1. Add the oil in a large pot over medium heat. Quickly add the ground beef, crumbling it in with your hands. 2. Sprinkle all the seasonings over the ground beef and stir to combine. Use a spatula or whisk to break up the meat as you stir so that it continues to crumble and there are no large chunks. 3. Cook, stirring occasionally, for 10 to 15 minutes. The beef will brown, then release some liquid; let that liquid boil away. Increase the heat to medium-high. Keep cooking and stirring until the beef is glossy and dark brown. Once you begin having to scrape it from the bottom of the pot, it's crispy. Turn off the heat. Squeeze in the lime juice and mix. 4. Serve hot! A little chopped fresh cilantro for garnish goes really well, but it's not necessary.

Per Serving:
calories: 326 | fat: 23g | protein: 24g | carbs: 6g | fiber: 1g | sugar: 2g | sodium: 576mg

Lamb and Quinoa Skillet Ragù

Prep time: 15 minutes | Cook time: 20 minutes | Serves 6

- 1 cup quinoa, rinsed well
- 2 cups filtered water
- 1 pound (454 g) ground lamb
- 3 garlic cloves, minced
- 1 yellow onion, diced
- 1 red bell pepper, diced
- 1 (28-ounce / 794-g) can
- diced tomatoes with their juice
- 1 cup minced fresh spinach leaves
- 2 teaspoons chili powder
- ½ teaspoon ground cumin
- ½ teaspoon smoked paprika
- Dash red pepper flakes

1. In a medium saucepan over high heat, bring the quinoa and the water to a boil. Cover the pan and reduce the heat to low. Simmer for 15 minutes. Remove from the heat and fluff with a fork. 2. Meanwhile, in a large skillet over medium heat, cook the lamb for 10 minutes, stirring occasionally to break up the meat. 3. Add the garlic, onion, and red bell pepper. Cook, stirring, for 5 minutes. 4. Stir in the tomatoes, spinach, chili powder, cumin, paprika, and red pepper flakes. Cover and cook for about 5 minutes, or until the lamb is fully cooked. 5. Remove the ragù from the heat and spoon over portions of quinoa.

Per Serving:
calories: 306 | fat: 13g | protein: 19g | carbs: 26g | fiber: 5g | sugar: 5g | sodium: 92mg

Pork Ragù

Prep time: 15 minutes | Cook time: 7 to 8 hours | Serves 4 to 6

- 1 pound (454 g) pork tenderloin
- 1 medium yellow onion, diced
- 1 red bell pepper, diced
- 1 (28-ounce / 794-g) can diced tomatoes
- 2 teaspoons chili powder
- 1 teaspoon garlic powder
- ½ teaspoon ground cumin
- ½ teaspoon smoked paprika
- Dash red pepper flakes
- 1 cup fresh spinach leaves, minced

1. In your slow cooker, combine the pork, onion, bell pepper, tomatoes, chili powder, garlic powder, cumin, paprika, red pepper flakes, and spinach. 2. Cover the cooker and set to low. Cook for 7 to 8 hours. 3. Transfer the pork loin to a cutting board and shred with a fork. Return it to the slow cooker, stir it into the sauce, and serve.

Per Serving:
calories: 292 | fat: 10g | protein: 36g | carbs: 15g | fiber: 3g | sugar: 8g | sodium: 532mg

Pork Chops with Gingered Applesauce

Prep time: 10 minutes | Cook time: 15 minutes | Serves 4

- 4 thin-cut pork chops
- ½ teaspoon sea salt
- ⅛ teaspoon freshly ground black pepper
- 6 apples, peeled, cored, and
- chopped
- ¼ cup packed coconut sugar
- ¼ cup water
- 1 tablespoon grated fresh ginger

1. Preheat the oven to 425ºF (220ºC). 2. Season the pork chops with the salt and pepper, put them on a rimmed baking sheet. Bake for about 15 minutes, or until the pork registers an internal temperature of 165ºF (74ºC) on an instant-read meat thermometer. 3. Meanwhile, in a large pot over medium-high heat, stir together the apples, sugar, water, and ginger. Cover and cook for about 10 minutes, stirring occasionally, until the apples have cooked into a sauce.

Per Serving:
calories: 442 | fat: 10g | protein: 35g | carbs: 56g | fiber: 8g | sugar: 39g | sodium: 301mg

Beef Sirloin Kebabs in Garlic Marinade

Prep time: 20 minutes | Cook time: 10 minutes | Serves 4

- 2 tablespoons olive oil, divided
- 1 tablespoon coconut aminos
- 1 tablespoon apple cider vinegar
- 1 tablespoon bottled minced garlic
- 1 tablespoon chopped fresh cilantro
- 1 pound (454 g) boneless top sirloin steak, trimmed of visible fat and cut into 1½-inch chunks
- 1 red onion, quartered and separated into layers
- 1 sweet potato, peeled, halved lengthwise, and each half cut into 8 pieces
- 8 medium button mushrooms

1. In a large bowl, stir together 1 tablespoon of olive oil, the coconut aminos, cider vinegar, garlic, and cilantro until well mixed. 2. Add the beef to the bowl and stir to coat the meat in the marinade. Cover the bowl and refrigerate for 1 hour to marinate. 3. Preheat the broiler. 4. Place an oven rack in the top quarter of the oven. 5. On 4 skewers, assemble the kebabs by alternating pieces of beef, onion, sweet potato, and mushrooms. 6. Lightly brush the vegetables with the remaining 1 tablespoon of olive oil, and arrange the kebabs on a baking sheet. 7. Broil the kebabs for 10 minutes for medium, turning once or twice, or until the beef is cooked to your desired doneness. Transfer the kebabs to a plate, and let them rest for 5 minutes before serving.

Per Serving:
calories: 319 | fat: 14g | protein: 37g | carbs: 10g | fiber: 2g | sugar: 3g | sodium: 86mg

Herbed Lamb Fillets with Cauliflower Mash

Prep time: 10 minutes | Cook time: 15 minutes | Serves 4

Cauliflower Mash:
- 1 large head cauliflower, florets broken into small chunks
- Filtered water, for cooking the cauliflower

Lamb:
- 2 (8-ounce / 227-g) grass-fed lamb fillets
- 1 teaspoon salt
- ½ teaspoon freshly ground

- 1 tablespoon ghee
- ½ teaspoon garlic powder
- ½ teaspoon salt
- Dash cayenne pepper

  black pepper
- 2 tablespoons avocado oil
- 1 teaspoon dried rosemary

Make the Cauliflower Mash: 1. In a large pot, combine the cauliflower and enough water to cover. Bring to a boil over high heat, and cook for 10 minutes. Drain, and transfer to a food processor (or blender). 2. Add the ghee, garlic powder, salt, and cayenne pepper. Pulse to a smooth consistency. Make the Lamb: 1. Season the lamb with the salt and pepper. 2. In a large skillet over medium-high heat, add the avocado oil and rosemary. 3. Add the lamb fillets to the skillet, spaced so they are not touching. Sear for 5 minutes, spooning the rosemary oil from the bottom of the pan over the lamb halfway through. Flip and continue to cook the lamb for 5 minutes, basting with the rosemary oil after about 2 minutes. 4. Transfer to a plate, and let rest for 5 minutes. 5. Slice the lamb into coins and serve with the cauliflower mash.

Per Serving:
calories: 289 | fat: 19g | protein: 34g | carbs: 8g | fiber: 3g | sugar: 1g | sodium: 931mg

Gyro Skillet Sausages

Prep time: 20 minutes | Cook time: 45 minutes | Makes 12 sausages

- 1 pound (454 g) 85% lean ground beef
- 1 pound (454 g) ground lamb
- 1 tablespoon dried oregano
- 2 teaspoons fine Himalayan salt
- 2 teaspoons ground black pepper
- 1 teaspoon ground cumin
- 1 small onion, roughly chopped
- ½ cup chopped fresh parsley or cilantro
- 2 large eggs
- 2 tablespoons coconut flour
- 1 tablespoon coconut oil, or more if needed

1. In a large bowl, mix together the ground beef and lamb using your hands. Add the oregano, salt, pepper, and cumin and mix thoroughly. Set aside. 2. Place the onions, parsley, and eggs in a food processor or blender. Pulse until the parsley and onion are finely minced and almost puréed. Add this to the meat mixture along with the coconut flour. Mix thoroughly. 3. Heat a large cast-iron skillet over medium heat. While it heats, shape the sausages: Take about ¼ cup of the meat mixture and roll it into a cylindrical shape no more than 2 inches in diameter and 3 inches long. Repeat with the rest of the meat mixture. 4. When the sausages are ready and the skillet is hot, heat the oil in the skillet. Add four sausages, or as many as will fit without crowding the pan, and cook for 15 minutes, using tongs to gently turn the sausages every 3 to 5 minutes so they brown on all sides. When they have a nice dark crust on all sides, transfer them to a paper towel–lined plate. 5. Repeat with the next two batches of sausages, adding more oil as needed between batches. There might be quite a bit of splatter, so use a splatter screen if you have one to avoid a mess. 6. Store leftovers in an airtight container in the fridge for up to 4 days. To reheat, bake in a preheated 350°F (180°C) oven for 5 minutes.

Per Serving:
calories: 312 | fat: 18g | protein: 32g | carbs: 2g | fiber: 2g | sugar: 0g | sodium: 598mg

Chocolate Chili

Prep time: 15 minutes | Cook time: 45 minutes | Serves 4 to 6

- 1 tablespoon extra-virgin olive oil
- 1 pound (454 g) lean ground beef
- 1 large onion, chopped
- 2 garlic cloves, minced
- 1 tablespoon unsweetened
- cocoa
- 1½ teaspoons chili powder
- 1 teaspoon salt
- ½ teaspoon ground cumin
- 2 cups chicken broth
- 1 cup tomato sauce

1. In a Dutch oven, heat the oil over high heat. Add the ground beef and brown well, about 5 minutes. 2. Add the onion, garlic, cocoa, chili powder, salt, and cumin and cook, stirring, for an additional minute. 3. Add the chicken broth and tomato sauce and bring to a boil. Reduce the heat to a simmer, cover, and cook, stirring occasionally, for 30 to 40 minutes. If the sauce becomes too thick as it cooks, add more chicken broth or water to thin it. 4. Ladle into bowls and serve.

Per Serving:
calories: 370 | fat: 27g | protein: 23g | carbs: 9g | fiber: 2g | sugar: 4g | sodium: 1010mg

Garlic-Mustard Steak

Prep time: 10 minutes | Cook time: 10 minutes | Serves 4

- ½ cup extra-virgin olive oil
- ½ cup balsamic vinegar
- 2 tablespoons Dijon mustard
- 2 garlic cloves, minced
- 1 teaspoon chopped fresh rosemary
- 1 teaspoon salt
- ¼ teaspoon freshly ground black pepper
- 4 (6-ounce / 170-g) boneless grass-fed steaks, about ½ inch thick

1. In a shallow baking dish, whisk together the olive oil, balsamic vinegar, Dijon, garlic, rosemary, salt, and pepper. 2. Add the steaks and turn them to coat well with the marinade. Cover and let the steaks marinate for 30 minutes at room temperature or up to 2 hours in the refrigerator. 3. Heat a large skillet over high heat. 4. Remove the steaks from the marinade and blot them with a paper towel to remove any excess marinade. 5. Cook the steaks, flipping once, until nicely browned, 2 to 3 minutes on each side. 6. Let the steaks rest for 5 minutes before serving.

Per Serving:
calories: 480 | fat: 31g | protein: 48g | carbs: 3g | fiber: 0g | sugar: 2g | sodium: 390mg

Pulled Pork Tacos

Prep time: 15 minutes | Cook time: 7 to 8 hours | Serves 4 to 6

- 1 teaspoon sea salt
- 1 teaspoon ground cumin
- 1 teaspoon garlic powder
- ½ teaspoon dried oregano
- ½ teaspoon freshly ground black pepper
- 3 to 4 pounds (1.4 to 1.8 kg) pork shoulder or butt
- 2 cups broth of choice
- Juice of 1 orange
- 1 small onion, chopped
- 4 to 6 corn taco shells
- Shredded cabbage, lime wedges, avocado, and hot sauce, for topping (optional)

1. In a small bowl, stir together the salt, cumin, garlic powder, oregano, and pepper. Rub the pork with the spice mixture, and put it in your slow cooker. 2. Pour the broth and orange juice around the pork. Scatter the onion around the pork. 3. Cover the cooker and set on low. Cook for 7 to 8 hours. 4. Transfer the pork to a work surface, and shred it with a fork. Serve in taco shells with any optional toppings you like.

Per Serving:
calories: 1156 | fat: 84g | protein: 84g | carbs: 12g | fiber: 2g | sugar: 1g | sodium: 942mg

Hearty Bolognese

Prep time: 15 minutes | Cook time: 7 to 8 hours | Serves 4 to 6

- 1 tablespoon extra-virgin olive oil
- 3 garlic cloves, minced
- ½ cup chopped onion
- ⅔ cup chopped celery
- ⅔ cup chopped carrot
- 1 pound (454 g) ground beef
- 1 (14-ounce / 397-g) can diced tomatoes
- 1 tablespoon white wine vinegar
- ⅛ teaspoon ground nutmeg
- 2 bay leaves
- ½ teaspoon red pepper flakes
- Dash sea salt
- Dash freshly ground black pepper

1. Coat the bottom of the slow cooker with the olive oil. 2. Add the garlic, onion, celery, carrot, ground beef, tomatoes, vinegar, nutmeg, bay leaves, red pepper flakes, salt, and black pepper. Using a fork, break up the ground beef as much as possible. 3. Cover the cooker and set to low. Cook for 7 to 8 hours. 4. Remove and discard the bay leaves. Stir, breaking up the meat completely, and serve.

Per Serving:
calories: 314 | fat: 21g | protein: 22g | carbs: 10g | fiber: 2g | sugar: 5g | sodium: 376mg

Macadamia-Dusted Pork Cutlets

Prep time: 10 minutes | Cook time: 10 minutes | Serves 4

- 1 (1 pound / 454 g) pork tenderloin, cut into ½-inch slices and pounded uniformly thin
- 1 teaspoon sea salt, divided
- ¼ teaspoon freshly ground black pepper, divided
- ½ cup macadamia nuts, pulsed in a blender or food processor to form a powder
- 1 cup full-fat coconut milk
- 2 tablespoons extra-virgin olive oil

1. Preheat the oven to 400ºF (205ºC). 2. Season the pork chops with ½ teaspoon of the salt and ⅛ teaspoon of the pepper. 3. In a shallow dish, stir together the macadamia nut powder, the remaining ½ teaspoon of salt, and the remaining ⅛ teaspoon of pepper. 4. In another shallow dish, whisk the coconut milk and olive oil to combine. 5. Dip the pork into the coconut milk and into the macadamia nut powder. Put it on a rimmed baking sheet. Repeat with the remaining pork slices. 6. Bake the pork for about 10 minutes, or until it registers an internal temperature of 165ºF (74ºC) measured on an instant-read meat thermometer.

Per Serving:
calories: 437 | fat: 33g | protein: 33g | carbs: 6g | fiber: 3g | sugar: 3g | sodium: 309mg

Lush Lamb and Rosemary Casserole

Prep time: 10 minutes | Cook time: 2 hours | Serves 4

- 1 tablespoon of olive oil
- 2 lean lamb fillets, cubed
- 1 onion, chopped
- 2 carrots,cubed
- 2½ cup kale
- 4 cups of homemade
- chicken stock
- 1 teaspoon dried rosemary
- 1 teaspoon of chopped parsley
- 2 cans rinsed and drained cannellini beans

1. In a large casserole dish, heat the olive oil on a medium high heat. 2. Add the lamb and cook for 5 minutes until browned. 3. Add the chopped onion and carrots. Leave to cook for another 5 minutes until the vegetables begin to soften. 4. Add the chicken stock, kale and rosemary. 5. Then cover the casserole and leave to simmer on a low heat for 1 to 2hours until the lamb is tender and fully cooked through. 6. Add the cannellini beans 15 minutes before the end of the cooking time. 7. Plate up and serve with the chopped parsley to garnish.

Per Serving:
calories: 335 | fat: 17g | protein: 24g | carbs: 23g | fiber: 5g | sugar: 8g | sodium: 427mg

Ground Beef Chili with Tomatoes

Prep time: 10 minutes | Cook time: 15 minutes | Serves 4

- 1 pound (454 g) extra-lean ground beef
- 1 onion, chopped
- 2 (28 ounces / 794 g) cans chopped tomatoes, undrained
- 2 (14 ounces / 397 g) cans kidney beans, drained
- 1 tablespoon chili powder
- 1 teaspoon garlic powder
- ½ teaspoon sea salt

1. In a large pot over medium-high heat, cook the beef and onion for about 5 minutes, crumbling the beef with a wooden spoon until it browns. 2. Stir in the tomatoes, kidney beans, chili powder, garlic powder, and salt. Bring to a simmer. Cook for 10 minutes, stirring.

Per Serving:
calories: 446 | fat: 24g | protein: 35g | carbs: 25g | fiber: 10g | sugar: 12g | sodium: 562mg

Pork Chops with Cooked Apple Salsa

Prep time: 20 minutes | Cook time: 25 minutes | Serves 4

- Salsa:
- 1 teaspoon olive oil
- ¼ cup finely chopped sweet onion
- ½ teaspoon grated fresh

Pork Chops:
- 4 (4-ounce / 113-g) boneless center-cut pork chops, trimmed and patted dry
- 1 teaspoon garlic powder
- 1 teaspoon ground

- ginger
- 2 apples, peeled, cored, and diced
- ½ cup dried raisins
- Pinch sea salt

- cinnamon
- Sea salt, to taste
- Freshly ground black pepper, to taste
- 1 tablespoon olive oil

Make the Salsa: 1. Place a medium skillet over medium heat and add the olive oil. 2. Add the onion and ginger. Sauté for about 2 minutes, or until softened. 3. Stir in the apples and raisins. Sauté for about 5 minutes, or until the fruit is just tender. Season the salsa with sea salt and set it aside. Make the Pork Chops: 1. Sprinkle the pork chops on both sides with the garlic powder, cinnamon, sea salt, and pepper. 2. Place a large skillet over medium-high heat and add the olive oil. 3. Add the seasoned chops and panfry for 7 to 8 minutes per side until just cooked through and browned, turning once. 4. Serve the chops with the cooked apple salsa.

Per Serving:
calories: 434 | fat: 32g | protein: 26g | carbs: 10g | fiber: 1g | sugar: 8g | sodium: 417mg

Pork Char Siu and Ramen

Prep time: 30 minutes | Cook time: 30 minutes | Serves 6

Char Siu:

- 1½ to 2 pounds (680 to 907 g) pork tenderloin
- 1 teaspoon fine Himalayan salt
- ½ cup blackberries
- 4 tablespoons coconut aminos, divided
- 3 tablespoons ghee
- 2 tablespoons coconut
- vinegar
- 1 tablespoon Dijon mustard
- 1 tablespoon fish sauce
- 2 teaspoons ginger powder
- 1 teaspoon Chinese five-spice powder
- 1 teaspoon garlic powder
- 2 teaspoons raw honey

Ramen:

- 6 cups bone broth
- 4 cloves garlic, minced
- 1 (1-inch) piece fresh ginger, peeled and minced
- 2 tablespoons sesame oil (optional)
- 1 teaspoon coconut aminos
- 1 teaspoon fish sauce
- 1 teaspoon fine Himalayan salt
- 6 cups shirataki noodles
- 6 large eggs (optional)
- ½ ounce (14 g) fresh cilantro or basil, trimmed, for garnish

1. Place the pork tenderloin in a freezer bag or airtight container. Sprinkle with the salt. 2. Heat a small saucepan over medium heat. Combine the blackberries, 2 tablespoons of the coconut aminos, ghee, vinegar, mustard, fish sauce, ginger powder, Chinese five-spice powder, and garlic powder in the saucepan. Bring to a simmer and cook, stirring occasionally, for 8 to 10 minutes. When the blackberries have turned red, mash them. 3. Pour the sauce through a fine-mesh sieve into a small bowl, using a spoon to mash the berries and scraping the sieve to get as much out as possible. Let the sauce cool to room temperature. 4. Add the sauce to the pork and rub it all over, then seal the bag or container. Place in the fridge to marinate for at least 3 hours or up to overnight. 5. Set the pork out to come to room temperature 30 minutes before cooking. Preheat the oven to 350ºF (180ºC). Line a sheet pan with parchment paper and place a baking rack on it. 6. Remove the pork loin from the marinade and place it on the rack, reserving the marinade. Mix the marinade with the remaining 2 tablespoons of coconut aminos and the honey. 7. Place the pork on the middle rack of the oven and roast for 15 minutes, then spoon half of the marinade over it.

Roast for another 7 to 10 minutes, until the internal temperature is 145ºF (63ºC). Spoon the remaining half of the marinade all over it. Broil for 2 minutes. 8. Remove the pork from the oven and let it rest for 5 minutes, then cut it into ¼-inch-thick slices. 9. While the pork roasts, prepare the ramen: In a large pot, mix the broth with the garlic, ginger, sesame oil (if using), coconut aminos, fish sauce, and salt. Bring to a simmer and cook for 8 minutes, then reduce the heat and keep warm until the pork is done. 10. Rinse the shirataki noodles in a fine-mesh sieve, drain, and set aside. 11. If including hard-boiled eggs, bring a large pot of water to a rapid boil. One at a time, add the eggs to the water. Boil for 7 minutes, then quickly drain all the water from the pot and cover the eggs with ice and cold water. Let them sit for 2 minutes. Peel the eggs under the cold water or under a fine stream of running water. Make sure to remove that fine film under the shell; this will ensure the egg whites won't break off. 12. Assemble the ramen bowls: Place 1 cup of noodles in each of six bowls, then add 1 cup of hot broth to each bowl. Add a hard-boiled egg (if using), a few sprigs of cilantro, and three or four slices of char siu pork. Serve hot and dig in! 13. The best way to store this is to pack each component of the meal in a separate airtight container. The pork will keep in the fridge for 3 to 4 days, the broth a week, and the eggs 5 days. Prepare the noodles to order.

Per Serving:
calories: 499 | fat: 22g | protein: 52g | carbs: 30g | fiber: 3g | sugar: 7g | sodium: 532mg

Beef and Bell Pepper Stir-Fry

Prep time: 5 minutes | Cook time: 10 minutes | Serves 4

- 1 pound (454 g) extra-lean ground beef
- 6 scallions, white and green parts, chopped
- 2 red bell peppers, chopped
- 2 tablespoons grated fresh ginger
- ½ teaspoon sea salt
- 3 garlic cloves, minced

1. In a large nonstick skillet over medium-high heat, cook the beef for about 5 minutes, crumbling it with a wooden spoon until it browns. 2. Add the scallions, red bell peppers, ginger, and salt. Cook for about 4 minutes, stirring, until the bell peppers are soft. 3. Add the garlic. Cook for 30 seconds, stirring constantly.

Per Serving:
calories: 171 | fat: 6g | protein: 25g | carbs: 5g | fiber: 1g | sugar: 2g | sodium: 372mg

Chapter 7

Snacks and Appetizers

Chapter 7 Snacks and Appetizers

Spinach and Kale Breaded Balls

Prep time: 15 minutes | Cook time: 30 minutes | Serves 4

- 2 cups frozen or fresh spinach, thawed and chopped
- 1 cup of frozen or fresh kale, thawed and drained
- ½ cup onion, finely chopped
- 1 garlic clove, finely chopped
- 3 tablespoons extra virgin olive oil
- 2 free range eggs, beaten
- ½ teaspoon ground thyme
- ½ teaspoon rubbed dried oregano
- ½ teaspoon dried rosemary
- 1 cup dry 100% wholegrain bread crumbs
- ½ teaspoon dried oregano
- 1 teaspoon ground black pepper

1. Preheat oven to 350ºF (180ºC). 2. Line a baking sheet with parchment paper. 3. In a bowl, mix the olive oil and eggs, adding in the spinach, garlic and onions and tossing to coat. 4. Add the rest of the ingredients, mixing to blend. 5. Use the palms of your hands to roll into 1 inch balls and arrange them onto the baking sheet. 6. Bake for 15 minutes, and then flip the balls over. 7. Continue to bake for another 15 minutes or until they're golden brown. 8. Serve and enjoy!

Per Serving:
calories: 262 | fat: 14g | protein: 10g | carbs: 26g | fiber: 4g | sugar: 3g | sodium: 289mg

Creamy Broccoli Dip

Prep time: 20 minutes | Cook time: 5 minutes | Makes about 2 cups

- 1 cup broccoli florets
- 1 garlic clove
- 1 scallion, coarsely chopped
- ¾ cup unsweetened almond yogurt, or coconut yogurt
- ½ avocado
- 1 tablespoon freshly squeezed lemon juice
- 1 teaspoon salt
- ½ teaspoon dried dill
- Pinch red pepper flakes

1. Fill a medium pot with 2 inches of water, place it over medium-high heat, and insert a steamer basket. 2. Add the broccoli to the steamer basket, cover, and steam for 5 minutes, or until the broccoli turns bright green. Remove the pan from the heat and drain the broccoli. 3. In a food processor, add the garlic, scallion, yogurt, avocado, lemon juice, salt, dill, and red pepper flakes. Pulse a few times until the mixture appears coarsely chopped. 4. Add the broccoli and process until well combined; the mixture should have some texture and not be completely puréed. Serve.

Per Serving:
calories: 82 | fat: 7g | protein: 1g | carbs: 7g | fiber: 4g | sugar: 1g | sodium: 628mg

Blueberry Nut Trail Mix

Prep time: 5 minutes | Cook time: 5 minutes | Serves 4

- 1 tablespoon extra-virgin olive oil
- 1 cup almonds
- Pinch of salt, to taste
- ½ teaspoon Chinese five-spice powder
- ½ cup dried blueberries

1. In a large nonstick skillet over medium-high heat, heat the olive oil until it shimmers. 2. Add the almonds, salt, and Chinese five-spice and cook for 2 minutes, stirring constantly. 3. Remove from the heat and cool. Stir in the blueberries.

Per Serving:
calories: 179 | fat: 16g | protein: 5g | carbs: 8g | fiber: 3g | sugar: 3g | sodium: 39mg

Simplest Guacamole

Prep time: 10 minutes | Cook time: 0 minutes | Makes about 3 cups

- 4 medium, ripe avocados, halved and pitted
- 1 teaspoon garlic powder
- ½ teaspoon salt

1. Scoop out the avocado flesh and put it in a medium bowl. 2. Add the garlic powder and the salt. With a fork, mash the avocados until creamy. 3. Serve immediately, or cover and refrigerate for up to 2 days.

Per Serving:
calories: 358 | fat: 32g | protein: 7g | carbs: 13g | fiber: 6g | sugar: 1g | sodium: 244mg

Fast and Fresh Granola Trail Mix

Prep time: 5 minutes | Cook time: 20 minutes | Serves 2

- 1 cup toasted almonds
- 1 tablespoon raw honey
- ½ cup cherries
- 1 cup granola

1. Preheat oven to 350ºF (180ºC). 2. Spread the almonds across a baking sheet. 3. Bake for five minutes and then add cherries and granola and toss. 4. Drizzle honey on top and toss again to coat before baking in oven for 10 to 15 minutes. 5. Remove to cool and serve.

Per Serving:
calories: 539 | fat: 27g | protein: 18g | carbs: 58g | fiber: 10g | sugar: 16g | sodium: 11mg

Sweet and Spicy Pepitas

Prep time: 10 minutes | Cook time: 30 minutes | Makes 2 cups

- 1 tablespoon chili powder
- 1 teaspoon ground cumin
- Pinch of cayenne pepper
- ½ teaspoon kosher salt
- ¼ teaspoon freshly ground black pepper
- 1 tablespoon organic canola oil
- 3 tablespoons maple syrup
- 1 egg white
- 2 cups raw pumpkin seeds

1. Preheat the oven to 300ºF (150ºC). Line a baking sheet with parchment paper. 2. Combine the chili powder, cumin, cayenne, salt, and black pepper in a small bowl. 3. Whisk the canola oil, maple syrup, and egg white in a large bowl. Add the spices and stir to combine. Add the pumpkin seeds and toss to coat. Spread the mixture on the prepared baking sheet. 4. Bake, stirring once, for 25 to 30 minutes. Let cool on the baking sheet. 5. Store in an airtight container at room temperature for up to 3 days.

Per Serving:
calories: 225 | fat: 10g | protein: 7g | carbs: 29g | fiber: 7g | sugar: 9g | sodium: 370mg

Homemade Trail Mix

Prep time: 5 minutes | Cook time: 0 minutes | Serves 14

- 1 cup pumpkin seeds
- 1 cup sunflower seeds
- 1 cup large coconut flakes
- 1 cup raisins
- 1 cup dried cranberries
- ½ cup cacao nibs (optional)

1. In a large bowl, stir together the pumpkin seeds, sunflower seeds, coconut, raisins, cranberries, and cacao nibs, if using. 2. Store, covered, in large jars in a cool, dry place, or portion into small containers for a quick grab-and-go option.

Per Serving:
calories: 183 | fat: 11g | protein: 5g | carbs: 19g | fiber: 3g | sugar: 12g | sodium: 24mg

Spicy Two-Bean Dip

Prep time: 10 minutes | Cook time: 0 minutes | Makes about 3½ cups

- 1 (14-ounce / 397-g) can black beans, drained and rinsed well
- 1 (14-ounce / 397-g) can kidney beans, drained and rinsed well
- 2 garlic cloves
- 2 cherry tomatoes
- 2 tablespoons filtered water
- 1 tablespoon apple cider
- vinegar
- 2 teaspoons raw honey
- 1 teaspoon freshly squeezed lime juice
- ¼ teaspoon ground cumin
- ¼ teaspoon salt
- Pinch cayenne pepper
- Freshly ground black pepper, to taste

1. In a food processor (or blender), combine the black beans, kidney beans, garlic, tomatoes, water, vinegar, honey, lime juice, cumin, salt, and cayenne pepper, and season with black pepper. Blend until smooth. Use a silicone spatula to scrape the sides of the processor bowl as needed. Cover and refrigerate before serving, if desired, or refrigerate for up to 5 days.

Per Serving:
calories: 166 | fat: 0g | protein: 9g | carbs: 34g | fiber: 8g | sugar: 5g | sodium: 404mg

Sweet Potato Chips

Prep time: 20 minutes | Cook time: 2 hours | Serves 4 to 6

- 2 large sweet potatoes, sliced as thin as possible
- 3 tablespoons extra-virgin
- olive oil
- 1 teaspoon sea salt

1. Preheat the oven to 250ºF (120ºC). 2. Position the rack in the center of the oven. 3. In a large bowl, toss the sweet potatoes slices with the olive oil. Arrange the slices in a single layer on two baking sheets. Sprinkle with the sea salt. 4. Place the sheets in the preheated oven and bake for about 2 hours, rotating the pans and flipping the chips after 1 hour. 5. Once the chips are lightly brown and crisp, remove them from the oven. Some may be a bit soft, but they will crisp as they cool. Cool the chips for 10 minutes before serving. 6. Serve immediately. The chips lose their crunch within several hours.

Per Serving:
calories: 267 | fat: 11g | protein: 2g | carbs: 42g | fiber: 6g | sugar: 1g | sodium: 482mg

Smooth Chia Pudding

Prep time: 10 minutes | Cook time: 0 minutes | Serves 4

- 1 cup mild bone broth
- 1 cup full-fat coconut milk
- 1 cup water
- ¼ cup cocoa powder
- ¼ cup steamed and then frozen cauliflower florets (about 3 florets)
- 2 teaspoon raw honey, or 20 drops liquid stevia
- 3 tablespoons chia seeds
- Pinch of fine Himalayan salt
- Fresh blackberries, for garnish (optional)

1. Place all of the ingredients in a high-powered blender. Blend on high until the chia seeds are pulverized and the mix is completely smooth and thick. 2. Pour the mixture into four 6-ounce (170-g) jars with lids, cover, and refrigerate for at least 4 hours to thicken. Garnish with blackberries before serving, if desired. Store in the refrigerator for up to 1 week.

Per Serving:
calories: 191 | fat: 17g | protein: 4g | carbs: 12g | fiber: 5g | sugar: 5g | sodium: 208mg

Pecan and Date Snack Bars

Prep time: 5 minutes | Cook time: 40 minutes | Serves 8

- 4 cups of dates, pitted and chopped
- 3 cups pecans

1. Preheat the oven to 350ºF (180ºC). 2. Put the dates in a bowl and cover them with water. 3. Leave for at least 20 minutes and then blitz the pecans in a food processor until they form a 'breadcrumb' texture. 4. Now, drain the water from the dates and then add to the processor until the nuts and fruit create a dough that easily needs together with your hands. 5. Line a baking sheet with parchment paper and then spread the dough onto the pan into a layer 2 inches thick. 6. Bake for 35 to 40 minutes or until cooked through and crispy on the top. 7. Remove to cool and slice into bars to serve.

Per Serving:
calories: 464 | fat: 27g | protein: 5g | carbs: 60g | fiber: 10g | sugar: 39g | sodium: 1mg

Quinoa Flatbread

Prep time: 5 minutes | Cook time: 30 minutes | Serves 10

- 1½ cups dry quinoa
- 2¼ cups water
- ¼ cup extra-virgin olive oil
- 1 teaspoon salt

1. Preheat the oven to 350ºF (180ºC). 2. Line a 9-by-13-inch baking pan (or a baking sheet with 1-inch sides) with parchment paper. 3. Using a spice grinder or high-speed blender, pulverize the quinoa into a fine meal. Transfer to a medium bowl. 4. Add the water, olive oil, and salt. Whisk well so there are no lumps. 5. Pour the batter into the prepared pan and smooth it. The batter will be quite wet. 6. Place the pan in the preheated oven and bake for 25 to 30 minutes, or until the flatbread is dry and lightly golden on top. 7. Cut into desired sizes and serve.

Per Serving:
calories: 171 | fat: 8g | protein: 5g | carbs: 21g | fiber: 2g | sugar: 0g | sodium: 292mg

Plantain Chips

Prep time: 10 minutes | Cook time: 20 minutes | Makes 2 cups

- 2 pounds (907 g) plantains, peeled and sliced thinly on the diagonal
- ¼ cup olive oil
- ½ teaspoon smoked paprika
- ½ teaspoon kosher salt

1. Preheat the oven to 375ºF (190ºC). Line two baking sheets with parchment paper. 2. Lay the plantain slices in a single layer on the prepared baking sheets. Brush the tops of the slices with half of the olive oil, then turn them over and brush the other side with oil. Sprinkle with the paprika and salt. 3. Roast for 18 to 20 minutes, turning halfway through, until the plantains are golden and crunchy. Let cool completely. 4. Store in an airtight container at room temperature for up to 3 days.

Per Serving:
calories: 397 | fat: 14g | protein: 3g | carbs: 59g | fiber: 5g | sugar: 24g | sodium: 300mg

Cinnamon-Spiced Apple Chips

Prep time: 15 minutes | Cook time: 1 hour | Makes 2 cups

- 2 tablespoons coconut sugar
- 1 teaspoon ground cinnamon
- 2 Granny Smith apples, cored and thinly sliced

1. Preheat the oven to 275ºF (135ºC). Line two baking sheets with parchment paper. 2. Combine the sugar and cinnamon in a small bowl. Place the apple slices on the prepared baking sheet and sprinkle with the cinnamon-sugar mixture. 3. Bake until dehydrated and lightly browned, about 1 hour. Remove from the baking sheet and allow to cool until crispy, about 15 minutes. 4. Store in an airtight container at room temperature for up to 1 week.

Per Serving:
calories: 132 | fat: 0g | protein: 1g | carbs:31 g | fiber: 5g | sugar: 24g | sodium: 3mg

Strawberry-Chia Ice Pops

Prep time: 20 minutes | Cook time: 0 minutes | Makes 6 ice pops

- 2 cup frozen unsweetened strawberries, thawed
- 1 tablespoon freshly squeezed lemon juice
- 1 (15-ounce / 425-g) can coconut milk
- 1 tablespoon chia seeds
- 1 teaspoon vanilla extract

1. Prepare six ice pop molds per the manufacturer's instructions. 2. In a medium bowl, stir together the strawberries, lemon juice, coconut milk, chia seeds, and vanilla. Let the mixture stand for 5 minutes so the chia seeds thicken slightly. This makes it easier to fill the molds. 3. Evenly divide the mixture among the molds. Place 1 ice pop stick in each mold. Freeze the pops for about 5 hours, or overnight, until solid.

Per Serving:

calories: 187 | fat: 17g | protein: 2g | carbs: 9g | fiber: 3g | sugar: 6g | sodium: 11mg

Cucumber-Yogurt Dip

Prep time: 15 minutes | Cook time: 0 minutes | Serves 4

- 1 cucumber, peeled and shredded
- 1 cup plain coconut yogurt
- 1 garlic clove, minced
- 1 scallion, chopped
- 2 tablespoons chopped fresh
- dill
- 1 teaspoon salt
- 2 tablespoons freshly squeezed lemon juice
- 2 tablespoons extra-virgin olive oil

1. Place the shredded cucumber in a fine-mesh strainer to drain. 2. In a small bowl, stir together the yogurt, garlic, scallion, dill, salt, and lemon juice. 3. Fold in the drained cucumber and spoon into a serving bowl. 4. Just before serving, drizzle with the olive oil.

Per Serving:

calories: 104 | fat: 9g | protein: 1g | carbs: 7g | fiber: 3g | sugar: 2g | sodium: 636mg

Roasted Apricots

Prep time: 10 minutes | Cook time: 30 minutes | Serves 4

- 20 fresh apricots, pitted and quartered
- 2 tablespoons coconut oil
- ⅛ teaspoon cardamom (optional)

1. Preheat the oven to 350ºF (180ºC). 2. In an ovenproof dish, toss the apricots with the coconut oil and cardamom, if using. 3. Place the dish in the preheated oven and roast for 25 to 30 minutes,

stirring occasionally.

Per Serving:

calories: 142 | fat: 8g | protein: 2g | carbs: 19g | fiber: 3g | sugar: 16g | sodium: 2mg

Chickpea Paste

Prep time: 15 minutes | Cook time: 0 minutes | Makes about 2 cups

- 1 (15-ounce / 425-g) can chickpeas, drained and rinsed
- ¼ cup extra-virgin olive oil
- ¼ cup fresh lemon juice
- ¼ cup minced onion
- 1 garlic clove, minced
- 1 teaspoon sea salt
- ½ teaspoon ground cumin
- ¼ teaspoon red pepper flakes

1. In a medium bowl, use a potato masher to mash the chickpeas until they are mostly broken up. 2. Add the olive oil, lemon juice, onion, garlic, salt, cumin, and red pepper flakes and continue mashing until you have a slightly chunky paste. Let sit for 30 minutes at room temperature for the flavors to develop, then serve.

Per Serving:

calories: 110 | fat: 8g | protein: 3g | carbs: 10g | fiber: 2g | sugar: 2g | sodium: 290mg

Sweet Potato Oat Muffins

Prep time: 10 minutes | Cook time: 20 to 25 minutes | Makes 12 muffins

1½ cups rolled oats

- 1 cup cooked sweet potato chunks or purée
- 1 cup nut milk of choice
- ⅓ cup coconut sugar
- ¼ cup almond butter
- 1 egg
- 2 tablespoons extra-virgin
- olive oil
- 1 teaspoon vanilla extract
- 1 teaspoon ground cinnamon
- 1 teaspoon baking powder
- ½ teaspoon baking soda
- ¼ teaspoon salt

1. Preheat the oven to 375ºF (190ºC). 2. Line a muffin tin with cupcake liners. 3. In a food processor (or blender), pulse the oats until a coarse flour is formed. Transfer the flour to a small bowl and set aside. 4. To the food processor (or blender), add the sweet potato, nut milk, coconut sugar, almond butter, egg, olive oil, vanilla, cinnamon, baking powder, baking soda, and salt. Pulse until smooth. 5. Slowly add the oat flour, pulsing until all ingredients are well incorporated. 6. Divide the batter among the 12 cupcake liners. 7. Bake for 20 to 25 minutes. Cool for 5 minutes.

Per Serving:

calories: 143 | fat: 7g | protein: 4g | carbs: 12g | fiber: 2g | sugar: 5g | sodium: 121mg

Super Healthy Sweet Potato Fries

Prep time: 10 minutes | Cook time: 30 minutes | Serves 2

- 2 large sweet potatoes, cut into thin strips
- 1 teaspoon of cumin
- 1 tablespoon of extra virgin
- olive oil
- ½ teaspoon of black pepper
- ½ teaspoon of paprika
- 1 dash of cayenne pepper

1. Preheat oven to 375ºF (190ºC). 2. Add the sweet potato strips into a large bowl. 3. Drizzle with some olive oil. 4. Sprinkle the rest of the ingredients over the top. 5. Toss together gently to evenly and fully coat the potatoes. 6. Get a baking sheet and arrange the coated potatoes into a thin layer. 7. Bake for around 30 minutes or until cooked through.

Per Serving:
calories: 149 | fat: 4g | protein: 3g | carbs: 28g | fiber: 5g | sugar: 6g | sodium: 134mg

Baked Apple and Walnut Chips

Prep time: 5 minutes | Cook time: 30 minutes | Serves 4

- 4 apples, peeled and thinly sliced
- 1 tablespoon cinnamon
- ¼ cup of walnut pieces for topping

1. Preheat oven to 375ºF (190ºC). 2. Layer the apple slices in a thin layer on a baking tray. 3. Dust with the cinnamon and top with walnut pieces. 4. Bake for 20 to 30 minutes or until crispy.

Per Serving:
calories: 132 | fat: 4g | protein: 1g | carbs: 27g | fiber: 6g | sugar: 19g | sodium: 2mg

White Bean Dip

Prep time: 15 minutes | Cook time: 0 minutes | Serves 4 to 6

- 1 (15-ounce / 425-g) can white beans, drained and rinsed
- 1 garlic clove
- 1 tablespoon tahini, or almond butter
- 3 tablespoons extra-virgin olive oil
- ¼ cup chopped pitted green olives
- 1 tablespoon chopped fresh parsley
- ¼ teaspoon salt
- 2 tablespoons freshly squeezed lemon juice

1. In a food processor, combine the white beans, garlic, and tahini.

With the machine running on low, slowly add the olive oil in a thin, steady stream. If the dip is too thick, thin with some water. 2. Add the olives, parsley, and salt. Pulse to combine. Stir in the lemon juice. 3. Spoon into a serving bowl and serve with raw vegetables and gluten-free crackers.

Per Serving:
calories: 239 | fat: 14g | protein: 9g | carbs: 25g | fiber: 6g | sugar: 0g | sodium: 358mg

Spiced Nuts

Prep time: 10 minutes | Cook time: 15 minutes | Makes about 2 cups

- 1 cup almonds
- ½ cup walnuts
- ¼ cup sunflower seeds
- ¼ cup pumpkin seeds
- 1 teaspoon ground turmeric
- ½ teaspoon ground cumin
- ¼ teaspoon garlic powder
- ¼ teaspoon red pepper flakes

1. Preheat the oven to 350ºF (180ºC). 2. Combine all the ingredients in a medium bowl and mix well. 3. Spread the nuts evenly on a rimmed baking sheet and bake until lightly toasted, 10 to 15 minutes. 4. Cool completely before serving or storing.

Per Serving:
calories: 180 | fat: 16g | protein: 6g | carbs: 7g | fiber: 3g | sugar: 1g | sodium: 5mg

Pumpkin and Carrot Crackers

Prep time: 10 minutes | Cook time: 15 minutes | Makes40 crackers

- 1⅓ cups pumpkin seeds
- ½ cup tightly packed shredded carrot (about 1 carrot)
- 3 tablespoons chopped fresh
- dill
- 2 tablespoons extra-virgin olive oil
- ¼ teaspoon salt

1. Preheat the oven to 350ºF (180ºC). 2. Line a baking sheet with parchment paper. 3. In a food processor, pulverize the pumpkin seeds into a fine meal. 4. Add the carrot, dill, olive oil, and salt. Pulse for 30 seconds to incorporate all. 5. Transfer the dough to the prepared sheet and pat it out into a rough rectangular shape. 6. Place another sheet of parchment over the dough. Roll the dough to about ⅛ inch thick. 7. Gently score the crackers with a knife or pizza cutter. 8. Place the sheet in the preheated oven and bake for 15 minutes, or until lightly golden. 9. Cool the crackers, separate them, and store in a sealed container.

Per Serving:
calories: 131 | fat: 12g | protein: 5g | carbs: 4g | fiber: 1g | sugar: 0g | sodium: 67mg

Crispy Thin Flatbread

Prep time: 10 minutes | Cook time: 20 minutes | Makes 2 crusts

- 4 large cold eggs
- ½ cup coconut oil, melted
- ½ teaspoon fine Himalayan
- salt
- ⅓ cup coconut flour, plus more if needed

1. Preheat the oven to 400ºF (205ºC). Line a baking sheet with parchment paper. 2. In a small bowl, whisk the eggs as you slowly pour in the coconut oil—it will become creamy. Then add the salt and stir to combine. Add the coconut flour and fold until a loose dough forms 3. The density of coconut flour can vary from brand to brand. If the dough does not take shape, add more flour a teaspoon at a time, waiting at least 30 seconds before adding the next teaspoon, until a pliable dough forms. 4. Separate the dough into 2 large balls. Use a spoon or spatula to spread each ball into a ¼-inch-thick, 8-inch round on the prepared baking sheet. 5. Bake for 15 to 20 minutes, until the center is firm and the edges are browned. Remove from the oven and let cool. 6. These flatbreads can be wrapped up tight and stored in the fridge for up to 4 days. To reheat, bake in a preheated 350ºF (180ºC) oven for 8 minutes.

Per Serving:
calories: 395 | fat: 35g | protein: 9g | carbs: 12g | fiber: 7g | sugar: 1g | sodium: 372mg

Mini Snack Muffins

Prep time: 20 minutes | Cook time: 15 to 20 minutes | Makes 24

- ¼ cup extra-virgin olive oil, plus extra for greasing
- 1 cup almond flour
- 1 cup brown rice flour
- 1 tablespoon baking powder
- ½ teaspoon salt
- 1 teaspoon ground cinnamon
- 4 eggs
- 1 cup shredded carrot
- 1 cup canned pumpkin

1. Preheat the oven to 375ºF (190ºC). 2. Line a mini-muffin tin with cupcake liners, or brush the tin with a little olive oil. 3. In a medium bowl, mix together the almond flour, brown rice flour, baking powder, salt, and cinnamon. 4. Add the eggs, carrot, pumpkin, and olive oil. Stir until well combined. 5. Scoop the batter into each muffin cup, filling each three-quarters full. 6. Place the tin in the preheated oven and bake for 15 minutes, or until the muffins are lightly browned. Remove from the oven and cool for 10 minutes before removing the muffins from the tin.

Per Serving:
calories: 65 | fat: 4g | protein: 2g | carbs: 7g | fiber: 1g | sugar: 1g | sodium: 66mg

Cashew Nuts and Broccoli Snack

Prep time: 10 minutes | Cook time: 25 minutes | Serves 4

- ½ cup cashews
- 2¼ cups water
- 2 tablespoons yellow curry powder
- 4 cups broccoli, sliced
- 2 tablespoons sunflower seeds

1. Preheat oven to the highest heat. 2. Layer the cashew nuts onto a dry baking tray and add to the oven for 5 to 10 minutes or until nuts start to brown. Turn whilst cooking to ensure even browning. 3. Remove to cool. 4. Meanwhile boil a pan of water on a medium heat and add the broccoli. 5. Cook on a simmer for 5 to 10 minutes or until cooked through. 6. Drain and place to one side. 7. Blend the water, curry powder, and sunflower seeds until smooth. 8. Crush the cashew nuts on a wooden chopping board or similar, using a sharp knife. 9. When ready to serve, top with roasted cashew nuts.

Per Serving:
calories: 45 | fat: 3g | protein: 3g | carbs: 4g | fiber: 3g | sugar: 0g | sodium: 18mg

Fried Hard-Boiled Eggs

Prep time: 10 minutes | Cook time: 15 minutes | Makes 12 eggs

- 12 large eggs
- 2 tablespoons avocado oil
- 1 teaspoon black sesame seeds
- ½ teaspoon fine Himalayan salt
- ½ teaspoon garlic powder
- ½ teaspoon ground black pepper

1. Bring a large pot of water to a rapid boil. One at a time, add the eggs to the boiling water. Boil the eggs for 8 minutes, then quickly drain all the water from the pot and cover the eggs with ice and cold water. Let them sit for 2 minutes. 2. Peel the eggs under the cold water or under a fine stream of running water. Make sure to remove that fine film under the shell; this ensures that the whites won't break off. Store the peeled eggs in the fridge for up to a week. 3. When you want a crispy egg, heat a cast-iron skillet over medium heat. As the skillet heats, toss two hard-boiled eggs with the oil, sesame seeds, salt, garlic powder, and black pepper in a shallow bowl. 4. When the skillet is hot, tip the eggs and all of the seasonings and oil into the skillet. Let the eggs cook for 2 to 3 minutes, then flip them over and cook the opposite side for 2 to 3 minutes. 5. Remove the eggs from the skillet. Cut them in half and spoon the avocado oil and sesame seeds from the skillet over them. Sprinkle with a little more salt. Enjoy!

Per Serving:
calories: 188 | fat: 14g | protein: 13g | carbs: 1g | fiber: 0g | sugar: 0g | sodium: 336mg

Curry-Spiced Nut Mix with Maple and Black Pepper

Prep time: 10 minutes | Cook time: 35 minutes | Makes 2 cups

- 1 cup raw cashew pieces
- ½ cup raw macadamia nuts, roughly chopped
- ½ cup raw pumpkin seeds
- 1 tablespoon fresh-pressed coconut oil
- 2 teaspoons maple syrup

- 2 teaspoons curry powder
- ½ teaspoon kosher salt
- ¼ teaspoon freshly ground black pepper
- Pinch of cayenne pepper

1. Preheat the oven to 300°F (150°C). Line a baking sheet with parchment paper. 2. Combine the cashews, macadamias, and pumpkin seeds in a large bowl. 3. In a medium saucepan over low heat, melt the coconut oil with the maple syrup, about 1 minute. Remove from the heat and pour over the nut mixture. Add the curry powder, salt, black pepper, and cayenne pepper and stir well to coat. Spread the mixture on the prepared baking sheet. 4. Bake, stirring once, until the nuts are light brown, 30 to 35 minutes. Let cool on the baking sheet. 5. Store in an airtight container at room temperature for up to 3 days.

Per Serving:

calories: 425 | fat: 34g | protein: 11g | carbs: 25g | fiber: 6g | sugar: 5g | sodium: 300mg

Mashed Avocado with Jicama Slices

Prep time: 15 minutes | Cook time: 0 minutes | Serves 4

- 2 ripe avocados, pitted
- 1 scallion, sliced
- 2 tablespoons chopped fresh cilantro
- ½ teaspoon ground turmeric

- Juice of ½ lemon
- 1 teaspoon salt
- ¼ teaspoon freshly ground black pepper
- 1 jicama, peeled and cut into ¼-inch-thick slices

1. In a small bowl, combine the scooped-out avocado, the scallion, cilantro, turmeric, lemon juice, salt, and pepper. Mash the ingredients together until well mixed and still slightly chunky. 2. Serve with the jicama slices.

Per Serving:

calories: 270 | fat: 20g | protein: 3g | carbs: 24g | fiber: 15g | sugar: 4g | sodium: 595mg

Chapter

8

Vegetables and Sides

Chapter 8 Vegetables and Sides

Crispy Oven-Roasted Broccoli with Italian Spice Trio

Prep time: 15 minutes | Cook time: 20 minutes | Serves 4

Italian Spice Trio:

- ◆ 2 tablespoons dried oregano
- ◆ 2 tablespoons fennel seeds
- ◆ ½ teaspoon crushed red pepper flakes
- ◆ 1 large or 2 small heads broccoli, cut into 1-inch
- florets
- ◆ ¼ cup extra-virgin olive oil
- ◆ 1 teaspoon kosher salt
- ◆ ¼ teaspoon freshly ground black pepper
- ◆ Zest and juice of 1 lemon

1. Make the spice trio: Combine the oregano, fennel seeds, and red pepper flakes in an airtight container. Store at room temperature for up to 1 month. 2. Place two racks in the lower third of the oven and preheat the oven to 450ºF (235ºC). Use the convection setting if available. Combine the broccoli, olive oil, 1 tablespoon of the spice trio, salt, pepper, and lemon zest in a large bowl. Stir to coat the broccoli evenly. Spread the broccoli evenly on two baking sheets. Roast for 10 minutes. 3.Remove from the oven and stir. Place the sheets on opposite racks and roast until the broccoli has caramelized and is just cooked through, 5 to 10 minutes. Stir in 1 teaspoon lemon juice, adding more to taste. Serve hot or at room temperature.

Per Serving:
calories: 120 | fat: 7g | protein: 5g | carbs: 13g | fiber: 6g | sugar: 3g | sodium: 324mg

Roasted Sweet Potatoes

Prep time: 15 minutes | Cook time: 20 minutes | Serves 4 to 6

- ◆ 2 tablespoons extra-virgin olive oil or melted coconut oil, plus more to brush the pans
- ◆ 3 large sweet potatoes, scrubbed and cut into thin wedges
- ◆ 1 teaspoon salt
- ◆ 1 teaspoon ground turmeric
- ◆ ½ teaspoon ground coriander
- ◆ ¼ teaspoon ground ginger
- ◆ ¼ teaspoon chipotle powder
- ◆ 1 lime

1. Preheat the oven to 400ºF (205ºC). Brush two rimmed baking sheets with olive oil. 2. Put the sweet potato wedges in a large bowl. Add 2 tablespoons of olive oil and toss to coat the potatoes. 3. In a small bowl, mix the salt, turmeric, coriander, ginger, and chipotle powder. Sprinkle the spice mix over the potatoes, mixing well to coat evenly. 4. Arrange the sweet potato wedges in a single layer on the prepared baking sheets. 5. Bake until the sweet potatoes are tender in the middle and slightly browned and caramelized on the edges, about 20 minutes. 6. Remove from the oven, squeeze lime juice over the wedges, and serve.

Per Serving:
calories: 150 | fat: 7g | protein: 2g | carbs: 20g | fiber: 3g | sugar: 4g | sodium: 640mg

Nut-Free Keto Bread

Prep time: 15 minutes | Cook time: 50 minutes | Makes 12 slices

- ◆ 6 large eggs, separated
- ◆ ⅓ cup coconut flour
- ◆ 1 teaspoon baking powder
- ◆ ½ teaspoon fine Himalayan salt
- ◆ ¼ cup flaxseed meal
- ◆ ½ cup filtered water
- ◆ ½ cup melted coconut oil
- ◆ 1 teaspoon poppy seeds, for garnish (optional)

1. Preheat the oven to 350ºF (180ºC). Line an 8½ by 4½-inch loaf pan with parchment paper. 2. Place the egg whites in the bowl of a stand mixer and beat on low until foamy, then bring up to medium speed and beat until soft peaks form. While the egg whites beat, prepare the rest of the recipe. (If you're using a handheld mixer instead of a stand mixer, beat the whites until soft peaks form, then set aside.) 3. Sift the coconut flour, baking powder, and salt into a large bowl. Whisk in the flaxseed meal. 4. In a small bowl, whisk together the egg yolks, water, and oil. Slowly pour the wet mixture into the dry mixture, whisking until fully combined. Use a spatula to fold in the beaten egg whites until you no longer see streaks of white. 5. Pour the dough into the prepared loaf pan and sprinkle with the poppy seeds (if using). Bake on the middle rack of the oven for 50 to 60 minutes, until the bread is golden brown on the outside and firm to the touch. 6. Remove the bread from the oven and let cool in the pan for an hour before unmolding and slicing. Store at room temperature in an airtight container or wrapped in plastic wrap for up to 5 days.

Per Serving:
calories: 269 | fat: 26g | protein: 8g | carbs: 3g | fiber: 2g | sugar: 1g | sodium: 204mg

Sautéed Spinach

Prep time: 5 minutes | Cook time: 5 minutes | Serves 4

- 1 tablespoons extra-virgin olive oil
- 1 (10-ounce / 283-g) package frozen chopped spinach, thawed and drained
- 1 garlic clove, minced
- 1 teaspoon salt
- ¼ teaspoon freshly ground black pepper
- 1 tablespoon fresh lemon juice

1. In a large skillet, heat the oil over high heat. 2. Add the spinach, garlic, salt, and pepper and sauté until the spinach is heated through, about 5 minutes. 3. Add the lemon juice, stir to combine, and serve.

Per Serving:
calories: 50 | fat: 4g | protein: 2g | carbs: 3g | fiber: 2g | sugar: 0g | sodium: 630mg

Cumin-Roasted Cauliflower

Prep time: 8 minutes | Cook time: 25 minutes | Serves 6

- 2 medium cauliflower heads, broken into florets
- 3 tablespoons melted coconut oil
- 2 tablespoons ground cumin
- 1 teaspoon ground coriander
- 1 teaspoon salt

1. Preheat the oven to 400ºF (205ºC). 2. In a large bowl, combine the cauliflower, coconut oil, cumin, coriander, and salt. Toss to coat. 3. Transfer the florets to a large roasting tray, or two baking sheets. 4. Place the tray in the preheated oven and bake for 25 minutes, or until the cauliflower is tender and beginning to brown on the edges.

Per Serving:
calories: 114 | fat: 7g | protein: 4g | carbs: 11g | fiber: 5g | sugar: 5g | sodium: 448mg

Brilliantly Beetroot Flavoured Ketchup

Prep time: 5 minutes | Cook time: 45 minutes | Serves 2

- 2 whole beetroots
- 1 juiced lemon
- 4 tablespoons sunflower seeds, soaked overnight
- 1 teaspoon mustard powder
- A pinch of black pepper to taste

1. Preheat oven 350ºF (180ºC). 2. Bake the beetroot for 30 to 40 minutes or until tender, and then peel and chop into cubes. 3. Add the rest of the ingredients and the beetroot into a blender and purée until smooth.

Per Serving:
calories: 144 | fat: 9g | protein: 5g | carbs: 13g | fiber: 4g | sugar: 7g | sodium: 93mg

Indian-Spiced Cauliflower

Prep time: 15 minutes | Cook time: 3 to 4 hours | Serves 4 to 6

- 1 large head cauliflower, leaves and large stem removed
- ½ medium onion, diced
- 2 tablespoons extra-virgin olive oil
- ½ teaspoon sea salt
- ½ teaspoon garlic powder
- ½ teaspoon ground ginger
- ½ teaspoon curry powder
- ¼ teaspoon ground turmeric
- ¼ teaspoon ground cumin
- ⅛ teaspoon cayenne pepper

1. Chop the cauliflower into florets, and place them in the slow cooker with the onion. 2. In a small bowl, combine the olive oil, salt, garlic powder, ginger, curry powder, turmeric, cumin, and cayenne. Whisk into a paste. Using a pastry brush or a spoon, spread the spice paste onto the cauliflower florets. 3. Cover the cooker and set to low. Cook for 3 to 4 hours and serve.

Per Serving:
calories: 121 | fat: 7g | protein: 4g | carbs: 13g | fiber: 6g | sugar: 5g | sodium: 354mg

Blanched Green Veggies with Radishes

Prep time: 15 minutes | Cook time: 5 minutes | Serves 4

- 1½ tablespoons olive oil
- 1 pound (454 g) asparagus spears, woody ends trimmed
- ½ pound (227 g) green beans, trimmed
- 1 cup fava beans (fresh or frozen and thawed)
- 1 cup peas (fresh or frozen and thawed)
- ½ cup whole radishes, trimmed
- 1 tablespoon rice vinegar
- Sea salt, to taste
- Freshly ground black pepper, to taste

1. Place a large skillet over medium heat and add the olive oil. 2. Add the asparagus, green beans, fava beans, and peas. Sauté for about 5 minutes, or until crisp-tender. 3. Add the radishes and rice vinegar, or and toss to combine. 4. Season the veggies with sea salt and pepper and serve.

Per Serving:
calories: 247 | fat: 6g | protein: 15g | carbs: 35g | fiber: 16g | sugar: 5g | sodium: 17mg

Grain-Free Fritters

Prep time: 5 minutes | Cook time: 20 minutes | Makes 12 fritters

- 2 cups chickpea flour
- 1½ cups water
- 2 tablespoons ground chia seeds
- ½ teaspoon salt
- 3 cups lightly packed spinach leaves, finely chopped
- 1 tablespoon coconut oil, or extra-virgin olive oil

1. In a medium bowl, whisk together the chickpea flour, water, chia seeds, and salt. Mix well to ensure there are no lumps. 2. Fold in the spinach. 3. In a nonstick skillet set over medium-low heat, melt the coconut oil. 4. Working in batches, use a ¼-cup measure to drop the batter into the pan. Flatten the fritters to about ½ inch thick. Don't crowd the pan. 5. Cook for 5 to 6 minutes. Flip the fritters and cook for 5 minutes more. 6. Transfer to a serving plate.

Per Serving:

calories: 318 | fat: 10g | protein: 15g | carbs: 45g | fiber: 15g | sugar: 7g | sodium: 222mg

Everything Flaxseed Meal Crackers

Prep time: 10 minutes | Cook time: 40 minutes | Makes 2 dozen crackers

- 2 cups flaxseed meal
- 1 cup water
- ½ cup apple cider vinegar or coconut vinegar
- 1 teaspoon dried dill weed
- 1 teaspoon dried rosemary needles
- 1 teaspoon fine Himalayan salt
- 1 teaspoon garlic powder
- 1 teaspoon ground black pepper
- 1 teaspoon poppy seeds
- 1 teaspoon sesame seeds

1. Preheat the oven to 350°F (180°C) convection or 375°F (190°C) bake. Line a baking sheet with parchment paper. 2. Place the flaxseed meal, water, and vinegar in a medium-sized bowl. Add the dill weed, rosemary, salt, garlic powder, pepper, and seeds and mix thoroughly until a thick paste forms. 3. Transfer the flaxseed meal paste to the prepared baking sheet and shape it into a square that's approximately 10 inches wide, ¼ inch thick, and smooth on top. Bake for 30 minutes, or until firm in the center. Remove from the oven, carefully cut the mass into squares, separate them a little bit, and bake for another 10 minutes. When they're done, the crackers will be dark brown, crispy, and hard to the touch. 4. Let the crackers cool to room temperature before storing in an airtight container in the pantry. They will keep for up to a week. If they soften, you can toast them at 400°F (205°C) for 5 minutes before enjoying.

Per Serving:

calories: 154 | fat: 12g | protein: 5g | carbs: 12g | fiber: 8g | sugar: 3g | sodium: 244mg

Savory Flax Waffles

Prep time: 5 minutes | Cook time: 20 minutes | Makes 4 waffles

- 4 large eggs
- ¼ cup coconut cream
- 1 tablespoon coconut vinegar
- 1 cup flaxseed meal
- ½ teaspoon fine Himalayan salt
- ½ teaspoon garlic powder
- ½ teaspoon ground black pepper
- ½ teaspoon onion powder

1. In a large bowl, whisk together the eggs, coconut cream, and vinegar until well combined. Add the flaxseed meal, salt, garlic powder, pepper, and onion powder and mix until a thick batter forms. 2. Preheat a waffle iron per the manufacturer's instructions. When it's ready, pour in about ¼ cup of the batter. Cook until crispy, about 5 minutes, depending on your appliance. Repeat with the remaining batter. 3. Serve immediately. Store leftovers in an airtight container in the fridge for up to 1 week. To reheat, toast in a preheated 400°F (205°C) oven for 4 minutes.

Per Serving:

calories: 249 | fat: 19g | protein: 12g | carbs: 9g | fiber: 8g | sugar: 1g | sodium: 260mg

Kale-Stuffed Mushrooms

Prep time: 15 minutes | Cook time: 28 minutes | Serves 4

- 16 large white button mushrooms, stemmed
- 2 teaspoons olive oil
- ½ cup finely chopped sweet onion
- 1 teaspoon bottled minced garlic
- 2 cups finely shredded kale
- 1 cup chopped water-packed canned artichoke hearts
- 1 teaspoon chopped fresh basil
- 1 teaspoon chopped fresh oregano
- ⅛ teaspoon sea salt

1. Preheat the oven to 375°F (190°C). 2. Arrange the mushroom caps, hollow-side up, on a baking sheet. 3. Place a large skillet over medium-high heat and add the olive oil. 4. Add the onion and garlic. Sauté for about 3 minutes, or until tender. 5. Stir in the kale, artichoke hearts, basil, oregano, and sea salt. Sauté for about 5 minutes, or until the kale is wilted. 6. With the back of a spoon, squeeze the liquid out of the filling into the skillet and evenly divide the mixture among the mushroom caps. 7. Bake for about 20 minutes, or until the mushrooms are tender. Serve warm.

Per Serving:

calories: 75 | fat: 3g | protein: 5g | carbs: 11g | fiber: 3g | sugar: 2g | sodium: 242mg

Sautéed Kale with Garlic

Prep time: 15 minutes | Cook time: 12 minutes | Serves 4

- 1 tablespoon olive oil
- 3 garlic cloves, thinly sliced
- 8 cups chopped kale
- 1 tablespoon balsamic vinegar
- ½ teaspoon ground nutmeg
- Sea salt, to taste

1. In a large skillet over medium heat, sauté the olive oil and garlic for about 4 minutes, or until the garlic is lightly caramelized and very fragrant. 2. Add the kale. Cover and sauté for about 5 minutes, or until the leaves have wilted. 3. Uncover and cook for about 3 minutes more until all the liquid has evaporated. 4. Stir in the balsamic vinegar, sprinkle with nutmeg, and season with sea salt.

Per Serving:
calories: 102 | fat: 4g | protein: 4g | carbs: 15g | fiber: 2g | sugar: 1g | sodium: 14mg

Maple-Dijon Brussels Sprouts

Prep time: 15 minutes | Cook time: 3 to 4 hours | Serves 4 to 6

- 1 pound (454 g) Brussels sprouts, ends trimmed
- 2 tablespoons maple syrup
- 1 tablespoon Dijon mustard
- ½ teaspoon garlic powder
- ½ teaspoon sea salt
- ¼ cup water

1. In your slow cooker, combine the Brussels sprouts, maple syrup, mustard, garlic powder, salt, and water. Toss together to distribute evenly. 2. Cover the cooker and set to low. Cook for 3 to 4 hours and serve.

Per Serving:
calories: 80 | fat: 0g | protein: 4g | carbs: 17g | fiber: 4g | sugar: 9g | sodium: 410mg

Easy Roasted Vegetables

Prep time: 20 minutes | Cook time: 25 minutes | Serves 4

- 2 zucchini, diced into 1-inch pieces
- 1 red bell pepper, diced into 1-inch pieces
- 1 yellow bell pepper, diced into 1-inch pieces
- 1 red onion, diced into
- 1-inch pieces
- 1 sweet potato, diced into 1-inch pieces
- 4 garlic cloves
- ¼ cup extra-virgin olive oil
- 1 teaspoon salt

1. Preheat the oven to 450ºF (235ºC). 2. Line a baking sheet with aluminum foil. 3. In a large bowl, toss together the zucchini, red bell pepper, yellow bell pepper, onion, sweet potato, garlic, olive oil, and salt. Spread the vegetables evenly on the prepared sheet. 4. Bake for 25 minutes, stirring halfway through.

Per Serving:
calories: 184 | fat: 14g | protein: 2g | carbs: 15g | fiber: 2g | sugar: 5g | sodium: 611mg

Cider-Baked Beets

Prep time: 15 minutes | Cook time: 25 minutes | Serves 6

- 4 medium golden beets, peeled and diced into 1-inch pieces
- 4 medium red beets, peeled and diced into 1-inch pieces
- ½ yellow onion, diced into 1-inch pieces
- ½ cup apple cider vinegar
- ½ cup extra-virgin olive oil
- 2 tablespoons coconut sugar
- ¼ teaspoon salt
- Freshly ground black pepper, to taste

1. Preheat the oven to 450ºF (235ºC). 2. Line a baking sheet with aluminum foil. 3. Spread the beets and onion into the prepared pan and drizzle with the vinegar and olive oil. 4. Sprinkle the coconut sugar and the salt onto the vegetables. Season with pepper and toss to coat. 5. Bake for 25 minutes, or until the beets caramelize around the edges and are fork-tender.

Per Serving:
calories: 233 | fat: 19g | protein: 2g | carbs: 18g | fiber: 2g | sugar: 12g | sodium: 184mg

Zucchini and Red Onion Salad with Olives

Prep time: 15 minutes | Cook time: 0 minutes | Serves 4

- 1 cup arugula
- 2 large zucchinis, thinly sliced
- ½ small red onion, thinly sliced
- 2 radishes, thinly sliced
- ½ cup pitted green olives, sliced
- 2 tablespoons extra-virgin olive oil
- 2 tablespoons fresh lemon juice
- 1 teaspoon salt
- ⅛ teaspoon red pepper flakes

1. In a medium bowl, combine the arugula, zucchini, red onion, radishes, and green olives. 2. Add the olive oil, lemon juice, salt, and red pepper flakes and toss to combine. Serve.

Per Serving:
calories: 120 | fat: 10g | protein: 2g | carbs: 7g | fiber: 3g | sugar: 4g | sodium: 870mg

Tangy Brussels Sprout, Onion and Apple Kebabs

Prep time: 15 minutes | Cook time: 20 minutes | Makes 12 kebabs

- 1 pound (454 g) Brussels sprouts, discolored exterior leaves removed and discarded
- 2 apples, diced into 1-inch pieces
- 2 small red onions, diced into 1-inch pieces
- 1 tablespoon avocado oil
- ⅓ cup fish sauce
- ¼ cup filtered water
- 3 tablespoons rice vinegar
- 2 tablespoons freshly squeezed lime juice
- 2 roughly chopped pitted dates
- 2 garlic cloves, minced
- Dash red pepper flakes
- Dash ground ginger

1. Preheat the oven to 400°F (205°C). 2. Carefully press a skewer through 1 Brussels sprout, 1 apple piece, and 1 onion piece, leaving ½ inch between each piece. Repeat until 12 skewers are evenly filled. Place the kebabs on a rimmed baking sheet. Roast for 20 minutes, or until thoroughly roasted, turning the skewers halfway through 3. While the vegetables roast, in a blender, combine the fish sauce, water, vinegar, lime juice, dates, garlic, red pepper flakes, and ginger. Pulse until smooth. 4. Remove the kebabs from the oven and drizzle with half the sauce. Serve immediately, with the remaining sauce as a dip.

Per Serving:
calories: 132 | fat: 3g | protein: 3g | carbs: 25g | fiber: 5g | sugar: 11g | sodium: 852mg

Homemade Avocado Sushi

Prep time: 20 minutes | Cook time: 15 minutes | Serves 4

- 1½ cups dry quinoa
- 3 cups water, plus additional for rolling
- ½ teaspoon salt
- 6 nori sheets
- 3 avocados, halved, pitted,
- and sliced thinly, divided
- 1 small cucumber, halved, seeded, and cut into matchsticks, divided
- Coconut aminos, for dipping (optional)

1. Rinse the quinoa in a fine-mesh sieve. 2. In a medium pot set over high heat, combine the rinsed quinoa, water, and salt. Bring to a boil. Reduce the heat to low. Cover and simmer for 15 minutes. Fluff the quinoa with a fork. 3. On a cutting board, lay out 1 nori sheet. Spread ½ cup of quinoa over the sheet, leaving 2 to 3 inches uncovered at the top. 4. Place 5 or 6 avocado slices across the bottom of the nori sheet (the side closest to you) in a row. Add 5 or 6 cucumber matchsticks on top. 5. Starting at the bottom, tightly roll up the nori sheet. sheet. Dab the uncovered top with water to seal the roll. 6. Slice the sushi roll into 6 pieces. 7. Repeat with the remaining 5 nori sheets, quinoa, and vegetables. 8. Serve with the coconut aminos (if using).

Per Serving:
calories: 557 | fat: 33g | protein: 13g | carbs: 57g | fiber: 15g | sugar: 2g | sodium: 309mg

Coconut-Almond Bake

Prep time: 10 minutes | Cook time: 25 minutes | Serves 4

- 1 tablespoon olive oil
- 1 sweet onion, chopped, or about 1 cup precut packaged onion
- 1 tablespoon grated fresh ginger, or 1 teaspoon ground ginger
- 2 teaspoons bottled minced garlic
- 1 cup canned lite coconut milk
- 1 cup water
- 1 cup quinoa, rinsed well
- ¼ cup chopped toasted almonds
- 1 scallion, white and green parts, chopped

1. Place a large saucepan over medium-high heat and add the olive oil. 2. Add the onion, ginger, and garlic. Sauté for about 3 minutes, or until softened. 3. Stir in the coconut milk, water, and quinoa. Bring the mixture to a boil. Reduce the heat to low, cover, and simmer for about 20 minutes, or until the quinoa is tender and the liquid has been absorbed. 4. Stir in the almonds and serve topped with the scallions.

Per Serving:
calories: 378 | fat: 24g | protein: 9g | carbs: 36g | fiber: 6g | sugar: 6g | sodium: 19mg

Baked Zucchini Fries

Prep time: 10 minutes | Cook time: 20 minutes | Makes about 12 fries

- ½ cup almond flour
- ½ teaspoon salt
- ½ teaspoon garlic powder
- ½ teaspoon freshly ground
- black pepper
- 1 medium zucchini, trimmed and halved widthwise
- 1 tablespoon avocado oil

1. Preheat the oven to 425°F (220°C). 2. Line a baking sheet with aluminum foil. 3. In a small bowl, mix the almond flour, salt, garlic powder, and pepper. 4. Cut each zucchini half into about 6 strips that resemble fries. Brush the strips with the avocado oil, and roll in the almond flour mixture until well coated. Evenly space the fries on the prepared pan. 5. Bake for 20 minutes, or until crispy.

Per Serving:
calories: 230 | fat: 21g | protein: 6g | carbs: 7g | fiber: 4g | sugar: 0g | sodium: 583mg

Buckwheat Tabbouleh

Prep time: 15 minutes | Cook time: 10 minutes | Serves 4

- 1 tablespoon olive oil
- ½ cup chopped red onion
- 2 teaspoons bottled minced garlic
- 2 cups cooked buckwheat
- Juice of 1 lemon (3 tablespoons)
- Zest of 1 lemon (optional)
- ½ cup chopped fresh parsley
- ¼ cup chopped fresh mint
- Sea salt, to taste

1. Place a large skillet over medium-high heat and add the olive oil. 2. Add the red onion and garlic. Sauté for about 3 minutes, or until translucent. 3. Stir in the buckwheat, lemon juice, and lemon zest (if using). Sauté for about 5 minutes, or until heated through. 4. Stir in the parsley and mint. Sauté for 1 minute more. 5. Remove from the heat and season with sea salt.

Per Serving:
calories: 184 | fat: 5g | protein: 6g | carbs: 34g | fiber: 5g | sugar: 2g | sodium: 9mg

Mustard Cauliflower Slices

Prep time: 5 minutes | Cook time: 0 minutes | Serves 2

- 2 cups cauliflower florets, finely sliced

Dressing:
- 1 teaspoon extra virgin olive oil
- 1 lemon, juiced
- 1 large garlic clove, minced
- 1 teaspoon wholegrain mustard

1. Get a large salad bowl and combine all of the ingredients. 2. Serve immediately so that the cauliflower remains crunchy!

Per Serving:
calories: 56 | fat: 3g | protein: 2g | carbs: 8g | fiber: 2g | sugar: 3g | sodium: 60mg

Slow-Roasted Sweet Potatoes

Prep time: 10 minutes | Cook time: 40 minutes | Serves 4

- Olive oil, for greasing the baking dish
- 3 sweet potatoes, peeled and cut into large chunks
- 1 tablespoon pure maple syrup
- ½ teaspoon ground allspice
- ½ teaspoon ground ginger
- ¼ teaspoon ground nutmeg
- Pinch sea salt
- ½ cup unsweetened apple juice

1. Preheat the oven to 350ºF (180ºC). 2. Lightly grease an 8-by-8- inch baking dish with olive oil. 3. In a large bowl, toss the sweet potatoes, maple syrup, all-spice, ginger, nutmeg, and sea salt until well mixed. Transfer the sweet potatoes to the prepared dish, and pour in the apple juice. 4. Cover the dish and bake the potatoes for about 40 minutes, or until very tender.

Per Serving:
calories: 295 | fat: 1g | protein: 4g | carbs: 70g | fiber: 9g | sugar: 10g | sodium: 56mg

Root Vegetable Loaf

Prep time: 25 minutes | Cook time: 1 hour | Serves 8

- 1 onion, finely chopped
- 2 tablespoons water
- 2 cups grated carrots
- 1½ cups grated sweet potatoes
- 1½ cups gluten-free rolled oats
- ¾ cup butternut squash purée
- 1 teaspoon salt

1. Preheat the oven to 350ºF (180ºC). 2. Line a loaf pan with parchment paper. 3. In a large pot set over medium heat, sauté the onion in the water for about 5 minutes, or until soft. 4. Add the carrots and sweet potatoes. Cook for 2 minutes. Remove the pot from the heat. 5. Stir in the oats, butternut squash purée, and salt. Mix well. 6. Transfer the mixture to the prepared loaf pan, pressing down evenly. 7. Place the pan in the preheated oven and bake for 50 to 55 minutes, uncovered, or until the loaf is firm and golden. 8. Cool for 10 minutes before slicing.

Per Serving:
calories: 169 | fat: 2g | protein: 5g | carbs: 34g | fiber: 6g | sugar: 3g | sodium: 442mg

Roasted Sweet Potatoes and Pineapple

Prep time: 15 minutes | Cook time: 25 minutes | Serves 4

- 3 tablespoons coconut oil
- 2 large sweet potatoes, or yams, peeled and cut into ½-inch pieces
- 1 cup fresh pineapple, cut into ½-inch pieces
- 2 teaspoons curry powder
- 1 teaspoon salt
- ¼ teaspoon freshly ground black pepper

1. Preheat the oven to 400ºF (205ºC). 2. In a microwave-safe bowl, melt the coconut oil in the microwave on high for about 1 minute. 3. In a large bowl, combine the sweet potatoes and pineapple. Add the melted coconut oil, curry powder, salt, and pepper. Toss to combine. 4. Spoon the mixture onto a rimmed baking sheet. Place the sheet in the preheated oven and roast for 20 to 25 minutes, or until the sweet potatoes are tender. 5. Serve warm or at room temperature.

Per Serving:
calories: 230 | fat: 11g | protein: 2g | carbs: 34g | fiber: 5g | sugar: 5g | sodium: 591mg

Burst Cherry Tomatoes with Garlic

Prep time: 10 minutes | Cook time: 20 minutes | Serves 6

- 1 pound (454 g) cherry tomatoes, halved
- 4 garlic cloves, minced
- 1 teaspoon dried basil
- (optional)
- 2 tablespoons extra-virgin olive oil
- Salt, to taste

1. Preheat the oven to 400ºF (205ºC). 2. Line a baking sheet with aluminum foil. 3. In a large bowl, mix the tomatoes, garlic, and basil (if using). Drizzle with the olive oil and toss to coat. Season generously with salt. Transfer to the prepared pan. 4. Bake for 15 to 20 minutes, or until the tomatoes collapse.

Per Serving:
calories: 46 | fat: 0g | protein: 2g | carbs: 10g | fiber: 3g | sugar: 2g | sodium: 4mg

Vegan Minestrone with Herb Oil

Prep time: 30 minutes | Cook time: 40 minutes | Serves 8

- 3 tablespoons olive oil
- 1 cup diced carrots
- ¾ cup diced celery
- 1 yellow onion, sliced
- Kosher salt, to taste
- 1 tablespoon tomato paste (optional if nightshade-sensitive)
- 2 garlic cloves, minced
- Pinch of crushed red pepper flakes

- 4 zucchini, diced
- 2 crookneck squash, diced
- 8 cups low-sodium vegetable broth
- 2 (14½ ounces / 411 g) cans diced San Marzano tomatoes
- 1 bunch rainbow chard, stems removed, coarsely chopped
- 2 (15 ounces / 425 g) cans cannellini beans, rinsed and drained

Herb Oil:
- ¼ teaspoon kosher salt
- 2 garlic cloves, peeled
- ½ cup extra-virgin olive oil
- ½ cup packed herbs, such as parsley, chives, basil, and mint

1. In a large stockpot or Dutch oven over medium heat, warm the olive oil. Add the carrots, celery, onion, and ½ teaspoon salt and cook, stirring frequently, until tender, about 10 minutes. Add the tomato paste (if using), garlic, and red pepper flakes and cook until the paste turns brick red, about 1 minute. Add the zucchini and squash and cook for 1 minute. Stir in the broth and tomatoes, bring to a boil over high heat, then turn the heat to medium-low and simmer uncovered for 15 minutes. Stir in the chard and simmer for 5 minutes longer. Stir in the beans and warm them for about 3 minutes. Season with salt. 2. In the meantime, make the herb oil: Place the salt and garlic in a small food processor or blender and process until the garlic is minced, about 20 seconds. Add the olive oil and herbs and blend until the oil is bright green, about 20 seconds. 3. Fill each bowl with soup and drizzle with 2 teaspoons of the herb oil to serve.

Per Serving:
calories: 250 | fat: 21g | protein: 7g | carbs: 13g | fiber: 4g | sugar: 5g | sodium: 400mg

Vegetable Spring Roll Wraps

Prep time: 20 minutes | Cook time: 0 minutes | Serves 6

- 10 rice paper wrappers
- 2 cups lightly packed baby spinach, divided
- 1 cup grated carrot, divided
- 1 cucumber, halved, seeded, and cut into thin, 4-inch-long strips, divided
- 1 avocado, halved, pitted, and cut into thin strips, divided

1. Place a cutting board on a flat surface with the vegetables in front of you. 2. Fill a large, shallow bowl with warm water—hot enough to cook the wrappers, but warm enough so you can touch it comfortably. 3. Soak 1 wrapper in the water and then place it on the cutting board. 4. Fill the middle of the wrapper with ¼ cup of spinach, 2 tablespoons of grated carrot, a few cucumber slices, and 1 or 2 slices of avocado. 5. Fold the sides over the middle, and then roll the wrapper tightly from the bottom (the side closest to you), burrito-style. 6. Repeat with the remaining wrappers and vegetables. 7. Serve immediately.

Per Serving:
calories: 246 | fat: 10g | protein: 4g | carbs: 36g | fiber: 6g | sugar: 4g | sodium: 145mg

Roasted Fingerling Potatoes

Prep time: 5 minutes | Cook time: 20 minutes | Serves 4 to 6

- 2 tablespoons extra-virgin olive oil, plus more to brush the baking sheet
- 1½ pounds (680 g) fingerling potatoes, scrubbed
- 1 teaspoon salt
- ¼ teaspoon freshly ground black pepper
- 1 tablespoon chopped fresh parsley or chives (optional)

1. Preheat the oven to 400ºF (205ºC). Brush a rimmed baking sheet with oil. 2. Put the potatoes in a large bowl. Add 2 tablespoons of oil and toss to coat the potatoes. 3. Toss the potatoes with the salt and pepper. 4. Arrange the potatoes in a single layer on the prepared baking sheet. 5. Bake until the potatoes are tender in the middle and slightly browned, about 20 minutes. 6. Remove from the oven, sprinkle with the parsley or chives (if using), and serve.

Per Serving:
calories: 180 | fat: 7g | protein: 3g | carbs: 27g | fiber: 4g | sugar: 2g | sodium: 610mg

Chapter 9

Vegetarian Mains

Chapter 9 Vegetarian Mains

Citrus Spinach

Prep time: 0 minutes | Cook time: 10 minutes | Serves 4

- 2 tablespoons extra-virgin olive oil
- 4 cups fresh baby spinach
- 2 garlic cloves, minced
- Juice of ½ orange
- Zest of ½ orange
- ½ teaspoon sea salt
- ⅛ teaspoon freshly ground black pepper

1. In a large skillet over medium-high heat, heat the olive oil until it shimmers. 2. Add the spinach and cook for 3 minutes, stirring occasionally. 3. Add the garlic. Cook for 30 seconds, stirring constantly. 4. Add the orange juice, orange zest, salt, and pepper. Cook for about 2 minutes, stirring constantly, until the juice evaporates.

Per Serving:
calories: 80 | fat: 7g | protein: 1g | carbs: 4g | fiber: 1g | sugar: 2g | sodium: 258mg

Sesame-Quinoa Cups

Prep time: 30 minutes | Cook time: 0 minutes | Serves 4

Dressing:
- ¼ cup olive oil
- 2 tablespoons rice vinegar
- 1 tablespoon raw honey
- ½ teaspoon grated fresh ginger
- ½ teaspoon ground cumin
- Sea salt, to taste

Cups:
- 1 cup cooked quinoa
- 1 cup shredded carrot
- 1 apple, cored and chopped
- 1 scallion, white and green parts, chopped
- ½ cup pumpkin seeds
- ¼ cup dried cranberries
- 1 tablespoon freshly squeezed lemon juice
- 1 large radicchio head, core removed, separated into 8 large leaves
- 1 tablespoon sesame seeds

Make the Dressing: In a small bowl, whisk the olive oil, rice vinegar, honey, ginger, and cumin. Season with sea salt and set it aside. Make the Cups: 1. In a large bowl, stir together the quinoa, carrot, apple, scallion, pumpkin seeds, cranberries, and lemon juice until well mixed. 2. Add the dressing and toss to mix well. 3. Spoon the rice mixture into the radicchio leaves, and serve topped with the sesame seeds.

Per Serving:
calories: 365 | fat: 23g | protein: 8g | carbs: 34g | fiber: 5g | sugar: 11g | sodium: 28mg

Roasted Broccoli and Cashews

Prep time: 10 minutes | Cook time: 20 minutes | Serves 4

- 6 cups broccoli florets
- 2 tablespoons extra-virgin olive oil
- 1 teaspoon salt
- 1 tablespoon coconut aminos
- ½ cup toasted cashews

1. Preheat the oven to 375ºF (190ºC). 2. In a large bowl, toss the broccoli with the olive oil and salt. Transfer the broccoli to a baking sheet, spreading it into a single layer. Place the sheet in the preheated oven and roast for 15 to 20 minutes, or until the broccoli is tender. 3. In a large bowl, toss the roasted broccoli with the coconut aminos and cashews, and serve.

Per Serving:
calories: 209 | fat: 15g | protein: 6g | carbs: 15g | fiber: 4g | sugar: 3g | sodium: 633mg

Tofu and Spinach Sauté

Prep time: 10 minutes | Cook time: 10 minutes | Serves 4

- 2 tablespoons extra-virgin olive oil
- 1 onion, chopped
- 4 cups fresh baby spinach
- 8 ounces (227 g) tofu
- 3 garlic cloves, minced
- Juice of 1 orange
- Zest of 1 orange
- ½ teaspoon sea salt
- ⅛ teaspoon freshly ground black pepper

1. In a large skillet over medium-high heat, heat the olive oil until it shimmers. 2. Add the onion, spinach, and tofu. Cook for about 5 minutes, stirring occasionally, until the onion is soft. 3. Add the garlic. Cook for 30 seconds, stirring constantly. 4. Add the orange juice, orange zest, salt, and pepper. Cook for 3 minutes, stirring, until heated through.

Per Serving:
calories: 128 | fat: 10g | protein: 6g | carbs: 7g | fiber: 2g | sugar: 3g | sodium: 266mg

Sweet Potato and Bell Pepper Hash with a Fried Egg

Prep time: 5 minutes | Cook time: 25 minutes | Serves 4

- 4 tablespoons extra-virgin olive oil, divided
- 1 onion, chopped
- 1 red bell pepper, chopped
- 4 cups cubed, peeled sweet potato
- 1 teaspoon sea salt, divided
- ⅛ teaspoon freshly ground black pepper
- 4 eggs

1. In a large nonstick skillet over medium-high heat, heat 2 tablespoons of the olive oil until it shimmers. 2. Add the onion, red bell pepper, and sweet potato. Season with ½ teaspoon of the salt and the pepper. Cook for 15 to 20 minutes, stirring occasionally, until the sweet potatoes are soft and browned. Divide the potatoes among 4 plates. 3. Return the skillet to the heat, reduce the heat to medium-low, and heat the remaining 2 tablespoons of olive oil, swirling to coat the bottom of the pan. 4. Carefully crack the eggs into the pan and sprinkle with the remaining ½ teaspoon of salt. Cook for 3 to 4 minutes until the whites are set. Gently flip the eggs and turn off the heat. Let the eggs sit in the hot pan for 1 minute. Place 1 egg on top of each serving of hash.

Per Serving:
calories: 384 | fat: 19g | protein: 10g | carbs: 47g | fiber: 8g | sugar: 16g | sodium: 573mg

Veggie Spring Rolls with Almond Dipping Sauce

Prep time: 20 minutes | Cook time: 0 minutes | Makes 10 rolls

Sauce:
- ½ cup almond butter
- 1 tablespoon coconut aminos
- 1 tablespoon coconut sugar
- 1 tablespoon freshly squeezed lime juice
- ¼ teaspoon garlic powder
- ¼ teaspoon red pepper flakes
- Dash ground ginger
- Filtered water, to thin

Rolls:
- 10 rice paper wrappers
- 1 large avocado, thinly sliced
- 1 red bell pepper, very thinly sliced
- ½ cup shredded carrots
- ½ cup julienned cucumber
- ½ cup shredded cabbage
- ¼ cup sliced scallion
- ¼ cup fresh cilantro leaves

Make the Sauce: In a small bowl, whisk the almond butter, coconut aminos, coconut sugar, lime juice, garlic powder, red pepper flakes, and ginger. If needed, add a little of the water to thin. Make the Rolls: 1. Prepare the rice paper wrappers according to the package instructions. 2. In a large bowl, gently combine the avocado, red bell pepper, carrots, cucumber, cabbage, scallion, and cilantro. On a clean work surface, divide the vegetables into 10 portions. 3. On a large plastic cutting board, lay out one wrapper and smooth any wrinkles. 4. Place 1 portion of veggies on the bottom third of the wrapper. Beginning at the bottom edge, roll it like a burrito until about three-fourths of the way to the top. Fold the side edges in, and continue to roll toward the top of the wrapper. 5. Repeat steps 3 and 4 with the remaining ingredients. 6. Serve the rolls with the dipping sauce alongside.

Per Serving:
calories: 176 | fat: 10g | protein: 5g | carbs: 21g | fiber: 3g | sugar: 2g | sodium: 54mg

Quinoa-Broccolini Sauté

Prep time: 10 minutes | Cook time: 10 minutes | Serves 4

- 1 tablespoon coconut oil
- 2 leeks, white part only, sliced
- 2 garlic cloves, chopped
- 4 cups chopped broccolini
- ½ cup vegetable broth, or water
- 1 teaspoon curry powder
- 2 cups cooked quinoa
- 1 tablespoon coconut aminos

1. In a large skillet over high heat, melt the coconut oil. Add the leeks and garlic. Sauté for 2 minutes. 2. Add the broccolini and vegetable broth. Cover the pan and cook for 5 minutes. 3. Stir in the curry powder, quinoa, and coconut aminos. Cook for 2 to 3 minutes, uncovered, or until the quinoa is warmed through. 4. Serve warm as a side dish, or at room temperature as a salad.

Per Serving:
calories: 273 | fat: 6g | protein: 11g | carbs: 44g | fiber: 6g | sugar: 5g | sodium: 54mg

Broccoli-Sesame Stir-Fry

Prep time: 10 minutes | Cook time: 10 minutes | Serves 4

- 2 tablespoons extra-virgin olive oil
- 1 teaspoon sesame oil
- 4 cups broccoli florets
- 1 tablespoon grated fresh ginger
- ¼teaspoon sea salt
- 2 garlic cloves, minced
- 2 tablespoons toasted sesame seeds

1. In a large nonstick skillet over medium-high heat, heat the olive oil and sesame oil until they shimmer. 2. Add the broccoli, ginger, and salt. Cook for 5 to 7 minutes, stirring frequently, until the broccoli begins to brown. 3. Add the garlic. Cook for 30 seconds, stirring constantly. 4. Remove from the heat and stir in the sesame seeds.

Per Serving:
calories: 134 | fat: 11g | protein: 4g | carbs: 9g | fiber: 3g | sugar: 2g | sodium: 148mg

Butternut Squash and Spinach Gratin with Lentils

Prep time: 15 minutes | Cook time: 20 minutes | Serves 4 to 6

- 1 tablespoon coconut oil
- 1 onion, peeled and chopped
- 2 garlic cloves, minced
- 1 small butternut squash, peeled, seeded, and cut into ½-inch cubes
- 4 cups packed spinach
- 1 teaspoon salt
- ½ teaspoon freshly ground black pepper
- 1 (13½-ounce / 383-g) can coconut milk
- 1½ or 2 cups vegetable broth
- 1 (15-ounce / 425-g) can lentils, drained and rinsed
- ¼ cup chopped fresh parsley
- 2 tablespoons chopped fresh sage
- ½ cup chopped toasted walnuts

1. Preheat the oven to 375ºF (190ºC). 2. In a large ovenproof skillet over high heat, melt the coconut oil. Add the onion and garlic. Sauté for 3 minutes. 3. Add the butternut squash, spinach, salt, and pepper. Sauté for 3 minutes more. 4. Stir in the coconut milk and just enough vegetable broth to cover the squash. Bring the liquid to a boil. 5. Add the lentils, parsley, and sage. Stir to combine. 6. Place the skillet in the preheated oven and bake the casserole for 15 to 20 minutes, or until the squash is tender. 7. Transfer the casserole to a serving dish and garnish with the walnuts.

Per Serving:
calories: 502 | fat: 37g | protein: 20g | carbs: 47g | fiber: 16g | sugar: 9g | sodium: 1063mg

Broccoli and Egg "Muffins"

Prep time: 10 minutes | Cook time: 20 minutes | Serves 4

- Nonstick cooking spray
- 2 tablespoons extra-virgin olive oil
- 1 onion, chopped
- 1 cup broccoli florets, chopped
- 8 eggs, beaten
- 1 teaspoon garlic powder
- ½ teaspoon sea salt
- ¼ teaspoon freshly ground black pepper

1. Preheat the oven to 350ºF (180ºC). 2. Spray a muffin tin with nonstick cooking spray. 3. In a large nonstick skillet over medium-high heat, heat the olive oil until it shimmers. 4. Add the onion and broccoli. Cook for 3 minutes. Spoon the vegetables evenly into 4 muffin cups. 5. In a medium bowl, beat the eggs, garlic powder, salt, and pepper. Pour them over the vegetables in the muffin cups. Bake for 15 to 17 minutes until the eggs set.

Per Serving:
calories: 207 | fat: 16g | protein: 12g | carbs: 5g | fiber: 1g | sugar: 2g | sodium: 366mg

Mushroom Egg Foo Young

Prep time: 10 minutes | Cook time: 20 minutes | Serves 2

- 1 tablespoon olive oil
- 1 cup sliced wild mushrooms
- 1 teaspoon bottled minced garlic
- 2 cups bean sprouts
- 2 scallions, white and green parts, chopped
- 6 eggs
- ¼ teaspoon sea salt
- 1 tablespoon chopped fresh cilantro

1. Place a large skillet or wok over medium heat and add the olive oil. 2. Add the mushrooms and garlic. Sauté for about 4 minutes, or until softened. 3. Add the bean sprouts and scallions. Sauté for 5 minutes, spreading the vegetables out in the skillet. 4. In a small bowl, beat the eggs and sea salt. Pour the eggs over the vegetables in the skillet, shaking so the egg seeps through the vegetables. Cook for about 5 minutes, or until the eggs are set on the bottom. 5. Cut the omelet into quarters and flip them over. Cook the egg foo young for about 3 minutes, or until the omelet is completely cooked through. 6. Serve two pieces per person.

Per Serving:
calories: 345 | fat: 23g | protein: 28g | carbs: 12g | fiber: 1g | sugar: 2g | sodium: 511mg

Kale Frittata

Prep time: 10 minutes | Cook time: 20 minutes | Serves 4

- 2 tablespoons extra-virgin olive oil
- 4 cups stemmed and chopped kale
- 3 garlic cloves, minced
- 8 eggs
- ½ teaspoon sea salt
- ¼ teaspoon freshly ground black pepper
- 2 tablespoons sunflower seeds

1. Preheat the broiler to high. 2. In a large ovenproof skillet over medium-high heat, heat the olive oil until it shimmers. 3. Add the kale. Cook for about 5 minutes, stirring, until soft. 4. Add the garlic. Cook for 30 seconds, stirring constantly. 5. In a medium bowl, beat the eggs, salt, and pepper. Carefully pour them over the kale. Reduce the heat to medium. Cook the eggs for about 3 minutes until set around the edges. Using a rubber spatula, carefully pull the eggs away from the edges of the skillet and tilt the pan to let the uncooked eggs run into the edges. Cook for about 3 minutes, until the edges set again. 6. Sprinkle with the sunflower seeds. Transfer the pan to the broiler and cook for 3 to 5 minutes until puffed and brown. Cut into wedges to serve.

Per Serving:
calories: 231 | fat: 17g | protein: 14g | carbs: 9g | fiber: 1g | sugar: 0g | sodium: 387mg

Thai Cabbage Bowl

Prep time: 20 minutes | Cook time: 15 minutes | Serves 4

- 1 tablespoon olive oil
- 1 sweet onion, chopped, or about 1 cup precut packaged onion
- 1 teaspoon bottled minced garlic
- 1 teaspoon grated fresh ginger
- 2 cups finely chopped cauliflower
- 2 cups shredded broccoli stalks, or packaged broccoli slaw
- 1 cup shredded sweet potato

- 1 carrot, shredded, or ½ preshredded packaged carrots
- 1 cup peas (fresh or frozen and thawed)
- 1 cup chopped fresh spinach
- 2 tablespoons apple cider vinegar
- 1 teaspoon ground cumin
- ½ teaspoon ground coriander
- ¼ cup pumpkin seeds
- ¼ cup dried cherries
- 4 large cabbage leaves

1. Place a large skillet over medium-high heat and add the olive oil. 2. Add the onion, garlic, and ginger. Sauté for about 3 minutes, or until softened. 3. Stir in the cauliflower, broccoli, sweet potato, and carrot. Sauté for about 8 minutes, or until the vegetables are tender. 4. Stir in the peas, spinach, cider vinegar, cumin, and coriander. Sauté for about 2 minutes more until the spinach has wilted. Remove the skillet from the heat. 5. Stir in the pumpkin seeds and dried cherries. Spoon the vegetable mixture into the cabbage leaves and serve.

Per Serving:
calories: 208 | fat: 8g | protein: 8g | carbs: 29g | fiber: 8g | sugar: 9g | sodium: 82mg

Braised Bok Choy with Shiitake Mushrooms

Prep time: 10 minutes | Cook time: 10 minutes | Serves 4

- 1 tablespoon coconut oil
- 8 baby bok choy, halved lengthwise
- ½ cup water
- 1 tablespoon coconut aminos
- 1 cup shiitake mushrooms,

- stemmed, sliced thinly
- Salt, to taste
- Freshly ground black pepper, to taste
- 1 scallion, sliced thinly
- 1 tablespoon toasted sesame seeds

1. In a large pan over high heat, melt the coconut oil. Add the bok choy in a single layer. 2. Add the water, coconut aminos, and mushrooms to the pan. Cover and braise the vegetables for 5 to 10 minutes, or until the bok choy is tender. 3. Remove the pan from the heat. Season the vegetables with salt and pepper. 4. Transfer the bok choy and mushrooms to a serving dish and garnish with the scallions and sesame seeds.

Per Serving:
calories: 285 | fat: 8g | protein: 26g | carbs: 43g | fiber: 18g | sugar: 21g | sodium: 1035mg

Herb Omelet

Prep time: 10 minutes | Cook time: 5 minutes | Serves 2

- 3 large eggs
- 1 tablespoon chopped fresh chives
- 1 tablespoon chopped fresh parsley

- 1 teaspoon ground turmeric
- ¼ teaspoon ground cumin
- ½ teaspoon salt
- 2 tablespoons extra-virgin olive, divided

1. In a medium bowl, whisk together the eggs, chives, parsley, turmeric, cumin, and salt. 2. In an omelet pan, heat 1 tablespoon of oil over medium-high heat. 3. Pour half of the egg mixture into the hot pan. 4. Reduce the heat to medium and let the eggs cook until the bottom starts to set. 5. Using a heat-proof spatula, gently move the eggs around the edges so the uncooked egg can spill over the sides of the cooked egg and set. 6. Continue to cook the omelet until just set, but still soft. Use the spatula to fold the omelet in half, then slide it out of the pan and onto a serving dish. 7. Repeat with the remaining egg mixture and 1 tablespoon of oil. Serve.

Per Serving:
calories: 240 | fat: 21g | protein: 11g | carbs: 1g | fiber: 0g | sugar: 1g | sodium: 310mg

Hummus Burgers

Prep time: 10 minutes | Cook time: 30 minutes | Serves 4

- 1 tablespoon extra-virgin olive oil, plus additional for brushing
- 2 (15-ounce / 425-g) cans garbanzo beans, drained and rinsed
- ¼ cup tahini
- 1 tablespoon freshly

- squeezed lemon juice
- 2 teaspoons lemon zest
- 2 garlic cloves, minced
- 2 tablespoons chickpea flour
- 4 scallions, minced
- 1 teaspoon salt

1. Preheat the oven to 375°F (190°C). 2. Brush a baking sheet with olive oil. 3. In a food processor, combine the garbanzo beans, tahini, lemon juice, lemon zest, garlic, and the remaining 1 tablespoon of olive oil. Pulse until smooth. 4. Add the chickpea flour, scallions, and salt. Pulse to combine. 5. Form the mixture into four patties and place them on the prepared baking sheet. Place the sheet in the preheated oven and bake for 30 minutes.

Per Serving:
calories: 408 | fat: 18g | protein: 19g | carbs: 43g | fiber: 12g | sugar: 2g | sodium: 625mg

Tomato Asparagus Frittata

Prep time: 10 minutes | Cook time: 10 minutes | Serves 4

- 2 tablespoons extra-virgin olive oil
- 10 asparagus spears, trimmed
- 10 cherry tomatoes
- 6 eggs
- 1 tablespoon chopped, fresh thyme
- ½ teaspoon sea salt
- ⅛ teaspoon freshly ground black pepper

1. Preheat the broiler to high. 2. In a large ovenproof skillet over medium-high heat, heat the olive oil until it shimmers. 3. Add the asparagus. Cook for 5 minutes, stirring occasionally. 4. Add the tomatoes. Cook 3 minutes, stirring occasionally. 5. In a medium bowl, whisk together the eggs, thyme, salt, and pepper. Carefully pour over the asparagus and tomatoes, moving the vegetables around so they are evenly spread in the pan. 6. Reduce the heat to medium. Cook the eggs for about 3 minutes until set around the edges. Using a rubber spatula, carefully pull the eggs away from the edges of the skillet and tilt the pan to let the uncooked eggs run into the edges. Cook for about 3 minutes, until the edges set again. 7. Carefully transfer the pan to the broiler and cook for 3 to 5 minutes until puffed and brown. Cut into wedges to serve.

Per Serving:
calories: 224 | fat: 14g | protein: 12g | carbs: 15g | fiber: 5g | sugar: 10g | sodium: 343mg

Mixed Vegetable Stir-Fry

Prep time: 30 minutes | Cook time: 11 minutes | Serves 4

- ¼ cup low-sodium vegetable broth
- 1 tablespoon coconut aminos
- 2 teaspoons raw honey
- 1 teaspoon grated fresh ginger
- 1 teaspoon bottled minced garlic
- 1 teaspoon arrowroot powder
- 1½ teaspoons sesame oil
- 1 cup sliced mushrooms
- 2 carrots, thinly sliced, or about 1 to 1½ cups precut packaged carrots
- 1 celery stalk, thinly sliced on an angle, or ½ cup precut packaged celery
- 2 cups broccoli florets
- 1 cup cauliflower florets
- 1 cup snow peas, halved
- 1 cup bean sprouts
- ¼ cup chopped cashews
- 1 scallion, white and green parts, chopped

1. In a small bowl, whisk the vegetable broth, coconut aminos, honey, ginger, garlic, and arrowroot powder until well combined. Set it aside. 2. In a large skillet or wok over medium-high heat, heat the sesame oil. 3. Add the mushrooms, carrots, and celery. Sauté for 4 minutes. 4. Stir in the broccoli, cauliflower, and snow peas. Sauté for about 4 minutes until crisp-tender. 5. Add the bean sprouts and sauté for 1 minute. 6. Move the vegetables to one side of the skillet and add the sauce. Cook for about 2 minutes, stirring until the sauce has thickened. Stir the vegetables into the sauce, stirring to coat. 7. Serve topped with the cashews and scallion.

Per Serving:
calories: 154 | fat: 6g | protein: 7g | carbs: 21g | fiber: 4g | sugar: 6g | sodium: 98mg

Tofu Sloppy Joes

Prep time: 10 minutes | Cook time: 15 minutes | Serves 4

- 2 tablespoons extra-virgin olive oil
- 1 onion, chopped
- 10 ounces (283 g) tofu, chopped
- 2 (14 ounces / 397 g) cans crushed tomatoes, 1 drained and 1 undrained
- ¼ cup apple cider vinegar
- 1 tablespoon chili powder
- 1 teaspoon garlic powder
- ½ teaspoon sea salt
- ⅛ teaspoon freshly ground black pepper

1. In a large pot over medium-high heat, heat the olive oil until it shimmers. 2. Add the onion and tofu. Cook for about 5 minutes, stirring occasionally, until the onion is soft. 3. Stir in the tomatoes, cider vinegar, chili powder, garlic powder, salt, and pepper. Simmer for 10 minutes to let the flavors blend, stirring occasionally.

Per Serving:
calories: 209 | fat: 10g | protein: 11g | carbs: 21g | fiber: 8g | sugar: 13g | sodium: 584mg

Sweet Potato Curry with Spinach

Prep time: 10 minutes | Cook time: 20 minutes | Serves 4

- 2 tablespoons extra-virgin olive oil
- 1 onion, chopped
- 4 cups cubed peeled sweet potato
- 4 cups fresh baby spinach
- 3 cups no-salt-added
- vegetable broth
- 1 cup lite coconut milk
- 2 tablespoons curry powder
- ½ teaspoon sea salt
- ⅛ teaspoon freshly ground black pepper

1. In a large pot over medium-high heat, heat the olive oil until it shimmers. 2. Add the onion. Cook for about 5 minutes, stirring, until soft. 3. Stir in the sweet potato, spinach, vegetable broth, coconut milk, curry powder, salt, and pepper. Bring to a simmer and reduce the heat to medium. Cook for about 15 minutes, stirring occasionally, until the sweet potatoes are soft.

Per Serving:
calories: 314 | fat: 11g | protein: 8g | carbs: 50g | fiber: 9g | sugar: 14g | sodium: 400mg

Chapter 10

Stews and Soups

Chapter 10 Stews and Soups

Classic Butternut Squash Soup

Prep time: 20 minutes | Cook time: 30 minutes | Serves 6

- 1 onion, roughly chopped
- 4½ cups plus 2 tablespoons water, divided
- 1 large butternut squash, washed, peeled, ends trimmed, halved, seeded, and cut into ½-inch chunks
- 2 celery stalks, roughly chopped
- 3 carrots, peeled and roughly chopped
- 1 teaspoon sea salt, plus additional as needed

1. In a large pot set over medium heat, sauté the onion in 2 tablespoons of water for about 5 minutes, or until soft. 2. Add the squash, celery, carrot, and salt. Bring to a boil. 3. Reduce the heat to low, Cover and simmer for 25 minutes. 4. In a blender, purée the soup until smooth, working in batches if necessary and taking care with the hot liquid. Taste, and adjust the seasoning if necessary.

Per Serving:
calories: 104 | fat: 0g | protein: 2g | carbs: 27g | fiber: 5g | sugar: 6g | sodium: 417mg

Chicken and Dumpling Soup

Prep time: 10 minutes | Cook time: 40 minutes | Serves 4

- 2 tablespoons avocado oil
- 1 medium onion, diced
- 3 ribs celery, diced
- 3 small radishes, diced
- 1 small carrot, sliced
- 4 cloves garlic, minced
- 1 pound (454 g) boneless,

Dumplings:

- 2 large eggs
- 2 tablespoons coconut oil
- 3 tablespoons coconut flour

- skinless chicken thighs
- 1 bay leaf
- 3 sprigs fresh oregano
- 4 cups bone broth
- 1 teaspoon fine Himalayan salt
- 1 teaspoon ground black pepper
- Pinch of fine Himalayan salt
- Pinch of ground nutmeg
- Fresh parsley, for garnish (optional)

1. Heat a 5-quart pot over medium heat. Pour in the avocado oil and add the onions, celery, radishes, carrots, and garlic. Sauté, stirring often, for 8 minutes, until the onions are aromatic and translucent. 2.

Push the sofrito to the side and place the chicken thighs flat on the bottom of the pot with the bay leaf and the oregano sprigs on top. Brown for 3 minutes on each side, then mix the chicken thighs well with the sofrito and pour in the broth. Stir in the salt and pepper. Bring the soup to a boil and cook for 20 minutes. 3. While the soup cooks, make the dumplings: In a medium-sized bowl, whisk together the eggs and coconut oil. Add the coconut flour, salt, and nutmeg and mix until a dry dough forms. Shape into eight equal-sized balls. 4. Reduce the heat to low and stir the soup, bringing it down to a simmer. Use tongs to gently tear apart the chicken thighs. 5. Carefully add the dumplings to the soup one at a time. Simmer for about 5 minutes, turning them over with tongs once. They're done when they begin to puff up a little—do not let them swell too much. 6. Remove the soup from the heat, garnish with fresh parsley if desired, and serve right away. Or store the soup in an airtight container in the refrigerator for up to 6 days. To reheat, bring to a simmer on the stovetop.

Per Serving:
calories: 430 | fat: 20g | protein: 48g | carbs: 13g | fiber: 6g | sugar: 2g | sodium: 539mg

Squash and Ginger Soup

Prep time: 10 minutes | Cook time: 20 minutes | Serves 4

- 2 tablespoons extra-virgin olive oil
- 1 onion, chopped
- 1 tablespoon grated ginger
- 4 garlic cloves, minced
- 6 cups vegetable broth
- 3 cups butternut squash or

- acorn squash
- ½ teaspoon sea salt
- ¼ teaspoon freshly ground black pepper
- ¼ cup coconut milk (optional)
- ¼ cup microgreens (optional)

1. In a large pot over medium-high heat, heat the olive oil until it shimmers. 2. Add the onion and ginger, and cook about 5 minutes, stirring occasionally, until onion is soft. 3. Add the garlic and cook for 30 seconds more, stirring constantly. 4. Add the vegetable broth, squash, salt, and pepper. Cook, covered, for about 10 minutes, until the squash is soft. 5. Carefully transfer to a blender. Blend and blend until smooth. 6. Serve garnished with the coconut milk and microgreens, if using.

Per Serving:
calories: 96 | fat: 7g | protein: 1g | carbs: 9g | fiber: 1g | sugar: 6g | sodium: 266mg

Thai Coconut Soup

Prep time: 15 minutes | Cook time: 25 minutes | Serves 8

- 1 tablespoon avocado oil
- 2 tablespoons peeled and minced fresh ginger
- 2 tablespoons minced garlic
- 2 stalks lemongrass, cut into large pieces
- 3 cups sliced baby bella mushrooms
- 2 tablespoons coconut aminos
- 2 tablespoons fish sauce
- 4 cups bone broth
- 2 (13½-ounce / 383-g) cans full-fat coconut milk
- 1 teaspoon fine Himalayan salt
- ¼ cup minced fresh cilantro, for garnish
- 3 to 4 sprigs basil, for garnish
- 2 limes, cut into wedges, for serving

1. Heat a large pot over medium heat. When it's hot, pour in the avocado oil. Then add the ginger, garlic, and lemongrass. Sauté, stirring often, for 2 to 3 minutes, until the garlic is lightly browned and aromatic. 2. Add the mushrooms and sauté, stirring often, for 5 to 6 minutes, until they have softened. Stir in the coconut aminos and fish sauce, mixing well and scraping up any bits of garlic or ginger that are stuck to the bottom of the pot. Pour in the broth and bring to a simmer. 3. Stir in the coconut milk and salt. Simmer for 10 minutes, then remove from the heat. Fish out the pieces of lemongrass. 4. Garnish with the minced cilantro and basil sprigs and serve with lime wedges on the side. Store leftovers in an airtight container in the fridge for up to 5 days. To reheat, bring to a simmer on the stovetop.

Per Serving:
calories: 217 | fat: 19g | protein: 4g | carbs:4 g | fiber: 3g | sugar: 1g | sodium: 514mg

Quick Miso Soup with Wilted Greens

Prep time: 10 minutes | Cook time: 5 minutes | Serves 4

- 3 cups filtered water
- 3 cups vegetable broth
- 1 cup sliced mushrooms
- ½ teaspoon fish sauce
- 3 tablespoons miso paste
- 1 cup fresh baby spinach, thoroughly washed
- 4 scallions, sliced

1. In a large soup pot over high heat, add the water, broth, mushrooms, and fish sauce, and bring to a boil. Remove from the heat. 2. In a small bowl, mix the miso paste with ½ cup of heated broth mixture to dissolve the miso. Stir the miso mixture back into the soup. 3. Stir in the spinach and scallions. Serve immediately.

Per Serving:
calories: 44 | fat: 0g | protein: 2g | carbs: 8g | fiber: 1g | sugar: 3g | sodium: 659mg

Curried Sweet Potato Soup

Prep time: 10 minutes | Cook time: 15 minutes | Serves 4

- 2 tablespoons extra-virgin olive oil
- 1 onion, chopped
- 4 cups cubed, peeled sweet potato
- 8 cups no-salt-added
- vegetable broth
- 1 teaspoon curry powder
- 1 teaspoon ground turmeric
- ½ teaspoon sea salt
- ⅛ teaspoon freshly ground black pepper

1. In a large pot over medium-high heat, heat the olive oil until it shimmers. 2. Add the onion. Cook for about 5 minutes, stirring occasionally, until soft. 3. Stir in the sweet potato, vegetable broth, curry powder, turmeric, salt, and pepper. Bring to a boil. Reduce the heat to medium and simmer for about 10 minutes until the sweet potato cubes are soft. 4. Carefully transfer to a blender and blend until smooth.

Per Serving:
calories: 253 | fat: 7g | protein: 3g | carbs: 45g | fiber: 7g | sugar: 2g | sodium: 261mg

Herbed Chicken Bone Broth

Prep time: 10 minutes | Cook time: 24 hours 30 minutes | Makes 8 to 10 cups

- 2 chicken carcasses
- 3 tablespoons apple cider vinegar
- 2 carrots, washed and roughly chopped
- 2 stalks celery, quartered
- 1 sweet onion, peeled and quartered
- 4 garlic cloves, smashed
- 4 fresh thyme sprigs
- 2 fresh rosemary sprigs
- 2 bay leaves

1. Preheat the oven to 350ºF (180ºC). 2. Place the chicken carcasses in a baking pan and roast for 30 minutes. Transfer the carcasses to a large stockpot. Add enough cold water to cover the carcasses by 2 inches, and the cider vinegar. Place the stockpot over high heat and bring to a boil. Reduce the heat to low and gently simmer for 18 hours, stirring every few hours. 3. Add the carrots, celery, onion, garlic, thyme, rosemary, and bay leaves, and bring to a boil again. Reduce the heat to low and simmer the broth for 6 hours more, stirring several times. 4. Remove the pot from the heat and let the broth cool slightly. 5. With tongs, remove and discard any large bones from the pot. Strain the broth through a fine-mesh sieve and discard any solid bits. 6. Pour the chicken broth into sealable containers and let it cool completely. 7. Refrigerate the broth for up to 7 days, or freeze for up to 3 months.

Per Serving:
calories: 60 | fat: 3g | protein: 1g | carbs: 0g | fiber: 0g | sugar: 0g | sodium: 36mg

Turkey Meatball Soup

Prep time: 15 minutes | Cook time: 15 minutes | Serves 6

Meatballs:

- 1 pound (454 g) ground turkey
- 1 tablespoon Dijon mustard
- 1 teaspoon dried basil
- 1 teaspoon garlic powder
- ½ teaspoon dried oregano

- ½ teaspoon salt
- ¼ teaspoon red pepper flakes
- Freshly ground black pepper, to taste
- 1 tablespoon ghee

Soup:

- 1 medium white onion, diced
- 2 carrots, diced
- 2 garlic cloves, minced
- ½ teaspoon dried thyme

- 6 cups vegetable broth
- 2 cups shredded kale leaves, stemmed and thoroughly washed
- 1 bay leaf

Make the Meatballs: 1. In a medium bowl, put the turkey, mustard, basil, garlic power, oregano, salt, and red pepper flakes, and season with pepper. With your hands, mix the ingredients until they are well combined. 2. Add the ghee to a stockpot over medium-high heat. Roll the meat mixture into 1-inch balls and layer across the bottom of the pot. Cook for about 2 minutes per side, until almost cooked through. Transfer the meatballs to a plate. Make the Soup: 1. To the stockpot, add the onion, carrots, garlic, and thyme. Cook for about 2 minutes, gently stirring, until the onions are translucent. 2. Add the broth, kale, bay leaf, and meatballs. Bring to a simmer, reduce the heat to medium-low, and simmer for about 15 minutes until the meatballs are cooked through and the kale has softened. Remove and discard the bay leaf. Serve hot.ely.

Per Serving:

calories: 259 | fat: 14g | protein: 26g | carbs: 9g | fiber: 2g | sugar: 4g | sodium: 734mg

Spiced Sweet Potato and Almond Soup

Prep time: 15 minutes | Cook time: 6 to 8 hours | Serves 4 to 6

- 4 cups vegetable broth, plus more if needed
- 1 (15-ounce / 425-g) can diced tomatoes
- 2 medium sweet potatoes, peeled and diced
- 1 medium onion, diced
- 1 jalapeño pepper, seeded and diced
- ½ cup unsalted almond

- butter
- ½ teaspoon sea salt
- ½ teaspoon garlic powder
- ½ teaspoon ground turmeric
- ½ teaspoon ground ginger
- ¼ teaspoon ground cinnamon
- Pinch ground nutmeg
- ½ cup full-fat coconut milk

1. In your slow cooker, combine the broth, tomatoes, sweet potatoes, onion, jalapeño, almond butter, salt, garlic powder, turmeric, ginger, cinnamon, and nutmeg. 2. Cover the cooker and set to low. Cook for 6 to 8 hours. 3. Stir in the coconut milk after cooking. 4. Using an immersion blender, purée the soup until smooth and serve.

Per Serving:

calories: 358 | fat: 23g | protein: 7g | carbs: 34g | fiber: 7g | sugar: 11g | sodium: 1066mg

Sweet Potato and Rice Soup

Prep time: 15 minutes | Cook time: 15 minutes | Serves 4 to 6

- 4 cups vegetable broth
- 1 large sweet potato, peeled and cut into 1-inch cubes
- 2 onions, coarsely chopped
- 2 garlic cloves, sliced thinly

- 2 teaspoons minced fresh ginger
- 1 bunch broccolini, cut into 1-inch pieces
- 1 cup cooked basmati rice
- ¼ cup fresh cilantro leaves

1. In a large Dutch oven over high heat, add the broth and bring to a boil. 2. Add the sweet potato, onion, garlic, and ginger. Simmer for 5 to 8 minutes, or until the sweet potato is cooked through. 3. Add the broccolini and simmer for an additional 3 minutes. 4. Remove the pan from the heat. Stir in the rice and cilantro.

Per Serving:

calories: 167 | fat: 2g | protein: 8g | carbs: 29g | fiber: 3g | sugar: 7g | sodium: 789mg

Zuppa Toscana

Prep time: 15 minutes | Cook time: 5 to 6 hours | Serves 4 to 6

- 4 cups vegetable broth
- 2 cups chopped de-ribbed kale
- 2 small sweet potatoes, peeled and diced
- 1 medium zucchini, diced
- 1 (15-ounce / 425-g) can cannellini beans, rinsed and drained well

- 1 celery stalk, diced
- 1 carrot, diced
- 1 small onion, diced
- ½ teaspoon garlic powder
- ½ teaspoon sea salt
- ¼ teaspoon red pepper flakes
- Freshly ground black pepper, to taste

1. In your slow cooker, combine the broth, kale, sweet potatoes, zucchini, beans, celery, carrot, onion, garlic powder, salt, and red pepper flakes, and season with black pepper. 2. Cover the cooker and set to low. Cook for 5 to 6 hours and serve.

Per Serving:

calories: 209 | fat: 1g | protein: 8g | carbs: 43g | fiber: 10g | sugar: 9g | sodium: 871mg

Chicken Chili with Beans

Prep time: 15 minutes | Cook time: 4 hours | Serves 6

- 2 tablespoons extra-virgin olive oil
- 2 onions, chopped
- 4 garlic cloves, minced
- 2 celery stalks, chopped
- 2 teaspoons ground cumin
- 1 teaspoon salt
- 1 teaspoon chipotle powder
- ½ teaspoon freshly ground black pepper
- 4 boneless skinless chicken
- breasts, cut into 1-inch pieces
- 1 teaspoon dried oregano
- 1 bay leaf
- 1 (28-ounce / 794-g) can chopped tomatoes
- 2½ cups chicken broth, plus additional as needed
- 2 (15-ounce / 425-g) cans white beans, drained and rinsed
- ¼ cup chopped fresh parsley, divided

1. In the slow cooker, combine the olive oil, onions, garlic, celery, cumin, salt, chipotle powder, pepper, chicken, oregano, bay leaf, tomatoes, chicken broth, and white beans. Set to high and cook for 4 hours. 2. If the mixture gets too thick, add a little more chicken broth or some water. 3. Garnish each serving with parsley. Serve alone or over cooked brown rice or quinoa.

Per Serving:
calories: 423 | fat: 13g | protein: 42g | carbs: 41g | fiber: 10g | sugar: 6g | sodium: 857mg

White Bean and French Onion Soup

Prep time: 15 minutes | Cook time: 7 hours | Serves 4 to 6

- 2 large onions, thinly sliced
- ¼ cup extra-virgin olive oil
- ¾ teaspoon sea salt
- 2 (14-ounce / 397-g) cans cannellini beans, rinsed and drained well
- 4 cups vegetable broth
- ½ teaspoon garlic powder
- ½ teaspoon dried thyme leaves
- 1 bay leaf
- Freshly ground black pepper, to taste

1. In your slow cooker, combine the onions, olive oil, and salt. 2. Cover the cooker and set to high. Cook for 3 hours, allowing the onions to caramelize. 3. Stir the onions well and add the beans, broth, garlic powder, thyme, and bay leaf, and season with pepper.

4. Re-cover the cooker and set to low. Cook for 4 hours. 5. Remove and discard the bay leaf before serving.

Per Serving:
calories: 328 | fat: 14g | protein: 11g | carbs: 39g | fiber: 10g | sugar: 7g | sodium: 968mg

Home-Style Red Lentil Stew

Prep time: 10 minutes | Cook time: 35 minutes | Serves 6

- 2 onions, peeled and finely diced
- 4 celery stalks, finely diced
- 6½ cups plus 2 tablespoons water, divided
- 3 cups red lentils
- 2 zucchini, finely diced
- 1 teaspoon dried oregano
- 1 teaspoon salt, plus additional as needed

1. In a large pot set over medium heat, sauté the onions and celery in 2 tablespoons of water for about 5 minutes, or until soft. 2. Add the lentils, zucchini, the remaining 6½ cups of water, the oregano, and salt. Bring to a boil. Reduce the heat to low. Cover and simmer for 30 minutes, stirring occasionally. 3. Taste, and adjust the seasoning if necessary.

Per Serving:
calories: 367 | fat: 1g | protein: 26g | carbs: 64g | fiber: 31g | sugar: 5g | sodium: 410mg

Easy Summer Gazpacho

Prep time: 10 minutes | Cook time: 0 minutes | Serves 4

- 6 large heirloom tomatoes, chopped
- ¼ cup extra-virgin olive oil
- ¼ cup fresh basil leaves
- 2 garlic cloves, minced
- Juice of 1 lemon
- Zest of 1 lemon
- ½ to 1 teaspoon hot sauce (optional)

1. In a blender, combine the tomatoes, olive oil, basil, garlic, lemon juice and zest, and hot sauce (if using). Pulse 20 times, in 1-second bursts, for a chunkier soup, or continue blending until smooth for a smoother texture.

Per Serving:
calories: 165 | fat: 13g | protein: 3g | carbs: 12g | fiber: 3g | sugar: 8g | sodium: 283mg

Gingered Chicken and Vegetable Soup

Prep time: 10 minutes | Cook time: 10 minutes | Serves 4

- 2 tablespoons extra-virgin olive oil
- 1 onion, chopped
- 2 red bell peppers, chopped
- 1 tablespoon grated fresh ginger
- 3 cups shredded rotisserie chicken, skin removed
- 8 cups no-salt-added chicken broth
- ½ teaspoon sea salt
- ⅛ teaspoon freshly ground black pepper

1. In a large pot over medium-high heat, heat the olive oil until it shimmers. 2. Add the onion, red bell peppers, and ginger. Cook for about 5 minutes, stirring occasionally, until the vegetables are soft. 3. Stir in the chicken, chicken broth, salt, and pepper. Bring to a simmer. Reduce the heat to medium-low and simmer for 5 minutes.

Per Serving:

calories: 341 | fat: 15g | protein: 40g | carbs: 11g | fiber: 1g | sugar: 8g | sodium: 577mg

Zesty Broccoli Soup

Prep time: 15 minutes | Cook time: 20 minutes | Serves 4

- 1 tablespoon ghee
- 1 medium white onion, diced
- 3 garlic cloves, minced
- 1 head broccoli, roughly chopped
- 1 carrot, chopped
- 1 celery stalk, diced
- 3 cups vegetable broth
- ½ teaspoon salt
- ½ teaspoon freshly squeezed lemon juice
- ½ teaspoon lemon zest
- Freshly ground black pepper, to taste

1. In a large soup pot over medium heat, melt the ghee. 2. Add the onion and garlic, and sauté for 5 minutes. 3. Add the broccoli, carrot, and celery, and sauté for 2 minutes. 4. Stir in the broth, salt, lemon juice, and lemon zest, and season with pepper. Bring to a simmer, and cook for about 10 minutes. Serve immediately.

Per Serving:

calories: 80 | fat: 4g | protein: 2g | carbs: 10g | fiber: 3g | sugar: 4g | sodium: 731mg

Winter Warming Chunky Chicken Soup

Prep time: 15 minutes | Cook time: 40 minutes | Serves 4

- 1 whole cooked free range chicken (no giblets)
- 1 bay leaf
- 5 cups of homemade chicken broth or water
- 1 onion, chopped
- 2 stalks of celery, sliced
- 3 carrots, chopped and peeled
- 2 parsnips, chopped and peeled
- Sprinkle of pepper to season

1. Add all of the ingredients minus the pepper into a large pot and boil on a high heat. 2. Once boiling, lower the heat and allow to simmer for 30 minutes, or until the chicken is piping hot throughout. 3. Remove the chicken and place on a chopping board. 4. Slice as much meat as you can from the chicken and remove the skin and bones. 5. Add it back into the pot and either serve right away as a chunky soup or allow to cool and whizz through the blender to serve. 6. Add black pepper to season and serve.

Per Serving:

calories: 576 | fat: 35g | protein: 44g | carbs: 19g | fiber: 5g | sugar: 6g | sodium: 203mg

Spicy Ramen Noodle Soup

Prep time: 15 minutes | Cook time: 0 minutes | Serves 4

- 8 ounces (227 g) buckwheat noodles or rice noodles, cooked
- 2 tablespoons sesame seeds
- ¼ cup thinly sliced cucumber
- ¼ cup sliced scallion
- ¼ cup chopped fresh cilantro
- 2 tablespoons sesame oil
- 2 tablespoons rice vinegar
- 1 tablespoon grated peeled fresh ginger
- 1 tablespoon coconut aminos
- 1 tablespoon raw honey
- 1 tablespoon freshly squeezed lime juice
- 1 teaspoon chili powder

1. In a large serving bowl, thoroughly mix the noodles, sesame seeds, cucumber, scallion, cilantro, sesame oil, vinegar, ginger, coconut aminos, honey, lime juice, and chili powder. Divide among 4 soup bowls and serve at room temperature.

Per Serving:
calories: 172 | fat: 9g | protein: 2g | carbs: 20g | fiber: 2g | sugar: 5g | sodium: 38mg

Spicy Lime-Chicken "Tortilla-Less" Soup

Prep time: 15 minutes | Cook time: 20 minutes | Serves 6

- 1 tablespoon avocado oil
- 3 garlic cloves, minced
- 1 medium white onion, diced
- 1 jalapeño pepper, seeded and minced
- 6 cups chicken broth or vegetable broth
- 1 pound (454 g) shredded cooked chicken
- 1 (14-ounce / 397-g) can diced tomatoes with their juice
- 1 (4-ounce / 113-g) can diced green chiles
- 3 tablespoons freshly squeezed lime juice
- 1 teaspoon chili powder
- 1 teaspoon ground cumin
- ½ teaspoon salt
- ¼ teaspoon cayenne pepper
- Freshly ground black pepper, to taste
- 1 avocado, sliced
- Fresh cilantro, for garnishing

1. In a large soup pot over medium heat, heat the avocado oil. 2. Add the garlic, onion, and jalapeño pepper, and sauté for 5 minutes. 3. Stir in the broth, chicken, tomatoes, green chiles, lime juice, chili powder, cumin, salt, and cayenne pepper, and season with black pepper. Bring to a simmer, and cook for 10 minutes. 4. Serve hot, topped with slices of avocado and garnished with cilantro.

Per Serving:
calories: 283 | fat: 7g | protein: 29g | carbs: 12g | fiber: 3g | sugar: 5g | sodium: 819mg

Chapter

11

Desserts

Chapter 11 Desserts

Strawberry Jam Thumbprint Cookies

Prep time: 15 minutes | Cook time: 15 minutes | Serves 6

- 1½ cups sunflower seeds
- 3 tablespoons coconut oil
- ¼ cup maple syrup
- ½ cup strawberry jam, divided

1. Preheat the oven to 350ºF (180ºC). 2. Line a baking sheet with parchment paper. 3. In a blender, food processor, or spice grinder, process the sunflower seeds into a fine meal. Transfer to a large bowl. 4. Add the coconut oil, mashing it into the sunflower meal with a spoon as if you are crumbling butter into flour. Stir in the maple syrup. Mix well. 5. Using a tablespoon measure, scoop the dough onto the prepared sheet, making 12 cookies. Gently press down on the cookies with the back of a wet spoon to flatten them. 6. With your thumb, make imprints in the center of each cookie. Fill each depression with 2 teaspoons of strawberry jam. 7. Place the sheet in the preheated oven and bake for 12 to 14 minutes. 8. Cool before eating.

Per Serving:
calories: 392 | fat: 19g | protein: 4g | carbs: 54g | fiber: 2g | sugar: 12g | sodium: 3mg

Chocolate-Coconut Brownies

Prep time: 15 minutes | Cook time: 35 minutes | Makes 16 brownies

- ½ cup gluten-free flour, such as Cup4Cup or Bob's Red Mill
- ¼ cup unsweetened alkalized cocoa powder
- ½ teaspoon sea salt
- 4 ounces (113 g) semisweet chocolate, coarsely chopped
- ¾ cup unrefined coconut oil
- 1 cup coconut sugar
- 4 eggs
- 1 teaspoon vanilla
- 4 ounces (113 g) semisweet chocolate chips (optional)

1. Preheat the oven to 350ºF (180ºC). Grease a 9-by-9-inch baking pan and line with parchment paper. 2. Combine the flour, cocoa powder, and salt in a medium bowl. Set aside. 3. In a double boiler or microwave, melt the chopped chocolate and coconut oil. Let cool slightly. Add the sugar, eggs, and vanilla, whisking until well combined. Whisk in the flour mixture. Fold in the chocolate chips (if using). Pour into the prepared pan. Bake until a toothpick inserted in the center of the brownies comes out clean, 20 to 25 minutes.

This will yield a somewhat gooey brownie. Continue to bake for 5 to 10 minutes if you prefer a drier brownie. 4. Let the brownies cool completely, then cut into squares. Store in an airtight container at room temperature for up to 3 days.

Per Serving:
calories: 382 | fat: 29g | protein: 6g | carbs: 28g | fiber: 4g | sugar: 15g | sodium: 180mg

Coconut Rice with Blueberries

Prep time: 15 minutes | Cook time: 10 minutes | Serves 4

- 1 (14 ounces / 397 g) can full-fat coconut milk
- 1 cup fresh blueberries
- ¼ cup coconut sugar
- 1 teaspoon ground ginger
- pinch sea salt
- 2 cups cooked brown rice

1. In a large pot over medium-high heat, combine the coconut milk, blueberries, sugar, ginger, and salt. Cook for about 7 minutes, stirring constantly, until the blueberries soften. 2. Stir in the rice. Cook for about 3 minutes, stirring, until the rice is heated through.

Per Serving:
calories: 469 | fat: 25g | protein: 6g | carbs: 60g | fiber: 5g | sugar: 19g | sodium: 76mg

Baked Fruit and Nut Pudding

Prep time: 10 minutes | Cook time: 1 hour | Serves 4

- 15 apricots
- 10 prunes
- 6 free range eggs
- 3 cups water
- 1 cup raw pecans or walnuts
- 2 tablespoons pure vanilla extract
- 2 broken cinnamon sticks

1. Preheat oven to 350ºF (180ºC). 2. In a large saucepan, boil the water on a high heat and then add the apricots, prunes, and cinnamon sticks before turning down the heat and simmering for 30 minutes. 3. Allow to cool. 4. Remove the cinnamon sticks and blend mixture, adding in the eggs and vanilla until smooth. 5. Add mixture to a glass oven dish and top with the nuts. 6. Oven bake for 30 minutes. 7. Cool and serve.

Per Serving:
calories: 353 | fat: 20g | protein: 14g | carbs: 31g | fiber: 6g | sugar: 14g | sodium: 101mg

Coconut-Blueberry Popsicles

Prep time: 15 minutes | Cook time: 0 minutes | Serves 6

- 1 cup fresh blueberries
- 1½ cups coconut milk
- ¼ cup maple syrup
- ¼ teaspoon cinnamon
- ⅛ teaspoon salt

1. In a small bowl, roughly mash the blueberries. 2. Divide the blueberry mixture among 6 ice pop molds. 3. In a medium bowl, mix together the coconut milk, maple syrup, cinnamon, and salt. 4. Pour the coconut milk mixture into the ice pop molds over the blueberries. 5. Freeze for at least 2 hours, or until solid.

Per Serving:
calories: 186 | fat: 14g | protein: 2g | carbs: 16g | fiber: 2g | sugar: 12g | sodium: 37mg

Lemon Lavender and Strawberry Compote

Prep time: 5 minutes | Cook time: 30 minutes | Serves 4

- 2 cups of strawberries, halved
- Juice and zest of 1 lemon
- 2 tablespoons raw honey
- 1 tablespoon lavender extract

1. Put all of the ingredients together into a saucepan and then simmer on a very low heat until the honey has been dissolved (15 to 20 minutes). 2. When the sauce starts to thicken, add the strawberries and simmer for 5 to 10 minutes. 3. Serve warm right away or allow to cool and drizzle over yogurt later on.

Per Serving:
calories: 67 | fat: 0g | protein: 1g | carbs: 15g | fiber: 2g | sugar: 13g | sodium: 2mg

Tangy Lemon Mousse

Prep time: 10 minutes | Cook time: 4 minutes | Serves 4

- ¼ cup water
- 2 teaspoons powdered gelatin
- 2 cups canned lite coconut milk
- ½ cup freshly squeezed lemon juice
- ¼ cup raw honey
- 2 tablespoons freshly grated lemon zest

1. Put the water in a small saucepan. Sprinkle the gelatin over the water and set it aside for 10 minutes to soften. 2. In a medium bowl, whisk the coconut milk, lemon juice, honey, and lemon zest until well combined. 3. Place the saucepan with the gelatin over low heat. Gently heat the gelatin for about 4 minutes, or until just dissolved. 4. Whisk the gelatin mixture into the coconut milk mixture, and refrigerate for about 2 hours until set. 5. Scoop the lemon mousse into serving bowls.

Per Serving:
calories: 348 | fat: 29g | protein: 3g | carbs: 25g | fiber: 3g | sugar: 22g | sodium: 20mg

Maple Carrot Cake

Prep time: 15 minutes | Cook time: 45 minutes | Serves 12

- ½ cup coconut oil, at room temperature, plus more for greasing the baking dish
- ¼ cup pure maple syrup
- 2 teaspoons pure vanilla extract
- 6 eggs
- ½ cup coconut flour
- 1 teaspoon baking soda
- 1 teaspoon baking powder
- 1 teaspoon ground cinnamon
- ½ teaspoon ground nutmeg
- ⅛ teaspoon sea salt
- 3 cups finely grated carrots
- ½ cup chopped pecans

1. Preheat the oven to 350ºF (180ºC). 2. Lightly grease a 9-by-13-inch baking dish with coconut oil and set it aside. 3. In a large bowl, whisk the ½ cup of coconut oil, maple syrup, and vanilla until blended. 4. One at a time, whisk in the eggs, beating well after each addition. 5. In a medium bowl, stir together the coconut flour, baking soda, baking powder, cinnamon, nutmeg, and sea salt. Add the dry ingredients to the wet ingredients, and stir until just combined. 6. Stir in the carrots and pecans until mixed. Spoon the batter into the prepared dish. 7. Bake for about 45 minutes, or until a toothpick inserted in the center comes out clean. 8. Cool the cake on a wire rack and serve.

Per Serving:
calories: 254 | fat: 21g | protein: 5g | carbs: 13g | fiber: 2g | sugar: 5g | sodium: 73mg

Chocolate-Avocado Pudding

Prep time: 10 minutes | Cook time: 0 minutes | Serves 4

- 12 Medjool dates, pitted
- 2 avocados, halved and pitted
- ½ cup cacao powder
- 1 cup coconut milk, divided

1. In a food processor, combine the dates, avocado flesh, cacao powder, and ¾ cup of coconut milk. Blend until smooth. If the pudding is too thick, add the remaining ¼ cup of coconut milk and blend well. 2. Refrigerate for 1 hour before serving.

Per Serving:
calories: 488 | fat: 36g | protein: 6g | carbs: 48g | fiber: 14g | sugar: 28g | sodium: 15mg

Blueberry Parfait with Lemon-Coconut Cream

Prep time: 10 minutes	Cook time: 0 minutes	Serves 4

Cream:

- 2 (14-ounce / 397-g) cans coconut milk, chilled
- 1 tablespoon pure maple syrup
- 1 tablespoon fresh lemon zest
- ½ teaspoon vanilla extract
- Dash salt

Parfait:

- 2½ cups fresh blueberries

Make the Cream: 1. In a large bowl, whip the coconut cream with an electric hand mixer for 2 minutes until small peaks form. 2. Add the maple syrup, lemon zest, vanilla, and salt, and whip for a few more seconds. Make the Parfait: 1. In 4 small glasses, alternate layers of whipped coconut cream and blueberries until the ingredients are all used. 2. Serve immediately.

Per Serving:
calories: 322 | fat: 24g | protein: 4g | carbs: 23g | fiber: 2g | sugar: 19g | sodium: 72mg

Honey Panna Cotta with Blackberry-Lime Sauce

Prep time: 10 minutes	Cook time: 5 minutes	Serves 6

- 2½ cups canned unsweetened coconut milk
- 2 teaspoons gelatin
- ¼ cup honey
- 1 vanilla bean, split and seeds scraped
- Kosher salt, to taste
- Blackberry-Lime Sauce:
- 2 cups blackberries
- Finely grated zest of ½ lime, plus 2 teaspoons lime juice
- 1 teaspoon raw coconut sugar

1. Place ½ cup of the coconut milk in a small bowl. Sprinkle the gelatin over the top and allow it to sit for about 2 minutes. 2. Place the remaining 2 cups coconut milk, the honey, vanilla bean and its seeds, and a pinch of salt in a medium saucepan. Warm over low heat, whisking occasionally, until bubbles form around the edge of the pan. Remove from the heat and let the mixture steep for 5 minutes. 3. Pour the coconut milk mixture through a fine-mesh strainer into a large bowl. Discard the vanilla bean. Whisk the gelatin mixture slowly into the warm coconut mixture until there are no lumps of gelatin. Divide evenly among six ½-cup ramekins or wineglasses. Cover and refrigerate until set, at least 4 hours or up to overnight. 4. Make the blackberry-lime sauce: Place the blackberries, lime zest, lime juice, and sugar in a medium bowl. Using a fork or pastry blender, gently mash the berries, leaving some large pieces of berry while allowing some of the juices to make a sauce. Set aside for at least 10 minutes, or cover and refrigerate up to overnight. 5. Spoon the sauce over each chilled panna cotta. Serve immediately.

Per Serving:
calories: 300 | fat: 24g | protein: 3g | carbs: 23g | fiber: 5g | sugar: 18g | sodium: 95mg

Mini Dark Chocolate-Almond Butter Cups

Prep time: 10 minutes	Cook time: 5 minutes	Makes 9 cups

- 6 ounces (170 g) dark chocolate, chopped
- ½ cup natural almond butter
- 2 tablespoons raw honey
- ½ teaspoon vanilla extract
- Dash salt

1. Line 9 cups of a mini muffin tin with mini paper liners. 2. In a small saucepan over low heat, slowly melt the chocolate. Use half of the chocolate among the mini muffin cups. Set the rest of the chocolate aside. 3. In a small bowl, stir together the almond butter, honey, and vanilla. Divide the mixture into 9 portions and roll each into a small ball. Drop 1 ball into each muffin cup. 4. Drizzle the remaining chocolate into each cup, covering the almond butter balls. 5. Sprinkle each lightly with the salt. 6. Refrigerate until solid.

Per Serving:
calories: 193 | fat: 16g | protein: 5g | carbs: 14g | fiber: 0g | sugar: 9g | sodium: 22mg

Warm Cinnamon-Turmeric Almond Milk

Prep time: 15 minutes	Cook time: 3 to 4 hours	Makes 4 to 6 cups

- 4 cups unsweetened almond milk
- 4 cinnamon sticks
- 2 tablespoons coconut oil
- 1 (4-inch) piece turmeric
- root, roughly chopped
- 1 (2-inch) piece fresh ginger, roughly chopped
- 1 teaspoon raw honey, plus more to taste

1. In your slow cooker, combine the almond milk, cinnamon sticks, coconut oil, turmeric, and ginger. 2. Cover the cooker and set to low. Cook for 3 to 4 hours. 3. Pour the contents of the cooker through a fine-mesh sieve into a clean container; discard the solids. 4. Starting with just 1 teaspoon, add raw honey to taste.

Per Serving:
calories: 133 | fat: 11g | protein: 1g | carbs: 10g | fiber: 1g | sugar: 7g | sodium: 152mg

Cranberry Compote

Prep time: 5 minutes | Cook time: 15 minutes | Serves 4

- 4 cups fresh cranberries
- ¼ cup honey
- 1 tablespoon grated fresh
- ginger
- juice of 2 oranges
- zest of 1 orange

1. In a large pot over medium-high heat, stir together the cranberries, honey, ginger, orange juice, and orange zest. Bring to a boil. Cook for about 10 minutes, stirring occasionally, until the cranberries begin to pop and form a sauce. Chill or serve immediately.

Per Serving:
calories: 172 | fat: 1g | protein: 1g | carbs: 39g | fiber: 6g | sugar: 30g | sodium: 1mg

Fruity Hot Milk

Prep time: 5 minutes | Cook time: 10 minutes | Serves 2

- 1 cup low fat coconut milk
- 3 bananas, sliced
- ½ cup fresh raspberries

1. In a pan simmer ingredients for 10 minutes on a medium-low heat. 2. Whizz up in a blender until smooth. 3. Serve warm or allow to cool and add ice cubes to serve as a chilled milkshake.

Per Serving:
calories: 450 | fat: 29g | protein: 5g | carbs: 50g | fiber: 9g | sugar: 27g | sodium: 20mg

Blueberry Crisp

Prep time: 15 minutes | Cook time: 20 minutes | Serves 4

- ½ cup coconut oil, melted, plus additional for brushing
- 1 quart fresh blueberries
- ¼ cup maple syrup
- Juice of ½ lemon
- 2 teaspoons lemon zest
- 1 cup gluten-free rolled oats
- ½ teaspoon ground cinnamon
- ½ cup chopped pecans
- Pinch salt

1. Preheat the oven to 350ºF (180ºC). 2. Brush a shallow baking dish with melted coconut oil. Stir together the blueberries, maple syrup, lemon juice, and lemon zest in the dish. 3. In a small bowl, combine the oats, ½ cup of melted coconut oil, cinnamon, pecans, and salt. Mix the ingredients well to evenly distribute the coconut oil. Sprinkle the oat mixture over the berries. 4. Place the dish in the preheated oven and bake for 20 minutes, or until the oats are lightly browned.

Per Serving:
calories: 497 | fat: 33g | protein: 5g | carbs: 51g | fiber: 7g | sugar: 26g | sodium: 42mg

Chocolate Fondue

Prep time: 10 minutes | Cook time: 5 minutes | Serves 6

- ½ cup cacao powder
- ¼ cup coconut oil
- ¼ cup maple syrup, or raw honey
- 4 cups fresh fruit for dipping (berries, bananas, pitted cherries, pineapple, etc.), sliced or cut into bite-size pieces

1. Create a makeshift double boiler: Fill a small pot with a few inches of water and place a metal bowl on top of the pot. Bring the water to a boil. 2. Put the cacao powder, coconut oil, and maple syrup into the bowl. Use oven mitts when handling the bowl, as it will be hot! 3. Stir the chocolate mixture until it melts, about 5 minutes. Transfer to a serving bowl or individual bowls for dipping.

Per Serving:
calories: 452 | fat: 16g | protein: 8g | carbs: 83g | fiber: 8g | sugar: 17g | sodium: 8mg

Seedy Cookie Dough Bites

Prep time: 12 minutes | Cook time: 0 minutes | Serves 6

- ⅔ cup pumpkin seeds
- ⅔ cup sunflower seeds
- ⅔ cup gluten-free rolled oats
- ¼ cup maple syrup
- 1 teaspoon vanilla extract
- ¼ cup cacao nibs, or dairy-free chocolate chips

1. Line a large plate with parchment paper. 2. In a food processor, combine the pumpkin seeds, sunflower seeds, and oats. Process into a fine meal. 3. Add the maple syrup and vanilla. Blend until combined. 4. Add the cacao nibs and pulse together. 5. Using a 1-tablespoon measure, roll 12-16 cookie balls with your hands. Place them on the prepared plate. 6. Freeze the dough balls for 30 minutes to firm. Transfer to a sealed container. Refrigerate.

Per Serving:
calories: 345 | fat: 19g | protein: 12g | carbs: 36g | fiber: 6g | sugar: 12g | sodium: 7mg

Coconut-Chocolate Clumps

- ¼ cup cacao powder
- ¼ cup maple syrup
- 3 tablespoons coconut oil

- 1 tablespoon cacao butter
- ½ cup unsweetened shredded coconut
- Pinch salt

1. Create a makeshift double boiler: Fill a small pot with a few inches of water and place a metal bowl on top of the pot. Bring the water to a boil. 2. Put the cacao powder, maple syrup, coconut oil, and cacao butter into the bowl. Use oven mitts when handling the bowl, as it will be hot! 3. Stir the chocolate mixture until it melts, about 5 minutes. 4. With the mitts, remove the bowl from the top of the pot. Stir in the shredded coconut. 5. Pour the chocolate mixture into candy molds. 6. Refrigerate or freeze until set.

Per Serving:

calories: 91 | fat: 8g | protein: 1g | carbs: 6g | fiber: 1g | sugar: 4g | sodium: 14mg

Vanilla Ice Cream

- 3 cups full-fat coconut milk
- ⅓ cup maple syrup

- 2 teaspoons vanilla extract
- ¼ teaspoon salt

1. In a large bowl, whisk together the coconut milk, maple syrup, vanilla, and salt. Alternately, use a blender to combine. 2. If using an ice cream maker, freeze according to the manufacturer's instructions. Transfer the ice cream to a sealed container and store in the freezer. 3. If not using an ice cream maker, pour the mixture into a container and freeze. You can also freeze some of the mixture in ice cube trays to add to smoothies.

Per Serving:

calories: 296 | fat: 24g | protein: 2g | carbs: 18g | fiber: 0g | sugar: 14g | sodium: 129mg

Chapter

12

Staples, Sauces, Dips, and Dressings

Chapter 12 Staples, Sauces, Dips, and Dressings

The Perfect Poached Egg

Prep time: 10 minutes | Cook time: 3 minutes | Serves 1

- 1 tablespoon white vinegar
- Kosher salt, to taste
- 1 fresh egg

1. Fill a small, shallow sauté pan with 1½ in water. Bring to a simmer, then add the vinegar and salt. Lower the temperature so the water is barely bubbling. You should see small bubbles rising to the surface rather than large bubbles popping on top. A rolling boil will cook the eggs too quickly. 2. Crack the egg into a small bowl or ramekin. (If the yolk breaks, cover the egg with plastic wrap and refrigerate to save for another use.) Gently tip the egg into the water. Cook until the white is barely opaque and the yolk is still runny inside, about 3 minutes. 3. Using a slotted spoon, gently lift the egg out of the water and place on a paper towel–lined plate. Use the towel to pat off any extra water, then transfer the egg to a dry dish. Serve immediately.

Per Serving:
calories: 66 | fat: 4g | protein: 6g | carbs: 0g | fiber: 0g | sugar: 0g | sodium: 141mg

Chipotle Black Beans

Prep time: 15 minutes | Cook time: 2 hours | Serves 10

- 2 cups dried black beans
- 3 tablespoons extra-virgin olive oil
- 1 red onion, diced
- 1 jalapeño, diced (optional if nightshade-sensitive)
- 2 garlic cloves, peeled and minced
- 1 tablespoon chili powder
- 1 teaspoon ground cumin
- ½ teaspoon dried oregano
- 2 tablespoons chipotles in adobo (optional if nightshade-sensitive)
- ¼ cup lime juice
- Kosher salt, to taste

1. Spread the beans on a baking sheet and discard any small stones or broken beans. Place the beans in a Dutch oven or heavy stockpot and cover with water by 2 inch. Allow to sit for at least 4 hours, or up to overnight. Drain the beans and set aside. 2. Place the same pot over medium heat. When it is hot, add the olive oil, onion, and jalapeño (if using). Cook, stirring occasionally, until the onion is soft, 5 to 7 minutes. Add the garlic and cook for 1 minute until fragrant. Add the chili powder, cumin, and oregano and stir until fragrant, about 1 minute. Stir in the beans, chipotles, and 6 cups water. Bring to a simmer, cover partially, and cook until the beans are tender, 1 to 1½ hours depending on the age of the beans. Stir in the lime juice and 1 teaspoon salt, then taste and add more salt if desired. 3. Store in an airtight container in the refrigerator for up to 1 week.

Per Serving:
calories: 159 | fat: 3g | protein: 9g | carbs: 26g | fiber: 7g | sugar: 1g | sodium: 178mg

Stir-Fry Sauce

Prep time: 5 minutes | Cook time: 0 minutes | Serves 4

- ¼ cup low-sodium soy sauce
- 3 garlic cloves, minced
- Juice of 2 limes
- 1 tablespoon grated fresh ginger
- 1 tablespoon arrowroot powder

1. In a small bowl, whisk together the soy sauce, garlic, lime juice, ginger, and arrowroot powder.

Per Serving:
calories: 24 | fat: 0g | protein: 1g | carbs: 4g | fiber: 0g | sugar: 2g | sodium: 587mg

Chia Jam

Prep time: 15 minutes | Cook time: 0 minutes | Makes about 3 cups

- 1 pound (454 g) ripe fresh berries
- 1 teaspoon vanilla extract
- 3 tablespoons chia seeds

1. In a food processor, purée the berries and vanilla until smooth. 2. Add the chia seeds and pulse for 10 seconds. 3. Place the jam in a pint jar (or two), seal tightly, and refrigerate. Consume within one week.

Per Serving:
calories: 10 | fat: 0g | protein: 0g | carbs: 2g | fiber: 1g | sugar: 1g | sodium: 0mg

Almost Caesar Salad Dressing

Prep time: 10 minutes | Cook time: 0 minutes | Makes about 1 cup

- ¾ cup extra-virgin olive oil
- 3 tablespoons apple cider vinegar
- 2 anchovy fillets
- 2 garlic cloves, minced
- ½ teaspoon salt
- Freshly ground black pepper, to taste

1. In a blender or food processor, purée the olive oil, cider vinegar, anchovies, garlic, salt, and pepper until smooth. 2. Refrigerate in an airtight container and use within one week.

Per Serving:

calories: 166 | fat: 19g | protein: 0g | carbs: 0g | fiber: 0g | sugar: 0g | sodium: 184mg

Rosemary-Apricot Marinade

Prep time: 15 minutes | Cook time: 0 minutes | Makes about 2 cups

- 1 cup chopped apricots, fresh or frozen
- ½ red onion, quartered
- ½ cup extra-virgin olive oil
- ¼ cup apple cider vinegar
- 2 garlic cloves
- 2 tablespoons raw honey or
- maple syrup
- 1 tablespoon Dijon mustard
- 2 teaspoons chopped fresh rosemary
- 1 teaspoon salt
- ¼ teaspoon freshly ground black pepper

1. In a blender or food processor, combine the apricots, onion, olive oil, cider vinegar, garlic, honey, Dijon mustard, rosemary, salt, and pepper. Process until smooth. (It's fine to see flecks of rosemary and red onion.) 2. Refrigerate in an airtight container for up to five days.

Per Serving:

calories: 69 | fat: 6g | protein: 0g | carbs: 3g | fiber: 0g | sugar: 3g | sodium: 159mg

Avocado-Dill Sauce

Prep time: 15 minutes | Cook time: 0 minutes | Makes about 1 cup

- 1 large, ripe avocado, peeled and pitted
- 2 teaspoons fresh dill
- 2 teaspoons freshly squeezed lemon juice
- ½ teaspoon sea salt
- Dash red pepper flakes
- Chopped veggies, for serving (if desired)

1. In a blender, combine the avocado, dill, lemon juice, salt, and red pepper flakes. Pulse until smooth. If the sauce is too thick, add water to thin as needed. Serve with chopped veggies (if using).

Per Serving:

calories: 301 | fat: 27g | protein: 4g | carbs: 19g | fiber: 12g | sugar: 2g | sodium: 1077mg

Beans

Prep time: 30 minutes | Cook time: 1 hour | Makes 2½ cups

- 8 ounces (227 g) dried beans
- Filtered water, for soaking and cooking
- Pinch salt
- Seasonings, such as bay leaves, garlic, onion, cumin (optional)

1. In a large glass bowl, cover the beans with water. Add the salt and let soak on the counter, covered, overnight. 2. Drain the beans and rinse well. Transfer to a large pot and add any seasonings you like (if using). 3. Cover the beans with 1 to 2 inches of water, place the pot over high heat, and bring to a boil. Reduce heat to low and simmer for 1 hour. 4. Check the beans for doneness; some varieties require longer cooking times. Continue to simmer, if needed, and check every 10 minutes until done. Use immediately in soups or chilis, or refrigerate in an airtight container for up to 1 week. Cooked beans can also be frozen for up to 3 months.

Per Serving:

calories: 153 | fat: 1g | protein: 10g | carbs: 28g | fiber: 7g | sugar: 0g | sodium: 42mg

Veggie Pâté

Prep time: 10 minutes | Cook time: 20 minutes | Makes 3 cups

- 2 carrots, cut into ½-inch pieces
- 1 large sweet potato, cut into ½-inch pieces
- 1 zucchini, cut into ½-inch pieces
- 1 onion, minced
- 2 garlic cloves, minced
- 2 tablespoons water
- ¾ teaspoon salt

1. Fill a pot with 2 inches of water and insert a steamer basket. Bring the water to a boil over high heat. 2. Add the carrots, sweet potato, and zucchini. Cover and steam for about 10 minutes, or until soft. 3. Meanwhile, in a medium skillet over medium heat, sauté the onion and garlic in the water for about 5 minutes, or until soft. 4. Allow all of the vegetables to cool once cooked. 5. In a food processor, combine the cooked carrots, sweet potato, zucchini, onion, and garlic. Add the salt. Blend until smooth. 6. Refrigerate for at least 1 hour before serving.

Per Serving:

calories: 25 | fat: 0g | protein: 1g | carbs: 6g | fiber: 1g | sugar: 2g | sodium: 162mg

Berry Vinaigrette

Prep time: 15 minutes | Cook time: 0 minutes | Makes about 1½ cups

- 1 cup berries, fresh or frozen, no added sugar (thawed if frozen)
- ½ cup balsamic vinegar
- ⅓ cup extra-virgin olive oil
- 2 tablespoons freshly squeezed lemon or lime juice
- 1 tablespoon raw honey or maple syrup
- 1 tablespoon lemon or lime zest
- 1 tablespoon Dijon mustard
- 1 teaspoon salt
- ½ teaspoon freshly ground black pepper

1. In a blender, purée the berries, balsamic vinegar, olive oil, lemon juice, honey, lemon zest, Dijon mustard, salt, and pepper until smooth. 2. Refrigerate in an airtight container for up to five days.

Per Serving:
calories: 73 | fat: 7g | protein: 0g | carbs: 3g | fiber: 0g | sugar: 2g | sodium: 210mg

Peperonata

Prep time: 15 minutes | Cook time: 50 minutes | Makes 4 cup

- 3 red bell peppers
- 2 yellow bell peppers
- 5 tablespoons extra-virgin olive oil, plus more for finishing (optional)
- Kosher salt, to taste
- 1 yellow onion, thinly sliced
- 1 small fennel bulb, core and stems removed, thinly
- sliced
- 3 garlic cloves, peeled and minced
- ¼ teaspoon crushed red pepper
- 2 tablespoons capers, rinsed and drained
- 2 tablespoons sherry vinegar
- Freshly ground black pepper

1. Place a rack in the top third of the oven and preheat the oven to 400°F (205°C). Line a baking sheet with parchment paper. 2. Place all the bell peppers in a medium bowl. Drizzle with 1 tablespoon of the olive oil, sprinkle with a generous pinch of salt, and toss until the peppers are well coated. Transfer to the prepared baking sheet. Roast for 15 minutes, turn the peppers, and continue roasting until the peppers are charred and soft, with their skins beginning to peel away, an additional 20 minutes. Return the peppers to a medium bowl, cover tightly with plastic wrap, and let sit for 10 minutes. When the peppers are cool enough to handle, remove the stems, skin, and seeds. Cut the flesh into rough strips and set aside. 3. In a large sauté pan over medium heat, warm the remaining 4 tablespoons olive oil. Add the onion and fennel and cook, stirring occasionally, until softened, 8 to 10 minutes. Add the garlic, crushed red pepper, and ½ teaspoon salt and cook, stirring

constantly, until fragrant, about 1 minute. Stir in the capers and vinegar and allow the vinegar to reduce for 1 minute. Remove from the heat. Stir in the roasted peppers. 4. Transfer to an airtight container. Taste and adjust the salt and pepper as desired. If using, finish with a generous drizzle of extra-virgin olive oil. 5. Store in the refrigerator for up to 1 week.

Per Serving:
calories: 224 | fat: 17g | protein: 3g | carbs: 17g | fiber: 4g | sugar: 5g | sodium: 430mg

Pistou

Prep time: 10 minutes | Cook time: 0 minutes | Makes 1½ cups

- 3 packed cups fresh basil leaves
- 6 cloves garlic, peeled
- ¾ cup avocado oil
- ½ cup shelled hemp seeds
- 1 teaspoon fine Himalayan salt
- 1 teaspoon garlic powder
- 1 teaspoon ground black pepper (optional)

1. Place all of the ingredients in a blender or food processor. Pulse until all of the basil and garlic is minced. 2. Blend on low for 20 to 30 seconds to smooth it out just a bit and bring the texture of the sauce together. Use a spatula to scrape it all out into a glass jar with a lid. Store in the fridge for up to 10 days.

Per Serving:
calories: 318 | fat: 33g | protein: 3g | carbs: 4g | fiber: 1g | sugar: 0g | sodium: 390mg

Chimichurri Sauce

Prep time: 15 minutes | Cook time: 0 minutes | Makes about 1 cup

- 1 cup fresh flat-leaf Italian parsley
- ½ cup fresh cilantro
- ½ cup extra-virgin olive oil
- ¼ cup white wine vinegar
- 3 garlic cloves, roughly chopped
- ½ teaspoon sea salt
- ½ teaspoon dried oregano
- ¼ teaspoon ground cumin
- Dash red pepper flakes
- Freshly ground black pepper, to taste

1. In a blender, food processor, or large bowl, combine the parsley, cilantro, olive oil, vinegar, garlic, salt, oregano, cumin, and red pepper flakes, and season with black pepper. Blend until smooth. Serve. Refrigerate any leftovers in an airtight container for up to 1 week.

Per Serving:
calories: 1018 | fat: 112g | protein: 4g | carbs: 14g | fiber: 5g | sugar: 1g | sodium: 1098mg

Creamy Sesame Dressing

Prep time: 5 minutes | Cook time: 0 minutes | Makes ¾ cup

- ½ cup canned full-fat coconut milk
- 2 tablespoons tahini
- 2 tablespoons freshly squeezed lime juice
- 1 teaspoon bottled minced garlic
- 1 teaspoon minced fresh chives
- Pinch sea salt

1. In a small bowl, whisk the coconut milk, tahini, lime juice, garlic, and chives until well blended. You can also prepare this in a blender. 2. Season with sea salt and transfer the dressing to a container with a lid. Refrigerate for up to 1 week.

Per Serving:
calories: 40 | fat: 4g | protein: 1g | carbs: 2g | fiber: 0g | sugar: 1g | sodium: 10mg

Lemon-Ginger Honey

Prep time: 10 minutes | Cook time: 0 minutes | Makes about 1 cup

- 1 cup water
- ¼ cup fresh lemon juice
- 2 tablespoons honey
- 2 teaspoons grated fresh ginger root

1. Combine all the ingredients in an airtight jar and shake until the honey is dissolved. 2. Refrigerate for 24 hours before using so the ginger can permeate the mixture. 3. Store in the refrigerator up to a week.

Per Serving:
calories: 20 | fat: 0g | protein: 0g | carbs: 5g | fiber: 0g | sugar: 4g | sodium: 0mg

Anti-Inflammatory Mayonnaise

Prep time: 10 minutes | Cook time: 0 minutes | Makes 1 cup

- 1 egg yolk
- 1 tablespoon apple cider vinegar
- ½ teaspoon Dijon mustard
- Pinch sea salt
- ¾ cup extra-virgin olive oil

1. In a blender or food processor, combine the egg yolk, cider vinegar, mustard, and salt. 2. Turn on the blender or food processor and while it's running, remove the top spout. Carefully, working one drip at a time to start, drip in the olive oil. After about 15 drops, continue to run the processor and add the oil in a thin stream until emulsified. You may adjust the amount of oil to adjust the thickness. The more oil you add, the thicker the mayonnaise will be. 3. Keep this refrigerated for up to 4 days in a tightly sealed container.

Per Serving:
calories: 169 | fat: 20g | protein: 1g | carbs: 0g | fiber: 0g | sugar: 0g | sodium: 36mg

Curried Black Pepper Vinaigrette

Prep time: 10 minutes | Cook time: 0 minutes | Makes ¾ cup

- ¼ cup lime juice
- 2 teaspoons honey
- 2 teaspoons curry powder, plus more as needed
- ½ teaspoon freshly ground
- black pepper
- ¼ teaspoon cayenne pepper
- ½ cup organic canola oil
- Kosher salt, to taste

1. Place the lime juice, honey, curry powder, black pepper, and cayenne in a small bowl. Whisk until smooth. Slowly whisk in the canola oil until combined. Season with salt. Taste, adding more salt or spice if desired. 2. Store in an airtight glass container in the refrigerator for up to 1 week. Whisk again just before serving to re-emulsify.

Per Serving:
calories: 173 | fat: 18g | protein: 0g | carbs: 3g | fiber: 1g | sugar: 2g | sodium: 388mg

French Vinaigrette

Prep time: 10 minutes | Cook time: 0 minutes | Makes ¾ cup

- 2 tablespoons Dijon mustard
- 2 teaspoons minced shallot
- ¼ cup sherry vinegar
- Kosher salt, to taste
- Freshly ground black pepper
- ½ cup extra-virgin olive oil

1. Place the Dijon mustard and shallot in a small bowl. Whisk in the vinegar. Add a generous pinch of salt and a fresh grinding of pepper. Allow the shallots to sit in the vinegar for about 5 minutes. Slowly whisk in the olive oil to create an emulsified vinaigrette. Taste, adding more salt and pepper if desired. 2. Store in an airtight glass container in the refrigerator for up to 1 week. Whisk again just before serving to re-emulsify.

Per Serving:
calories: 166 | fat: 18g | protein: 0g | carbs: 1g | fiber: 0g | sugar: 0g | sodium: 446mg

Creamy Lentil Dip

Prep time: 10 minutes | Cook time: 15 minutes | Makes 3 cups

- 1 cup dried green or brown lentils, rinsed
- 2½ cups water, divided
- ⅓ cup tahini
- 1 garlic clove
- ½ teaspoon salt, plus additional as needed

1. In a medium pot, combine the dried lentils with 2 cups of water. 2. Bring to a boil over high heat. Reduce the heat to low and cook for 15 minutes, or until the lentils are tender. If there is water remaining in the pot, drain the lentils. 3. In a food processor, combine the lentils, the remaining ½ cup of water, tahini, garlic, and salt. Blend until smooth and creamy. 4. Taste, and adjust the seasoning if necessary.

Per Serving:
calories: 101 | fat: 4g | protein: 5g | carbs: 11g | fiber: 6g | sugar: 0g | sodium: 107mg

Mediterranean Rub

Prep time: 5 minutes | Cook time: 0 minutes | Makes ¾ cup

- ¼ cup packed coconut sugar
- 3 tablespoons dried oregano leaves
- 2 tablespoons dried thyme leaves
- 1 tablespoon dried tarragon
- 1 teaspoon dried marjoram
- 1 teaspoon dried dill
- 1 teaspoon dried basil

1. In a small bowl, stir together the coconut sugar, oregano, thyme, tarragon, marjoram, dill, and basil until well blended. 2. Store the seasoning in a sealed container for up to 1 month.

Per Serving:
calories: 5 | fat: 0g | protein: 0g | carbs: 1g | fiber: 0g | sugar: 1g | sodium: 1mg

Lemony Mustard Dressing

Prep time: 10 minutes | Cook time: 0 minutes | Makes about 1½ cups

- 1 cup extra-virgin olive oil
- ¼ cup fresh lemon juice
- 1 tablespoon honey
- 1 teaspoon Dijon mustard
- 1 shallot, sliced
- 1 teaspoon grated lemon zest
- 1 teaspoon salt
- ¼ teaspoon pepper

1. In a blender or food processor, combine the olive oil, lemon juice, honey, Dijon, shallot, lemon zest, salt, and pepper. Process until smooth. 2. Refrigerate in an airtight container for up to 5 days.

Per Serving:
calories: 180 | fat: 20g | protein: 0g | carbs: 2g | fiber: 0g | sugar: 2g | sodium: 220mg

Fiesta Guacamole

Prep time: 15 minutes | Cook time: 0 minutes | Makes 3 cups

- 3 medium Hass avocados, halved, pitted, and peeled
- 3 small radishes, sliced
- 3 large strawberries, diced
- 3 cloves garlic, minced
- 1 green onion, sliced
- ½ bunch fresh cilantro (about 1½ ounces / 43 g), minced
- Juice of 2 lemons
- 2 teaspoons fine Himalayan salt
- 1 tablespoon extra-virgin olive oil

1. Place all the ingredients in a large bowl. Use a whisk or pestle to mix and mash them together until you have a chunky guacamole. 2. If it's not all going to be consumed right away, transfer it to an airtight container, drizzle olive oil on it, set a sheet of plastic wrap on the top so that it sticks directly to the guacamole—this will help keep the avocado from turning brown—and then put the lid on. Store in the fridge until ready to enjoy, but no more than 4 days.

Per Serving:
calories: 215 | fat: 18g | protein: 4g | carbs: 5g | fiber: 3g | sugar: 1g | sodium: 354mg

Avocado-Herb Spread

Prep time: 10 minutes | Cook time: 0 minutes | Makes 1 cup

- 1 avocado, peeled and pitted
- 2 tablespoons freshly squeezed lemon juice
- 2 tablespoons chopped fresh parsley
- 1 teaspoon chopped fresh
- dill
- ½ teaspoon ground coriander
- Sea salt, to taste
- Freshly ground black pepper, to taste

1. In a blender, pulse the avocado until smoothly puréed. 2. Add the lemon juice, parsley, dill, and coriander. Pulse until well blended. 3. Season with sea salt and pepper. 4. Refrigerate the spread in a sealed container for up to 4 days.

Per Serving:
calories: 53 | fat: 5g | protein: 1g | carbs: 2g | fiber: 2g | sugar: 0g | sodium: 5mg

Caramelized Onions

Prep time: 10 minutes | Cook time: 55 minutes | Makes 2¼ cups

- 3 tablespoons olive oil
- 3 large yellow onions, thinly sliced
- 1 teaspoon kosher salt

1. In a large sauté pan over medium-low heat, warm the olive oil. Add the onions and salt and cook, stirring often, until the onions start to wilt, about 10 minutes. When the onions begin to caramelize, stir frequently, scraping the browned bits from the bottom on the pan so the natural sugars do not burn. 2. Continue to cook, stirring frequently, until the onions are a deep brown, about 45 minutes. 3. Store in an airtight container in the refrigerator for up to 3 days.

Per Serving:

calories: 60 | fat: 5g | protein: 1g | carbs: 5g | fiber: 1g | sugar: 2g | sodium: 260mg

Pickled Onions

Prep time: 10 minutes | Cook time: 0 minutes | Makes 2 cups

- ½ cup lime juice
- ¼ cup warm water
- 1 teaspoon coconut sugar
- ½ teaspoon kosher salt
- 1 red onion, halved and thinly sliced
- 1 jalapeño, sliced (optional if nightshade-sensitive)

1. Place the lime juice, water, sugar, and salt in a medium bowl and whisk to dissolve the salt. Submerge the onion and jalapeño (if using) in the liquid. Allow them to sit for 2 hours until slightly pickled. Store in an airtight container in the refrigerator for up to 1 week.

Per Serving:

calories: 14 | fat: 0g | protein: 0g | carbs: 4g | fiber: 0g | sugar: 2g | sodium: 292mg

Parsley Chimichurri

Prep time: 5 minutes | Cook time: 0 minutes | Makes 1 cup

- 1 cup coarsely chopped fresh parsley
- ½ cup fresh mint leaves
- ¼ cup olive oil
- 2 tablespoons freshly squeezed lemon juice
- 2 teaspoons bottled minced garlic
- Pinch sea salt

1. In a blender or food processor, combine the parsley, mint, olive oil, lemon juice, garlic, and sea salt. Pulse until the herbs are very finely chopped and the ingredients are well mixed. 2. Refrigerate the mixture in a sealed container for up to 1 week.

Per Serving:

calories: 61 | fat: 6g | protein: 1g | carbs: 1g | fiber: 1g | sugar: 0g | sodium: 9mg

Toasted Coconut Sunbutter

Prep time: 10 minutes | Cook time: 8 minutes | Makes 1½ cups

- 1½ cups sunflower seeds
- 1½ cups large-flake unsweetened coconut
- ⅛ teaspoon salt

1. Preheat the oven to 350ºF (180ºC). 2. On a baking sheet, spread the sunflower seeds and coconut. 3. Place the sheet in the preheated oven and bake for 6 to 8 minutes. Keep a close watch, as the seeds and coconut can burn quickly. 4. Remove from the oven and cool. 5. In a food processor, combine the seeds, coconut, and salt. Blend until smooth and creamy, scraping down the sides as needed. 6. Pour into a sealable jar.

Per Serving:

calories: 66 | fat: 7g | protein: 1g | carbs: 3g | fiber: 2g | sugar: 1g | sodium: 31mg

Creamy Turmeric Dressing

Prep time: 15 minutes | Cook time: 0 minutes | Serves 4 to 6

- ¼ cup extra-virgin olive oil
- 2 tablespoons water
- 2 tablespoons freshly squeezed lemon juice
- 1½ tablespoons raw honey
- 1 tablespoon apple cider vinegar
- 1 teaspoon ground turmeric
- 1 teaspoon Dijon mustard
- ½ teaspoon ground ginger
- ¼ teaspoon sea salt
- Pinch freshly ground black pepper

1. In a small bowl, combine the olive oil, water, lemon juice, honey, vinegar, turmeric, mustard, ginger, salt, and pepper. Whisk well to combine. Keep refrigerated in an airtight container.

Per Serving:

calories: 151 | fat: 14g | protein: 0g | carbs: 8g | fiber: 0g | sugar: 7g | sodium: 176mg

Green Olive Tapenade

Prep time: 10 minutes | Cook time: 0 minutes | Makes about 1 cup

- 1 cup pitted green olives
- 2 garlic cloves
- ¼ cup extra-virgin olive oil
- ¼ cup freshly squeezed lemon juice
- Pinch dried rosemary
- Salt, to taste
- Freshly ground black pepper, to taste

1. In a food processor, combine the olives, garlic, olive oil, lemon juice, and rosemary. Season with salt and pepper. Process until the mixture is almost smooth; a little chunky is fine. 2. Refrigerate in an airtight container. The tapenade will keep for several weeks.

Per Serving:

calories: 73 | fat: 8g | protein: 0g | carbs: 2g | fiber: 1g | sugar: 0g | sodium: 201mg

Lemon-Dijon Mustard Dressing

Prep time: 5 minutes | Cook time: 0 minutes | Makes about 6 tablespoons

- ¼ cup extra-virgin olive oil
- 2 tablespoons freshly squeezed lemon juice
- 1 teaspoon Dijon mustard
- ½ teaspoon raw honey
- 1 garlic clove, minced
- ¼ teaspoon dried basil
- ¼ teaspoon salt

1. In a glass jar with a lid, combine the olive oil, lemon juice, mustard, honey, garlic, basil, and salt. Cover and shake vigorously until the ingredients are well combined and emulsified. Refrigerate for up to 1 week.

Per Serving:

calories: 128 | fat: 13g | protein: 0g | carbs: 1g | fiber: 0g | sugar: 1g | sodium: 160mg

Appendix 1: Measurement Conversion Chart

VOLUME EQUIVALENTS(DRY)

US STANDARD	METRIC (APPROXIMATE)
1/8 teaspoon	0.5 mL
1/4 teaspoon	1 mL
1/2 teaspoon	2 mL
3/4 teaspoon	4 mL
1 teaspoon	5 mL
1 tablespoon	15 mL
1/4 cup	59 mL
1/2 cup	118 mL
3/4 cup	177 mL
1 cup	235 mL
2 cups	475 mL
3 cups	700 mL
4 cups	1 L

VOLUME EQUIVALENTS(LIQUID)

US STANDARD	US STANDARD (OUNCES)	METRIC (APPROXIMATE)
2 tablespoons	1 fl.oz.	30 mL
1/4 cup	2 fl.oz.	60 mL
1/2 cup	4 fl.oz.	120 mL
1 cup	8 fl.oz.	240 mL
1 1/2 cup	12 fl.oz.	355 mL
2 cups or 1 pint	16 fl.oz.	475 mL
4 cups or 1 quart	32 fl.oz.	1 L
1 gallon	128 fl.oz.	4 L

TEMPERATURES EQUIVALENTS

FAHRENHEIT(F)	CELSIUS(C) (APPROXIMATE)
225 °F	107 °C
250 °F	120 °C
275 °F	135 °C
300 °F	150 °C
325 °F	160 °C
350 °F	180 °C
375 °F	190 °C
400 °F	205 °C
425 °F	220 °C
450 °F	235 °C
475 °F	245 °C
500 °F	260 °C

WEIGHT EQUIVALENTS

US STANDARD	METRIC (APPROXIMATE)
1 ounce	28 g
2 ounces	57 g
5 ounces	142 g
10 ounces	284 g
15 ounces	425 g
16 ounces (1 pound)	455 g
1.5 pounds	680 g
2 pounds	907 g

Appendix 2: The Dirty Dozen and Clean Fifteen

The Environmental Working Group (EWG) is a nonprofit, nonpartisan organization dedicated to protecting human health and the environment Its mission is to empower people to live healthier lives in a healthier environment. This organization publishes an annual list of the twelve kinds of produce, in sequence, that have the highest amount of pesticide residue-the Dirty Dozen-as well as a list of the fifteen kinds of produce that have the least amount of pesticide residue-the Clean Fifteen.

THE DIRTY DOZEN

- The 2016 Dirty Dozen includes the following produce. These are considered among the year's most important produce to buy organic:

Strawberries	Spinach
Apples	Tomatoes
Nectarines	Bell peppers
Peaches	Cherry tomatoes
Celery	Cucumbers
Grapes	Kale/collard greens
Cherries	Hot peppers

- *The Dirty Dozen list contains two additional items kale/collard greens and hot peppers-because they tend to contain trace levels of highly hazardous pesticides.*

THE CLEAN FIFTEEN

- The least critical to buy organically are the Clean Fifteen list. The following are on the 2016 list:

Avocados	Papayas
Corn	Kiw
Pineapples	Eggplant
Cabbage	Honeydew
Sweet peas	Grapefruit
Onions	Cantaloupe
Asparagus	Cauliflower
Mangos	

- *Some of the sweet corn sold in the United States are made from genetically engineered (GE) seedstock. Buy organic varieties of these crops to avoid GE produce.*

Appendix 3: Recipes Index

A

Allergen-Free Breakfast Cookies	12
Almost Caesar Salad Dressing	91
Anti-Inflammatory Mayonnaise	93
Apple-Turkey Burgers	30
Avocado Boat Breakfast	17
Avocado Toast with Greens	12
Avocado-Dill Sauce	91
Avocado-Herb Spread	94

B

Baked Apple and Walnut Chips	59
Baked Fruit and Nut Pudding	84
Baked Halibut with Avocado Salsa	39
Baked Salmon with Oregano Pistou	37
Baked Zucchini Fries	67
Balsamic-Glazed Chicken Thighs with Steamed Cauliflower	31
Balsamic-Glazed Turkey Wings	30
Basic Beans	19
Basic Quinoa	21
Beans	91
Beef and Bell Pepper Fajitas	48
Beef and Bell Pepper Stir-Fry	53
Beef Sirloin Kebabs in Garlic Marinade	50
Beefy Lentil and Tomato Stew	48
Berry Vinaigrette	92
Black Bean Chili with Garlic and Tomatoes	20
Blanched Green Veggies with Radishes	64
Blueberry Crisp	87
Blueberry Nut Trail Mix	55
Blueberry Parfait with Lemon-Coconut Cream	86
Blueberry-Millet Breakfast Bake	14
Braised Bok Choy with Shiitake Mushrooms	74
Brilliantly Beetroot Flavoured Ketchup	64
Broccoli and Egg "Muffins"	73
Broccoli-Sesame Stir-Fry	72
Brown Rice with Bell Peppers	19
Buckwheat Granola	14
Buckwheat Tabbouleh	68
Burst Cherry Tomatoes with Garlic	69
Butternut Squash and Spinach Gratin with Lentils	73

C

Caramelized Onions	95
Carne Molida	49
Cashew Nuts and Broccoli Snack	60
Chia Breakfast Pudding	13
Chia Jam	90
Chia Pudding with Oats, Strawberries, and Kiwi	11
Chia-Coconut Porridge	13
Chicken and Broccoli Stir-Fry	27
Chicken and Dumpling Soup	77
Chicken Bone Broth	26
Chicken Breast with Cherry Sauce	33
Chicken Chili with Beans	80
Chicken Kofta Kebabs	31
Chicken Salad with Green Apples and Grapes	25
Chicken Satay and Grilled Zucchini	27
Chicken Skewers with Mint Sauce	24
Chickpea Paste	58
Chimichurri Sauce	92
Chipotle Black Beans	90
Chocolate Chili	51
Chocolate Fondue	87
Chocolate-Avocado Pudding	85
Chocolate-Coconut Brownies	84
Cider-Baked Beets	66
Cilantro-Lime Chicken Drumsticks	25
Cinnamon-Spiced Apple Chips	57
Citrus Spinach	71
Classic Butternut Squash Soup	77
Coconut Chicken	32
Coconut Crab Cakes	37
Coconut Rice with Blueberries	84
Coconut-Almond Bake	67
Coconut-Blueberry Popsicles	85
Coconut-Braised Chicken	26
Coconut-Braised Curried Chicken	25
Coconut-Chocolate Clumps	88
Coconut-Crusted Cod with Mango-Pineapple Salsa	41
Coconutty Brown Rice	20
Cod with Ginger and Black Beans	41
Country Captain'S Chicken	30
Cranberry Compote	87

Creamy Broccoli Dip 55
Creamy Lentil Dip 94
Creamy Sesame Dressing 93
Creamy Turmeric Dressing 96
Crispy Chicken Milanese with Hollandaise 29
Crispy Oven-Roasted Broccoli with Italian Spice Trio 63
Crispy Thin Flatbread 60
Cucumber-Yogurt Dip 58
Cumin-Roasted Cauliflower 64
Curried Black Pepper Vinaigrette 93
Curried Sweet Potato Soup 78
Curry-Glazed Salmon with Quinoa 43
Curry-Spiced Nut Mix with Maple and Black Pepper 61

D

Daring Shark Steaks 35

E

Easy Chicken and Broccoli 32
Easy Roasted Vegetables 66
Easy Summer Gazpacho 80
Everything Flaxseed Meal Crackers 65

F

Fast and Fresh Granola Trail Mix 56
Fennel Baked Salmon 42
Fiesta Guacamole 94
Fish and Vegetable Casserole 40
Fish En Papillote 36
Five-Spice Cod Broth 40
French Vinaigrette 93
Fricase De Pollo 32
Fried Hard-Boiled Eggs 60
Fruity Hot Milk 87

G

Garlicky Tofu Scramble 13
Garlic-Mustard Lamb Chops 48
Garlic-Mustard Steak 51
General Tso's Chicken 24
German Chocolate Cake Protein Oats 14
Gingered Chicken and Vegetable Soup 81
Golden Beet and Spinach Frittata 11

Golden Coconut Pancakes 17
Grain-Free Fritters 65
Green Olive Tapenade 96
Grilled Rib-Eye And Summer Succotash 47
Grilled Salmon Packets with Asparagus 38
Ground Beef Breakfast Skillet 11
Ground Beef Chili with Tomatoes 52
Gyro Skillet Sausages 50

H

Hearty Bolognese 51
Herb Omelet 74
Herbed Chicken Bone Broth 78
Herbed Harvest Rice 20
Herbed Lamb Fillets with Cauliflower Mash 50
Homemade Avocado Sushi 67
Homemade Trail Mix 56
Home-Style Red Lentil Stew 80
Honey Panna Cotta with Blackberry-Lime Sauce 86
Hummus Burgers 74

I

Indian Butter Chickpeas 19
Indian-Spiced Cauliflower 64

K

Kale Frittata 73
Kale-Stuffed Mushrooms 65
Korean Beef Lettuce Wraps 47

L

Lamb and Quinoa Skillet Ragù 49
Lazy Moco 45
Lemon and Garlic Chicken Thighs 29
Lemon Lavender and Strawberry Compote 85
Lemon-Dijon Mustard Dressing 96
Lemon-Ginger Honey 93
Lemony Mustard Dressing 94
Lentil-Lamb Ragu 46
Lentils with Tomatoes and Turmeric 20
Lime-Salmon Patties 38
Lulu's Iced Coffee 12
Lush Lamb and Rosemary Casserole 52

M

Macadamia-Dusted Pork Cutlets	52
Manhattan-Style Salmon Chowder	39
Maple Carrot Cake	85
Maple-Cinnamon Granola	16
Maple-Dijon Brussels Sprouts	66
Maple-Tahini Oatmeal	13
Mashed Avocado with Jicama Slices	61
Mediterranean Chicken Bake	28
Mediterranean Quinoa with Peperoncini	19
Mediterranean Rub	94
Meditteranean Vegetable Frittata	12
Mini Dark Chocolate-Almond Butter Cups	86
Mini Fruit Muffins	16
Mini Snack Muffins	60
Mixed Vegetable Stir-Fry	75
Morning Millet	13
Mushroom Egg Foo Young	73
Mushroom Risotto with Spring Peas	22
Mushroom Turkey Thighs	33
Mustard Cauliflower Slices	68

N

Nut-Free Keto Bread	63
Nutmeg and Cherry Breakfast Quinoa	12

P

Pan-Seared Haddock with Beets	37
Pan-Seared Rib-Eye with Arugula	48
Parsley Chimichurri	95
Party Meatballs	46
Pecan and Date Snack Bars	57
Pecan-Crusted Trout	42
Peperonata	92
Persian Herb Frittata	14
Pickled Onions	95
Pistou	92
Plantain Chips	57
Pork Char Siu and Ramen	53
Pork Chops with Cooked Apple Salsa	52
Pork Chops with Gingered Applesauce	49
Pork Ragù	49
Protein Fried Rice	46
Protein Scotch Eggs	16

Pulled Pork Tacos	51
Pumpkin and Carrot Crackers	59

Q

Quick Miso Soup with Wilted Greens	78
Quinoa Flatbread	57
Quinoa Florentine	20
Quinoa-Broccolini Sauté	72

R

Red Lentil Curry with Cauliflower and Yams	21
Roast Chicken with Lemon and White Beans	28
Roasted Apricots	58
Roasted Broccoli and Cashews	71
Roasted Fingerling Potatoes	69
Roasted Leg of Lamb	45
Roasted Salmon and Asparagus	35
Roasted Sweet Potatoes	63
Roasted Sweet Potatoes and Pineapple	68
Root Vegetable Loaf	68
Rosemary Chicken	33
Rosemary-Apricot Marinade	91
Rosemary-Lemon Cod	36
Russian Kotleti	25

S

Salmon and Asparagus Skewers	39
Salmon Baked with Leeks and Fennel	36
Salmon with Quinoa	43
Santa Barbara Migas	15
Sardine Donburi	35
Sautéed Kale with Garlic	66
Sautéed Sardines with Cauliflower Mash	39
Sautéed Spinach	64
Savory Beef Meatloaf	45
Savory Flax Waffles	65
Scrumptious Scallops with Cilantro and Lime	41
Seared Honey-Garlic Scallops	41
Seared Scallops with Greens	38
Seedy Cookie Dough Bites	87
Sesame Chicken Stir-Fry	28
Sesame Mahi-Mahi and Fruit Salsa	40
Sesame Miso Chicken	32
Sesame-Quinoa Cups	71
Sesame-Tuna with Asparagus	38

Shredded Jerk Chicken	31	
Shrimp with Cinnamon Sauce	43	
Shrimp with Spicy Spinach	35	
Simple Steel-Cut Oats	15	
Simplest Guacamole	55	
Slow-Roasted Sweet Potatoes	68	
Smoked Salmon Scrambled Eggs	15	
Smooth Chia Pudding	57	
Sole with Vegetables in Foil Packets	42	
Southwest Turkey-Stuffed Bell Peppers	28	
Spanish Rice	21	
Spiced Nuts	59	
Spiced Trout and Spinach	40	
Spicy Chicken Drumsticks	29	
Spicy Lime-Chicken "Tortilla-Less" Soup	82	
Spicy Ramen Noodle Soup	82	
Spicy Two-Bean Dip	56	
Spinach and Kale Breaded Balls	55	
Squash and Ginger Soup	77	
Stir-Fry Sauce	90	
Strawberry Jam Thumbprint Cookies	84	
Strawberry-Chia Ice Pops	58	
Super Healthy Sweet Potato Fries	59	
Sweet and Spicy Pepitas	56	
Sweet Potato and Bell Pepper Hash with a Fried Egg	72	
Sweet Potato and Rice Soup	79	
Sweet Potato Chips	56	
Sweet Potato Curry with Spinach	75	
Sweet Potato Oat Muffins	58	
Sweet Potato-Ground Turkey Hash	15	

T

Tangy Brussels Sprout, Onion and Apple Kebabs	67
Tangy Lemon Mousse	85
Thai Cabbage Bowl	74
Thai Coconut Soup	78
Thai Red Curry with Tofu and Green Beans	22
The Perfect Poached Egg	90
Thin-Cut Pork Chops with Mustardy Kale	47

Toasted Coconut Sunbutter	95
Tofu and Spinach Sauté	71
Tofu Sloppy Joes	75
Tomato Asparagus Frittata	75
Tropical Coconut Delight	11
Turkey Larb Lettuce Wraps	26
Turkey Meatball Soup	79
Turkey Meatballs in a Muffin Tin	24
Turkey Sloppy Joes	26
Turkey-Cranberry Sausage with Sage	17
Turkey-Thyme Meatballs	30
Tuscan Chicken	27

V

Vanilla Ice Cream	88
Vegan "Frittata"	16
Vegan Minestrone with Herb Oil	69
Vegetable Spring Roll Wraps	69
Veggie Pâté	91
Veggie Spring Rolls with Almond Dipping Sauce	72

W

Warm Cinnamon-Turmeric Almond Milk	86
Warming Gingerbread Oatmeal	15
Wasabi Salmon Burgers	37
White Bean and French Onion Soup	80
White Bean Dip	59
White Fish with Mushrooms	42
Whitefish Chowder	36
Winter Warming Chunky Chicken Soup	81

Z

Zesty Broccoli Soup	81
Zucchini and Red Onion Salad with Olives	66
Zuppa Toscana	79

Made in the USA
Columbia, SC
25 October 2024

45068864R00059